She Believed She Could

A Journey of Self Discovery
One Day at a Time

Sharon K. Angelici
© 2019

Copyright 2019 by Sharon K. Angelici

Cover Art by Taylor Rose

First Edition

All rights to this publication and its characters are reserved. This publication may not be reprinted, reproduced, transmitted or utilized in any form or means now known or hereinafter invented, including but not limited to photocopying, recording or any type of data storage and/ or retrieval system, without express written permission in writing from the author.

Write with Light Publications Colorado, USA

ISBN: 9798846389441
ISBN: 978-1-970289-37-4
ISBN: 978-1733626514

Library of Congress Number: 2019944710

Dedication

For my husband, my daughter and my son. You inspire me and I'm grateful for the minutes, days and years of living this adventure called life. I'm glad you are mine.

For my Aussie family, including our rescued Greyhound fur babies. I cannot imagine my life without you in it. Your courage led me to find my own. We have done incredible things with all this love.

For my father, you taught me to work hard and to always wear gloves. The days we fought for mom together were the hardest I've ever lived. I wish we had won. I love you always.

To Hillary, you know and that's all that matters. It's the only thing that matters. #whynot

To my mother, this story begins and ends because you inspired me to be more. Even after your heart stopped beating, and the days felt impossible, you made me believe. If wishes were reality, you'd be holding this book in your beautiful hands drinking a cup of my dandelion tea.

To all my people, you know who you are. When the adventures seemed insurmountable you were there to inspire me. I didn't do this on my own. Thank you for being with me on this journey.

Intro

I Had No Idea

I was so cocky in mid-August of 2017. I made a public decree that I would do 365 new things for 365 consecutive days. I wasn't thinking about the how or where. If I'm honest I wasn't thinking at all.

I was inspired. My niece is a travel writer and blogger. She'd just returned from China after two years of service with the Peace Corps.

Her accomplishments inspired me, and I gobbled up the voyages and triumphs of travel bloggers around the globe. I lived vicariously through random posts and websites and stumbled upon a wild and adventurous couple. They'd challenged one another to the ultimate year of experiences. The idea activated every curious bone in my body.

Months before reading that blog, I was in the mountains of Colorado on retreat. I was riding a spiritual and emotional high and I had changed. I felt connected to myself, my family and home life and this new balance invigorated me as I approached my 49th year of life.

I was indifferent about celebrating my birthday, but I couldn't believe that the reflection in the mirror was a year away from turning fifty. I felt young and fit and I wondered how a half-century of life had happened to me.

I'm not sure what I was thinking when I announced my plan on social media. I should have spent more time looking at the "how" of it before making a public request for first time adventure and experience ideas. In an instant

I was responsible for filling 365 days. It didn't take long for emails and messages to post to my accounts and although I stipulated real achievable ideas some suggestions went off in wild and crazy directions. A few people missed the condition that I had to accomplish the adventure in 24 hours.

I was intimidated and I questioned my ability to achieve all 365 days long before the year began. Fear; It was real and abundant. That's when I knew I had to put myself to the test. I wasn't going to let it define me.

I crafted a plan… sort of. I color coded an alphabetized and numbered list and on day one I felt like my 113 original ideas would be a great start. I'd recruited family, friends and co-workers who wanted to be involved in this journey. Some hesitation faded as confidence grew, when I started to believe, I was certain I could get through this.

Even with my loose plan I understood the year needed meticulo, organization. I shopped for a pocket journal and discovered after about a month that this was a brilliant idea. I numbered each day starting on my 49th birthday and tracked as much as I could: miles traveled, dollars spent, if I planted a rock and when I accomplished my 60-second plank.

I planned to write about everything, as each bit of information might be important this blog became a journal about my life. As the days turned to weeks and the calendar shaded over with achievements, I realized they fell into five categories; what I'd read, what I'd done, what I saw, what I made and what I ate.

That's how I organized the year and that's how the book chapters came to be. This was an organic experience from the moment it was conceived, and meticulous record keeping was important to my story telling.

I created a page on my website dedicated to sharing all my individual firsts. The grid pattern was also a visual reminder of what I planned to accomplish. On day one it was daunting. I set up my blog site and had a goal to share every experience no matter how big or small. 365 new things in 365 days shared with 365 consecutive blog posts. What could be difficult about this?   So cocky!

Part One

I Read This

On day one of my journey, I wanted to do something so spectacular that it would attract attention and people would want to follow me throughout the year. It needed to be amazing. I thought I could zip line or take a balloon ride; maybe even bungee jump off a bridge but day one came fast, and it was more like a spring rain than a thundering storm.

My journey began as I read about the love and loss experienced by another writer. Rupi Kaur's Milk and Honey was my day one experience. It was also a realization that each 24-hour period would be a blessing and a curse. I tried not to think about tomorrow. When I did, the year of firsts seemed impossible to achieve. Looking back at this decision it set a tone and created an anthem for the next 365 days.

I had no idea when I started to read this book that the message would inspire me through some very difficult days. Rupi's writing is tragic and triumphant, so much like my 365-day challenge would become.

I used a few books during the 365 days and most fed a broader view of my world. On day 40 I read the study of numerology. I am a curious person by nature. Whenever I find a book about magical beliefs and ideas, I buy it and say, "someday I'll teach myself."

I try to keep an open mind to new experiences and the possibility of more. My 40th day started with very simple calculations involving my name and I proceeded to spend hours writing out my life in numbers. It felt prophetic and as I look back at the notes, I understand that some things are beyond simple explanation and on occasion seeds are planted that might bring strength. My numerology notebook transitioned to something very different, as 2017 became 2018. I had no idea what would come.

This is the first piece of research that I lost during many long days of adventure. Lesson Learned: keep the journals and paperwork organized.

On day 51, while waiting in court to hear the verdict after a long trial, I read a book about the unique qualities of my hand. The guide to palmistry is part of that personal library and something I've wanted to understand. I had this book for years, always saying, "someday I'll read that, and I'll know." The wait's over, this was the day.

I sat alone in the wood and stone hallway staring at my palm; I can only imagine what people passing by were thinking. I was oblivious. I scribbled notes and traced lines and continued until I was interrupted. I'm not sure I would remember much about day 51 if I hadn't had specific intentions to accomplish something new. When I was allowed in the courtroom everything faded. I realized a few days later that my 365-day challenge would become the journal I didn't know I would need.

I started to realize how big this experience was, but I had no idea it would keep me from curling in a ball and giving up. My mother's illness was diagnosed on day 91. I was compelled to stop and focus on medical care. From the moment I shared this 365-day idea with her she was part of the planning team. A few days after her surgery she asked me to read the blogs she'd missed. She wanted me to continue my adventures. Who I am and how I was changed in the grey of that hospital room.

In the weeks following her diagnosis my personal experiences took second place to mom. I got creative. If I could find a way for us to accomplish an adventure from her hospital bed, we did it.

She was joy. On day 100 after long hours of doctors and nurses I sat with my mother. It was late and most of my extended family had come and gone for the day. The alarms of the bedside monitors were silent, but mom was wide-awake. I asked if she'd like to hear a story. Her response, "why not." This became her answer to just about everything and although it might have appeared passive, I always felt it meant, "Bring it on!"

I chose the only book in the room, *"The Tales of Beedle the Bard."* My mother was an enthusiastic Harry Potter fan, and this book would make an appropriate bedtime story. Until that day I'd never read to my mother with such intimacy. When I close my eyes, I can still see the two of us side by side and looking back my heart was breaking with every word I read. As I finished the book her eyes were closed and if tears hadn't been visible, I would have thought she was at rest. This experience changed me. For the very first time in our 49-year relationship mom was looking to me for care.

She was my rock. She taught me how to read and showed me the joy that could come from complete immersion in a perfect story. She followed all my writing and wasn't shy about sharing how proud she was to have an author in her family.

My hospital mornings continued and on the 106th day I brought another book. This how-to tutorial about the art of reading runes accompanied by a bag of engraved rocks spilled out across the tiny rolling hospital table. I studied the message on the tray.

My first impression was confusion and impossibility. As I reflect on this experience, I recognize the skill that is necessary to use runes. After a few hours of study, I know the basics and even now I would have to refer to the book for help, but it was a moment to ask questions to the universe, I'm not sure about the actual answers.

The next hundred days were the most difficult of my life. I'm certain that this 365-day experience was inspired by a higher power because on day 214 my mother died. It was sudden and unexpected; in fact, we were determined to fight for a long time… as a family.

I spent the days following her death sorting through all her things; unfinished dreams in boxes, wishes scrawled across pieces of paper and projects tucked inside manila file folders, all of which originated from her shelves of books. My mother was an educated woman and devoted to filling her mind with information. She had ambitious crafting projects and gardening that accumulated into enough for two lifetimes. I understand where my curiosity comes from.

While going through the mountains of unfinished projects I found a tiny book she'd tucked away. *"50 ways to a better you, for Dummies"* was an interesting find and it felt as if mom was delivering messages to me from the afterlife. It's a little book and the very first tip inside…Talk To Someone.

This was sound advice and possibly the most precious to come at a very vulnerable time. I don't know why mom bought this book or if she ever read it but finding it when I did sent a message that I needed to hear. Losing her was devastating. It still is. She was my go-to, my sounding board and a partner in satisfying a long list of curiosities even before the 365-day challenge began.

She's a hard habit to break and I had no clue when this adventure began that she would feed me with so many ideas. On day 243 I used a cookbook that I'd purchased for my mother after an incredible adventure in Colorado. In March of 2017 I was in the mountains to work with a professional educator to develop *Dear Kane; what I wish we would have said* into a teaching curriculum. It's still a work in progress but while I was there the hostess made our meals using the *Thug Kitchen* cookbook.

This publication is a serious commitment to food and vulgarity and as I stood in Deb's kitchen I was wrecked with laughter. I thought of my mom and had to send a copy to her. Without hesitation, I ordered it from the app on my phone. A few days later I got a message from mom, and she could hardly contain her feelings about my gift. She loved the sentiment even if it was a bit crude. She was funny that way, always a lady but sometimes a little bit wild. As day 243's experience played out I didn't bake so much as I prepared a recipe for tea smoothies. It felt right, as tea was a huge part of my mother's life.

Almost 100 days passed before another book entered my year. It's not like I wasn't reading but I just had all my energies focused on the next 24 hours and there wasn't much time to get sidetracked. I downloaded the Qúran to my kindle. I don't know why this book intrigues me; in fact, I'm not a huge fan of organized religion.

Is there some great truth that I discovered? If I'm honest it didn't change my life, but I didn't read the entire book in one day. I did use a how-to guide to read it. I learned that this book is "word for word" what came from their prophet. No translations or interpretations are allowed and as a religion the book that is read today is the same as it was in the beginning. I'm intrigued by the history of the Qúran.

In a strange turn of events and because I had a long plane ride from Scotland, my final book was about the Formation of Scripture. Looking back, it is very odd for me to have read either the Qúran or a book about scripture, but I did. It also makes sense that as firsts they would be a part of this year.

The Formation of Scripture was another book that mom planted in my life. She was quite the gardener even when there weren't any green things involved. This was actually not a book, but an 80-page pamphlet written in 1967. I wasn't even born. In fact, it was published one year prior almost to the day.

Why would mom plant this little book in my life? Years ago, on one of our many excursions we had a discussion about religion. She was usually behind the wheel of her huge car, and I was biting my nails as a passenger. Her driving always made me nervous and it's incredible to think she was behind the wheel just days before her illness was discovered.

She mentioned this pamphlet during our conversation and planned to look for her copy so I could read it. I'd forgotten about the conversation until that little 80-page document showed up in my mailbox. I'll admit I was a little pissed because it looked like religious solicitation and what was worse is that it smelled like something that came out of a dirty wet basement. Remember 1967?

This was my experience on day 357. I'd been holding on to this book for a long time. Mom and I never got to have that conversation again, so it felt right to read it in honor of her faith journey. She led by example. She was humble and based her life on science, faith and information. That message became so clear as I sat in my airplane seat. I scribbled notes in pencil. I don't know why.

In 365 days, I read and used 10 books written by people I've never met. Their thoughts and ideas became important parts of my own adventure. They inspired, humbled and offered guidance through less than a dozen days but left a permanent mark on my humanity. I'm grateful to my mother for stressing the importance of reading and for sharing ideas through artistic expression and I'm humbled by the power of words.

Part Two

I Did This

Putting 365 individual accomplishments in to five categories so that I could have five chapters happened as organically as my 365-day challenge. From the beginning the number 365 was daunting and even the best planner could not "event calendar" their way through this. I did ninety percent of this entire year on the fly. Yes, I'm confessing that there was hardly ever a plan and this is how most days went.

Wake up.
Think, "What is my plan?"
Sob in my pillow because I don't have one.
Research.
GO!

For the most part I did this 365 times. Relief came when my adventure involved a coconspirator, which actually happened on day four, but I'm skipping ahead.

My very first "I did it" was using a glass pen. This stunning writing instrument was a present my son bought for me at a Renaissance Festival. It's beautiful and I'd looked at them many times but would never buy one for myself. It is a treasured gift not because of the physical item but because my son paid attention to the little things and knew it would be special. He's a beautiful soul and a cherished artistic partner.

My experience with that pen was also my first 365-day YouTube video. I made about 45 of them. For better or worse I became a YouTuber even though to date the pen adventure only has 25 views. After a few days I learned that most of this year was going to be me against myself. If people were reading, that was wonderful, but getting through all the tasks I'd set didn't leave much room for anything else. I had no idea what was coming, no one ever does.

The problem with accomplishing a task on the fly is the margin for error that's inevitable with the lack planning. I organized my pen and ink with a few sheets of paper. I set up a camera and once it was rolling, I had no idea what to write, or draw.

If you watch the video, you'll see that I hesitate because "no plan panic" set in quick. Remember it's the third day. I've got 362 more of these to go and I'm freaking out in front of my camera. It happens in one second, but I can still remember how it felt. Lesson learned on day three, give me a bit of a breath and have a strategy before the beginning.

I tried to make a plan for the fourth day by doing a car repair. My daughter hit a deer on the way to school and although the damage was minor the lights needed to be replaced. It seemed like the perfect idea to fix it now. How hard could it be? Remember that plan?

The phone rings, it's my husband and coconspirator. We've been together for twenty-six years and after that much time as a couple there should be an unspoken level of understanding.

I love this man. He's gentle and kind and would climb with me to the top of the world, but his inquiry was the last I ever expected to hear. "Do you have a dress?" he asks. The question was silly, I haven't worn a dress in years and the size I am today is not even close to the size I was when I bought the dusty thing in the back of my closet. I asked him why and he said we were going to a formal dinner, and it was a "surprise."

I reminded him that it was day four and I was busy.

"Drop everything!" My husband is an amazing human being. He supported this entire crazy year in every way. I don't think he understood what he was asking. I'm not a girly girl. I have never been a girly girl and dresses are 100% not my thing.

Day four turned into a shopping experience I never wanted nor desired. I had a few hours to find a dress. It's ridiculous for anyone to expect that I could do this without help. Yes, I went dress shopping alone for a formal event that I didn't know anything about. It's day four and I'm skeptical that day 365 will ever arrive. I went to a half dozen stores, picked through hundreds of items and found three that I thought might pass as formal. I bought them all, but you know what happens after you buy a dress? Shoes.

The big reveal was that the event was a fundraiser for the Boys and Girls club, and the keynote speaker was Evander Holyfield. The dinner was amazing, and I met the boxing champ who spoke about his humble beginnings and shared the path to success aided by this generous organization. The speech inspired me, and the evening planted the thought that "I can accomplish this."

I did have a chance to do that car repair the next day. After a few hours of YouTube videos, crawling around on the ground and some basic electrical wiring those lights were connected. I'm five days in and I've already experienced highs and lows, so I'm expecting this will be quite the roller coaster of a year.

For my eleventh experience I attended Light fest. In my dreams I had an idealized image of lanterns drifting magically across the night sky. The reality was almost the same. We arrived early enough to set up chairs, eat a picnic and listen to the music on the stage below us.

It was a festival, and we were waiting for the sun to go down so the lanterns could go up. I didn't consider what would happen to those glowing puffballs after they floated away. The fire department was on the scene so I figured they just burned up and what was left would biodegrade.

I was wrong. The lanterns aren't as earth friendly as I had hoped, and the fuel (candle) burns just long enough for them to rise and drift about one hundred yards.

I was disappointed as I walked back to my car; the sight of the deflating lanterns strewn across the parking lot made me terribly sad. All I could see was the waste and I felt guilty for contributing to it. This was one of the first disappointments during the year. It opened my eyes to how I would use resources and think twice when planning future projects. I could accomplish this experience without stomping an eco-unfriendly footprint all over creation.

Day 27 was a ghastly misadventure of vanity. For 49 years I have avoided professional facial hair removal of every kind. It made sense to try it during this 365-day journey. This has to be in the top five of the most regretted experiences of the year.

Threading my eyebrows was the challenge of the day. I'm not a hairy person but for some reason my eyebrows grow all over the place. I had no idea how true this was until a woman started pulling them out with a piece of string. This was torture and I regretted it right after that first tiny hair was ripped out. I couldn't escape. It's like feeling the pains of childbirth and saying, nope not doing it. Once I started this endeavor I had to finish because half a hairy face is totally noticeable. I should have researched this process.

I should have listened to my instincts when they told me to be natural and keep those little hairs and just pull the bristly ones. Lesson learned.

Throughout the next 365 days I learned how to play a lot of games. Many were opportunities to include people I love and also learn pastimes they are passionate about. On day 31 my adventures in miniature war gaming began. This was time I spent with my daughter, and it was priceless.

It's not very often that parents are invited in and it's time I will hold close and cherish as the space and distance of adulthood push us in different directions. My daughter is an artist when it comes to assembly and finishing tiny little war machines. I know that over the years hundreds of these mini soldiers have entered my home. I didn't understand the game, and to be honest I still don't get it, but the sense of community that is a result is what's important. On day 114 the club members invited me inside their game room to play Space Hulk. I felt honored to learn to play and witness the family of people who support the human being my child has become. Passion is important even when the goal is fun.

In October of 2017 the game of Pickle ball attracted an interesting crowd to my local fitness center. The court space to play this game was offered five days a week and for two hours a plastic whiffle ball was smashed back and forth like a schoolyard game of tennis. I had no idea when I walked into the gym that the sweet Sr. crowd of people I greeted most days were unrelenting competitive pickle ballers.

I was schooled and I usually come to win. For two hours I got my butt kicked by this seasoned crowd. I wasn't ready. It was adorable at first, they were sweet and patient and forgiving when I made a scoring error or missed a ball in bounds. They gave me about fifteen minutes and then launched me into the fray. Pickle ball was fun and competitive and exhausting. I went to the local sporting goods store to buy a paddle of my own. I played a few more times after day 13 but time and new adventures prevented me from achieving those tournament goals.

The pickle ball fatigue was nothing compared to my day 70 adventure. It was one of the most physical and as it began I had no idea how difficult it would be to chop down a tree using only an axe. I'll explain that this tree was already dead and although there wasn't any reason to worry about it falling over, I seized this opportunity to experience a hand-felled tree.

It started out well. I had a plan. We sharpened the double-bladed axe and set up cameras to record the action. I created a safe distance for the tech setup and fixed my attack on this knotty old pine. It took a long time and my son helped when my arms got tired. The idea was to chop one side and then the other and it would drop in the direction with an elegant crackling of limbs and timber!

It didn't happen that way at all. I chipped away at the trunk of that tree like a beaver cutting the base for a dam. I thought it would never drop and when I gave it a casual shove it cracked and fell fast. It did scare me and the YouTube video is evidence of my 70th day. Five days later I used a chainsaw for the first time to cut up this 30' length of pine. I've always been afraid of using a chainsaw, but I faced that fear head on and diced that tree into manageable campfire logs.

It felt amazing.

On day 98 I took a chance on virtual reality gaming. It was a disaster for so many reasons, the obvious one being my tendency toward motion sickness. VR was a gift for Christmas and my son, being the adventurer, invited me to take a chance on this first. "How hard could it be?"

I am a child of the '80's. I cut my video gaming teeth on the Atari 2600. The controller had one button and a single huge joystick, and my gaming soundtrack music came from the skipping 78 on the record player. This is where my skill at gaming began and ended.

VR gaming has more technology before I even get the headgear in place. This adventure would be simple: maneuver through the home screen of the test game. The HOME SCREEN was a teaching tool for the actual game. I didn't even make it inside of the actual game! Less than 30 minutes of play and I was curled in a ball on the couch trying not to puke from flying a fake plane.

Disaster.

I am not a virtual reality gamer, but I didn't give up on the technology all together. On day 288 I put that headset back on to defuse VR bombs in the challenging game of "*Keep talking and no one explodes.*" This brought my family of four together for puzzle solving fun and to test our communication skills. I had a pretty solid belief that we would enjoy the evening.

On day 127 we used those same communication skills to free ourselves from an escape room. It wasn't our first time playing together as a family and as I reflect on our adventures, I realize how much their support got me to day 365. I didn't do this alone.

In total for the year, I counted 158 new "Did it" experiences. I drove my first Jeep and cracked a geode with a giant guillotine. I learned how to lay flooring in my bathroom and hang Dura rock in a shower. I became a minister to perform a rainbow wedding and welded rubber roofing. I learned how to play Hakuna Matata on the ukulele. I did so many new and exciting things, but they happened fast.

2018 rolled in and I fulfilled another long time wish. On one of the coldest New Year's days in recent history I participated in the Polar Plunge. It was subzero and as much as I'd planned for the adventure, I was not prepared for a wind chill of -25.

I am not designed to be in water at any temperature. I don't enjoy beaches or pools or getting wet in anything larger than my bathtub. I threw all those anxieties aside and marched into Lake Michigan a few minutes before the noon starting gun.

I fell back into the freezing water and jumped up with a rush of adrenalin that lasted long enough for my shorts to freeze to my thighs. Of all the 365-day challenges I would never do this again, but I have no regrets about doing it once.

For a brief moment I felt invincible until my fingertips numbed and I crawled over to a campfire someone built before taking their plunge. I stripped out of my wet clothes and into sweats but didn't remove the swimsuit underneath. BIG MISTAKE! By the time I made it to my car I had ice forming around my inner thighs.

A suggestion: if you're going to make a frigid plunge, be prepared to strip naked on a beach. A special shout out goes to: David, Davie, Kathy & Jim for being my beachfront pit crew and cheering squad.

I didn't accomplish this year of challenges without help and as the year progressed, I had opportunities to serve as an aid, teacher and assistant. One of the first volunteer experiences was to collect and sort toys for the Royal Family Kids Kenosha organization.

I've given my time to a lot of charities in my life. I was raised in a house where community service was essential. Both of my parents gave their talents to others and since children do what they see that continued thru me. When I heard about Royal Family Kids I wanted to help. Their goal: to give children in foster care a summer camp adventure. The week is funded by donations and that was part of what we collected while I was volunteering on day 18.

My history with this organization began when we sponsored a child for a week of camp. As a thank you we were invited to their talent show. The experience changed me. It's sobering to think that one week can have such an impact on the life of the children who attend. Thank you,

RFK and all of the volunteers who give to our local foster kids.

In contrast to my Royal Family Kids experience I had a ride along with the Lake Geneva Fire department on day 91. This was an adventure I'd always wanted. My dear friend Diana helped organize this experience and after passing the volunteer test I was in for the day. Part of me wanted this adventure to be packed with first encounters but that would also mean hardships for others. It turned out to be a mix of duties and emergencies.

I was nervous and excited to have my very first experience inside the station. The guys were generous and as we ran through the daily routine I was waiting for something to happen.

I spent my early twenties studying law enforcement but when it comes to fire and rescue the job is definitely different. It takes a very special heart to run toward danger and give 100%. It is also incredibly selfless to be present through life and death. Our only emergency run for the day wasn't critical but it was an exercise in how the job is unpredictable. Those who choose to serve their community in emergency services humble me.

I'm still in awe of the people I spent the day with, but I haven't been back. Just after 10pm that evening I received a call that my mom was ill. In the same 24 hour time period I was a volunteer and a passenger in an ambulance going to the hospital. As I recall this day, there were uncountable unknowns, and it was the beginning of so many endings.

I've never been an outspoken political person. This year was my first opportunity to hear people speak their truth in community protest.

The women's march was held on a chilly winter day and it was my 123rd experience. I brought my family along and as I stood in the courtyard of the city center in Milwaukee I was struck by the magnitude of the day. There were women along the steps, in the street and huddled in unity. I've never felt so proud and safe in a crowd. The speeches were short and diverse. The common thread in every message: there is strength in unity and women need to take back their power.

We marched through the city and along the way we bumped shoulders with people who are tired of being second class. I wanted more from the day and although the rally inspired me to march, I had hoped the experience would lead to change.

One of my favorite volunteer moments of the year was my time with children at a STEAM event. Science, Technology, Engineering, Arts and Mathematics are the focus of the program emphasizing the need to engage young minds to become future innovators.

My first thought about this 244th experience was why aren't we teaching this already? How do we compete with global education programs that see these as obvious skill sets? Steam is the future, and I was excited to volunteer for the day.

The event was set up in stations and I spent the time building with Knex construction toys. This was an absolute first for me and I think I had as much fun as the children.

I was an observer for a few hours, and it was interesting to watch problem solving when a child played with the toys for the first time. Some children were natural leaders and taught others how to connect the pieces and assemble vehicles, machines and structures. Eventually I was convinced to build with a curious child and her suggestions led to an adorable windmill that stayed on the table for the rest of the afternoon.

STEAM programs are essential and after spending the day teaching and learning I am convinced that every school needs a program like this and not just for a single day.

As the year drew closer to day 365, I escaped to the mountains of Colorado. I learned how to keep bees and collect honey from the hive. I also learned what it means to get a bee in your bonnet. My bee-keeping sister Kathy asked if I was allergic. I think we should have had that conversation before smoking those buzzing honey makers out of their house. I'm very glad to report that I am not allergic.

On day 79 I learned how to tie flies for fishing. I knew that I would make my way out to the mountain and stream filled state to learn how to catch fish with them. On day 313 I learned how to buy and assemble all the equipment necessary to hook the little swimmers and on day 314 I was a successful fly fisherperson. It was the beginning of a beautiful relationship with fishing.

For 120 days I would juggle mom's hospital stay with my personal challenges. For so many reasons those moments felt like the last, but mom didn't want me to quit. She wanted me to finish even if it meant learning to juggle in her dim lit hospital room.

On day 223 I watched as my mother's ashes were placed in their permanent home. I don't know how I survived the day and it's mostly a blur. I stood in the church where I was baptized, received my first communion and grew into a person of faith. My mother was there for all those moments and, as I struggled with the organization of religion, mom was there too. It felt so different to be in this church without her present and my heart ached.

I read from the bible my father gave to me. The words I read are associated with weddings by tradition, but they were most appropriate for my mother's funeral. The reading spoke of patience and kindness, humility and love. I'm summarizing but reading it was more about helping the people in that church come to understand that she was extraordinary and that it is possible for a human being to live as the physical presence of love.

I never expected to say goodbye to my mother so soon. When her urn was locked inside the columbarium everything changed. I couldn't see the granite stone that marked her final place of rest. I couldn't see the point of finishing the day; I wasn't sure how to get through what was left of the year. I questioned everything and I still do.

Mom died on Saturday, April 21st, 2018. Mother's Day was three weeks away. I wasn't prepared to experience her death and a celebration of our first connection. Today as those anniversaries loom, I still fight the urge to call her for tea and to talk about anything.

When I started this adventure, I planned for it to end in the outback of Australia at Uluru. I've read that it is one of the most sacred spaces and I have dreamed of visiting it for years. What a perfect location to end this journey of mind, body and spirit. It didn't happen. The ability to travel was exhausted by medical days, time off for mourning and funerals.

After mom's death I wanted to go to a place we'd talked about visiting, The Lavender farm in Northern Wisconsin. The plan was to spend a day walking among the flowers my mother loved, surrounded by the healing aroma of lavender. I called to make a reservation for a tour. My heart broke when they explained that the final crop had been harvested and their tours ended that same weekend.

I was crushed. I didn't have another plan. My days inched away, and I learned how to play a bagpipe practice cantor that chased the living beings out of my house. I shot a crossbow and climbed to the top of Wallace Monument in Scotland. The end was near, and I still didn't have a big ah ha finale moment.

I had the beginning, an unbelievable middle but somehow, I'd lost focus on how it would end.

Part Three

I Saw This

365 days meant 365 opportunities to see something new. Having open eyes is important when setting out on a year of first-time experiences. When I stop to reflect, I saw all 365 days but some of them were very specific eye-opening firsts.

In 2002 we rescued a scruffy, weary-souled Siberian husky. When I looked at his face, I saw one blue eye and one brown and when my husband David brought him home, I was scared to death. I saw a wild wolf. He howled like a feral beast.

His name was Jake, and he turned out to be a giant gentle creature. He was sweet and smart and loved his forever home. He died the winter of 2016, and I still miss his presence. When I got the opportunity on day 48 to visit a no kill shelter, I was excited, it was because of this no-kill mentality that we adopted our fur baby. The facility I visited had a recent remodel and the puppies and dogs were still at the old facility.

This was divine intervention as I'm certain it prevented me from adopting a new dog. The few hours I spent in the kitty corrals were delightful and I wanted to take a half dozen home. I donated in Jake's name, which put me on the mailing list.

The facility recruits local teens to help with the animals and it's beautiful to witness the tenderness that's exchanged. A few of the young volunteers were kind enough to share their favorite cats with me. It was an emotional experience and I'm fortunate it was a part of my year.

A few days after ground level with furry friends I ascended the peak of my first lakeside tower. My 54th experience was a tour of a lighthouse. It's obvious that I've never been to one, but I had no explanation why I'd waited so long.

The day was dreary which gave the entire visit a romantic feel. My ticket admission included a guided tour and an interesting lesson on the history of lighthouses. I know people who obsess about visiting them and until this adventure I couldn't relate.

I'm not a historian but having the responsibility of keeping that light going, navigating people to their homes is incredibly romantic. Entering the tower was a little frightening. The steel staircase was narrow, and the treads were open. I looked down through as I climbed; it was an exercise in mind over matter, and the romance was dead.

Each level of the lighthouse tower transitioned to a different stairway until I was climbing up a skinny ladder. I imagine the lighthouse keeper was very fit and the view was amazing even as I white-knuckle gripped the hand railing. It would have been the absolute perk of the job.

I understand the excitement about getting to the top, but I was happy to get down and enjoy the rest of the property. This could have been a "saw it" experience if it wasn't for that first time climb to the top. After 54 days I was beginning to see that overcoming fear would be an active part of the year to come.

In 1986 I took an Astronomy class. I was a Sr. in high school, and the instructor was a retired NASA engineer. He had hundreds of stories and led us on an adventure through the darkness of a Texas marsh to view Haley's Comet. It was heart stopping and I still remember the joy I felt when I turned that spectacle of science into focus.

Once in a lifetime experiences aren't always possible and when I heard about the Super Blue Blood Moon that was coming on day 134, I created a plan to see it.

The date, January 31st of 2018, all the reports suggested an early morning viewing to the west. I have a very long driveway, so I set up my camera. I watched the shadow of the earth fall against the moon. It was beautiful.

As the eclipse continued it dropped below the height of my tree line.

I grabbed all my camera equipment, hopped in my car in search of an open area to continue watching. I saw the colors change as I navigated the country road, just as I pulled into a huge parking lot the clouds rolled in to cover the entire event.

I was disappointed and not sure I'd captured the experience on camera. It was frustrating to have this once in a lifetime experience lost in the cover of clouds. I sat for a long time. The weather was mild for a January morning, and I hoped that the clouds would disappear, and I'd get one more glance.

It wasn't meant to be. I did capture a few images and although they might night be super, blue or bloody they are a reminder that nothing is ever perfect.

If there was an experience that made me feel comfortable in my skin, it was my time as a volunteer at Clexacon in Las Vegas. I've been a volunteer for many things, but I've never been involved with a convention that's focused on positive representation of the LGBTQ community in media.

I'm a huge fan of science fiction and followed the TV series Buffy the Vampire Slayer when it aired in the late 90's early 2000's. As a closeted bisexual woman, I was devastated when midway through the sixth season a popular queer character was murdered by gun violence. It was a huge shift from the genre.

You don't kill vampires with guns and the lazy storytelling played right in to the Bury you Gays trope that is common in LGBTQ story telling. Up until recent years queer stories ended in death. In 2016 after too many BYG deaths on TV, the series "the 100" killed off a fan favorite lesbian character with gun violence. Fans were outraged and in response organized a convention to raise awareness and bring an end to the harmful trope.

I'm proud of my time as a volunteer and the opportunity to listen to actresses, writers, artists and show runners express their support and dedication to this call for change.

I had 40 "Saw It" experiences. If you ask what was the most devastating, it was witnessing my mother's therapy treatment.

The first day was an exploration of my weakness and her strength. As the nursing staff worked with casual care I stood behind the concrete wall watching them handle her fragile body.

Two weeks prior technicians made a plastic mask of her head. It was locked over her face to hold her in still while they administered their treatment. The dimples in the frame pinpointed the focus. Watching the machine rotate around her head still haunts me. I don't know why I went in and I've never spoken about how horrible it made me feel to see her so sick.

She was a fighter, an inspiration and on occasion she slept through the process. On this day she was awake and all I wanted to do was stand beside her and hold her hand. She never talked about how it made her feel, and I'd hoped one day we could discuss it. It wasn't meant to be, and I'm haunted by day 146.

Sixty-eight days later my mother died from complications of a common illness. The entire twenty-four hours of this day are a blur, and I look back at my blog for help remembering the details.

She passed away in the early morning, alone in her bed. I like to believe she fell asleep and let her spirit float away in peace. I have no memory of writing my blog post for that day. I sat beside her body and looked out her window. The snow on the ground was melting and I wished I'd brought a bird feeder so she could feel like she was at home.

I had all these thoughts in the moments of denial that followed. I watched them roll the body bag out of her room. I closed my eyes and tried to erase the stain of soiled wheel marks trailing after mom's body down the long hallway of the nursing home. I packed up all the comforts we'd brought in for her care. Tears were heavy and I realized later that I had become her memory keeper. The absence of my mother is enormous, and the loss is the major regret I will carry away from this 365-day experience.

The real challenge for me was to go on.

My first-born graduated from college on day 235. After five long years: a major in Philosophy, Anthropology and History and a certificate in ethics. I sat in the auditorium and watched hundreds of students cross that stage. My pride and joy was near the end and I just wanted to jump from the bleachers and hug her like crazy. If losing my mother created an abundance of sorrow, watching this commencement brought double the volume of joy. It came at a time when so much seemed to be going wrong. A few days later she got the letter of acceptance to study Philosophy in Scotland, a dream becoming reality after so many years of hard work.

In an effort to escape the reminders of my mother's passing I took a trip to Seattle. I had quite a few adventures in the city. I found the courage to ride the elevator to the observation deck of the space needle. It was the very first time I'd ever been to the top of any building like it.

In the spring of 2018, the Space Needle was under construction, and I managed to get a backstage tour. The service elevator took me to the first level, and I was able to walk out on the glass framed viewing deck. My heart was pounding, and the view of the city was amazing. I would love to return to see the completed renovation.

When this year began my plan was loose and I was so cocky about how I'd get through 365 days. Sometimes an adventure fell right into my lap as it did on my 345th day.

While driving home from shopping, I caught something from the corner of my eye. It didn't register at first but when my brain processed the Weiner mobile parked in a lot, I made a frenzied U-turn to get back to the location. One huge life dream comes true. This was "the thing" of my childhood and I wanted to see it up close. I was 10 again. My kids were with me to witness the freak-out.

I was full-on fangirling over a giant orange hotdog on wheels. My son explained the 365-day experience to the attendant, and he let me inside. I couldn't sit in the driver's seat but that didn't matter... I WAS IN!

I got a weenie whistle and a sticker as a souvenir of the experience. I don't eat hot dogs but my kids each had one for me. It was and still is one of my favorite spontaneous 365-day adventures.

I had 40 chances to see my life in a new way. Sometimes we look at the people and places around us but we don't see them. I felt the rhythm as musicians played and walked the halls of quirky museums looking at dreams come to reality.

Did they change me? Some of them did and they opened my eyes to a view of the world that was missing from my soul.

.

Part Four

I Made This

365 days, 365 opportunities to create a mile of messes. On day one I felt like I had time to sort out how to make my new experiences come to life for the people who were following my progress. I learned how to do 105 new things and sometimes they lingered for days in my kitchen, on my counter and in my cupboard.

In an attempt to deal with some pricy mass-produced addictions, I researched food experiments. My day 6 challenge was an adventure to brew kombucha. Prior to this challenge I was purchasing a single bottle of this drink for about $4. After a bit of research, I discovered how simple it is to ferment a never-ending supply. The reality of this process is that it takes a scoby (Symbiotic Culture of Bacteria and Yeast) to grow a scoby, and you need a scoby to brew kombucha. I purchased a bottle of chunky fizzy tea fungus, shaking it to determine if it had as abundant bits left after the commercial filtering process.

I turned that $4 container into months of delicious digestive joy. I've been brewing this drink for over a year and have amassed a huge jar of symbiotic culture. I can't seem to give it away. Everything happens at room temperature in the darkness of my pantry. With little effort I can maintain a steady brew. It's tangy and a bit like vinegar if I'm not careful, so there's no danger that anyone in is sneaking a sip.

Before it began, I thought this yearlong adventure would be exciting. My belief that after the day ended I could move on to something new gave the illusion of simplicity. I had a problem with this concept on day 7 when I made my first batch of paper.

I was only one week into the 365-day experience, and I couldn't stop liquefying my shredded recycle and squeezing it back in to rippled sheets of paper. I spent the next fourteen days finishing my daily adventure so that I could make more paper. I averaged about 10 pieces per day and accumulated an inspiring stack of textured sheets. I intended to make invitations for a woman's day party. That plan disappeared on day 92 when mom's diagnosis turned everything upside down.

I made my first cheesecake at age 49 mostly because I find it disgusting and hoped that mixing it from scratch would help to enhance the flavor. It didn't, even though I bought rich ingredients and used decadent chocolate. I gave it to my husband, and his coworkers enjoyed this edible first and looked forward to future culinary experiences.

As I continued to experiment with mouthwatering creations, I came to respect my taste buds and their instincts, but it didn't prevent me from testing the boundaries. After all, I had 365 days to fill.

I nurtured fungus in the cool damp environment of my basement, and the massive portabellas satisfied an experience that I'd wanted to try for years. I purchased a kit from my local farm that included spores and fertilizer. Yes, I bought a box of fungus and poop.

If that's not an adventure I don't know what is. A few weeks after "the grow" began I went to a goat farm and learned how tricky it is to milk these stinky feisty creatures. Fresh raw goat's milk smells one hundred percent like the barn that they live in and after this olfactory overload I wasn't sure if I could make this milk into the cheese that I wanted to try.

After a bit of research and conversation with the farmer I settled on a ricotta style cheese. It was tasty and the process of curdling goat's milk was simple. I timed the cheese making around the day I would pick my first mushrooms. I made the most delicious portabella steaks smothered in balsamic vinegar and warm goat cheese. It was satisfying and after only a few weeks I felt empowered to keep the culinary adventures going. It was a perfect balance between disgusting and delicious.

On day 55 I learned how simple it is to make candy sprinkles for cakes and ice cream. The real trick is patience and as I pointed out in many of my blog posts, I've never been known for my ability to wait. The result was magical and tasty. A few days later I baked my first Bundt cake. I sprinkled the top with the candy I'd made. It was as if I'd planned the entire thing, perfect.

I was beginning to understand that the mystery behind "creating" wasn't mysterious at all. How would I accomplish a new adventure? I had to let go of expectations, dive in and see what happened.

Perhaps I was good at following directions or just lucky but as the year progressed, I had more success than failure. My day-one list was beginning to dwindle but there were still plenty of unknowns to go. I took aim at all the promises to, "do this one day," in hopes of hitting the target.

"I've always wanted to," became a battle cry as I learned how to spin wool into yarn. I waited for so long, but the truth is I didn't have a single hobby that required the use of yarn. I'm not usually so practical about learning new things, but I'm glad I waited.

I've got 365 days to fill and day 69 felt like the perfect time to twirl a bit of yarn. I used a drop spindle and I'm the first to admit that this looks easier than it is. I should mention that I have an incredible ability to take a wonderful spool of cord, yarn, thread or string and turn it into a jumbled tangled mess. This might also explain my reason for avoiding yarn spinning because one poor drop and that stuff tangles up into an unusable pile. I started over many times until my spindle was full. I knew that day 72 would be the second step in yarn making so I built my own niddy noddy. Don't laugh, this is a thing and it's an ancient one. My crisscross of plastic tubing would hold the twisted wool taught as I submerged the entire thing in water. Soaking and drying fixes the twist and locks it all together. I made an adorable ball of yarn.

I was fortunate that my day 125 egg noodles didn't tangle together in a mound of goo. The instructions were pretty simple and after the mystery vanished noodle making was fun.

My kitchen creation required yolks only, so I used the leftover egg whites to bake meringue cookies the following day. As I added positive food experiments to the year, I'd planned to use all my new delights to make a meal for the people who'd encouraged me along the way. The intention was there but when my mother became ill and lost her battle this plan mirrored my spirit and fell apart.

On October 16th I found a colorful rock in the parking lot at work. It was painted bright yellow and said, "You are my sunshine." Finding that simple rock brought me joy and I set it on the desk planning to plant it somewhere else. My coworker suggested I use it as my 365-day experience. I'd never abandoned decorated rocks before and decided it was a great idea. Because accomplishing a single task in twenty-four hours wasn't enough, I would incorporate a colorful stone into the rest of my year.

I wanted to put a 365-day spin on this experience, so I collected about 100 rocks of my own, painted them with rainbows and left one behind every time I had an experience away from home. I used the #365rockdays on each stone and put up pictures on Instagram. It was a fun idea, and it added a bit of a challenge.

I would smack myself for this later as there were a few times I forgot the rock and had to return to the scene of the adventure. I traveled for the next 300+ days with a box, container and baggie filled with rainbow painted rocks. Thanks Emily.

Those stones became a part of my travel arsenal. If I was on the road, I had a box of rocks. I counted out just enough to cover a short trip to Ohio where I was fortunate enough to spend a few days behind the scenes at their Renaissance Fair.

The bowyer helped me build my own bow, which became the fierce portion of my book cover. It was an educational experience, and I learned about the craftsmanship behind this art. The following day my son taught me how to build and fletch my own arrows.

He is an adventurer and as a homeschooling family we've cut, created and twisted many projects together and until recently my role was teacher. On this adventure he tilted the table and taught me what he'd learned as an apprentice. Our relationship as child and parent evolved into peers. I can't think of anything more fulfilling as a mom.

To keep things in perspective I was spending most of my days with my mother and when I could bring an adventure along with me to the hospital I would. On day 136 I decided to make spring flowers to brighten up her dreary nursing home room.

She was a master gardener and loved mothering her plants. Her spring gardens were beautiful, and she rooted flowers in the grass just to sprinkle color all around her yard. Mom helped me with my paper tulips; maybe she knew that I was trying to get her to use her left hand.

It doesn't matter now but my goal was wellness and bringing spring into her dingy nursing home space. We talked about gardens as her hands spread across the pieces of paper. She watched more than she helped and when we were done, we had two small pails of paper tulips sitting on her windowsill. The colorful bouquet was my hope that winter was coming to an end.

The weather in the spring of 2018 was unpredictable, but I wanted to tap my trees to make Maple syrup. I purchased supplies in October, but the drilling would have to wait until the spring thaw. When the heat of the sun hits the south side of the tree the sap begins to run.

I watched hours of videos and put together storage containers to collect over 30 gallons of liquid gold. Except it isn't gold and I had no idea how much space 30 gallons would require; it was my good fortune that the temperature was cold enough to keep my sap outside. Every shelf of the refrigerator was packed. I collected for about seven days and set up my backyard grill to start the boiling process.

I asked a few questions to local syrup makers and discovered I could boil off my sap using a Nesco cooking pan. (Thank you Heather) This was a game changer. I wouldn't have to sit outside in the cold to watch liquid boil. My house was humid and after 16 hours of continuous bubbling I reduced 30 gallons of sap down to four quarts of delicious maple syrup. My house smelled like pancakes.

If you've ever shopped for real 100% pure maple syrup, you'll notice the price first. I understand why. It's time consuming to make and requires a lot of attention. I want to do it again, but empty nesters don't eat a lot of syrup. I did cook a few pints on day 358 to boil maple sugar treats. Candy making is not a skill I have, and I didn't want to waste a lot of syrup, but the final result was delicious.

Changing tree sap to syrup wasn't my only conversion experience. With the help of my blacksmithing partner/son I had exciting creation experience. Over the course of a few days, he taught me how to use an angle grinder for a stock removal. I cut an old cleaver into a chopping knife. The goal was to create a piece I could use in my kitchen.

On day 77 I made micarta to use as material for the knife handle. He taught me how to weld, and I made a beveling jig to put a cutting edge on that same blade. On day 84 I had a beautiful, finished knife that barely cut paper.

I didn't know how to hone the edge to make it sharp, so my father taught me how to use a whetstone on day 219. We started slow and I watched his weathered hands drag across the well-worn stone. He was more patient than I and after a few hours the blade was complete. I'm proud to say that no blood was shed during this adventure. The knife is beautiful even if it is a bit heavy.

Some might think that knives and making sharp things is like playing with fire; after this year of experiences, I'd have to agree. There is nothing more exciting than watching flames flicker and who hasn't wanted to touch fire? During the 365-day challenge I tangled with fire on a few occasions. I made flaming balls that I could hold in my hands. At a party a few years ago, I watched a friend use them and this was a definite to-do on my list for the year.

A few days after holding my hot balls of fire I experimented with flaming arrows. What was my ultimate plan? I wanted to shoot that flickering stick, using the bow I helped make on day 37, and if my aim was true, I'd ignite a huge bonfire. Creating the flaming arrow was tricky. My first attempt with lighter fluid and string ended with fire in the sky. The entire assembly fell apart midair. I thought about the success of my orange candle on day 122 and decided to soak my cloth in liquefied coconut oil. I wrapped thin wire and the old t-shirt around the arrow shaft and as the oil returned to solid form it held together.

I tested the flame, and it burned for a few minutes before falling apart. I built it again and the launch sent a perfect blaze across the yard and into the target. I never had that bonfire but one day I will, and I'll light it up from halfway across the yard.

Fire, fire everywhere and as the holidays came around and I brought a classic Christmas tune to life when I roasted chestnuts on an open fire, although the idea seemed nostalgic, I didn't acquire a taste for that nut.

I continued to eliminate suggestions from that day-one list of firsts. I made soap and bath bombs, body butter, lip balm and dandelion salve. Each concoction was an experiment with natural ingredients like bee's wax, coconut oil and cocoa butter and I have a supply that will last for quite a while. I used peppermint and lavender both of which create sense memories that remind me of a year filled with victories and defeats.

In mid-January I walked into a stained-glass class thinking I could accomplish this project in a single day. I looked at the pile of templates and decided to make something to brighten mom's dreary hospital room.

On day 124 I accomplished the first step by learning how to cut glass. I loved it and hated it at the same time. I'm happy to say I did not bleed once. A few days later I learned how to clean, snip and grind that glass to join them together like a puzzle. On day 150 I foiled the edge of every piece. It would be over 100 days before I returned to solder this project together. It was no longer a gift, but a reminder. Mom passed away before seeing the final result and my heart wasn't in it to go back. It's a memory of what is lost. I returned to the shop to pick up the finished piece on Mother's Day 2019. The shop owner, Penny, guarded it well.

Day 362 was my mother's 80th birthday and our plan to celebrate together wasn't meant to be. This was almost as difficult as reading at her funeral. I spent the entire day creating something to honor the woman who taught me to be the woman I am. The plan to build a floating lantern was one of the original 113 and became the perfect tribute to mom.

Over the span of the year, I learned how to make all the components I would need to assemble an eco-friendly lantern to float in my pond. The base was a string tied raft of sticks collected in the yard. I made natural glue on day 330 by cooking tree sap into pine pitch. I used soft balsa wood to support my homemade paper panels. The most important element of my lantern was illumination.

On day 122 I learned how to make a candle using an orange peel and coconut oil. I assembled this tiny floating raft and waited for the sun to set. I was impatient but the final result was beautiful. The lantern floated. The mosquitoes were intense as the sun set so I sat in my car and watched it drift across the water. The lamp stayed lit for hours and drifted across the pond for five days. It felt like the perfect farewell to this woman who made me believe I could make it to the end.

As the days grew to weeks and months, I realized that many of these personal firsts were about breaking boundaries created by my fear of failure. I wasn't frightened to make cold brew or candy sprinkles but failing to do it right was a hurdle to overcome. I had no idea how many people were following or reading my daily posts, but I wanted to be successful for them and for myself. I was an experiment. The person who started this adventure was evolving, 24 hours at a time.

Part Five

I Ate This

Food experiences, Challenges, Adventures.

I'm using all three categories because some days the things I ate fell into one or all of them.

On my second day of this year, I was led to an adorable coffee house to have my very first nitrogen infused cold brewed coffee. The truth is I love coffee almost as much as I like beer. The two are delicious and make my taste buds happy.

The most incredible part of my nitro experience was the decadent dark roasted flavor. I didn't anticipate how active this cup of coffee would be and as it rested on the counter it behaved like a fresh poured glass of Dark Irish Guinness Stout. If you haven't had the experience of a draft pour of this brew you should and then place the glasses together and watch. It's amazing. A top-notch drink and I felt like my very first "ate it" adventure was setting a standard that I hoped I could keep.

In the next few hundred days I ate some tasty fruit. During the planning moments of this year, I thought about blending all my food experiences into a lunch or dinner and inviting all my best friends to attend. That never happened but the possibility still exists.

Not all the fruits of the earth are created equal. I learned this on day 12. I had a sticky battle with Jackfruit. I should have spent more time researching this food, lesson learned. Jackfruit is an enormous piece of prickly sticky fruit. Aside from weighing ten pounds it also requires hours of time to clean and prepare for eating. Over half of the inside of the jackfruit isn't edible without tons of cooking and seasoning and time.

I had 24 hours, so I focused on the basics. It makes a horrible "quick" snack. Did I mention sticky? This is ridiculously messy. The piece of fruit that I bought was only a slice of the 10-pound whole and I had no idea when I unwrapped it that it would be like handling glue. After dissecting to find the edible fruit I had to figure out how to wash my hands. As an example, my 20-ounce slice yielded about 2 ounces of edible fruit.

In the end I used acetone to remove most of the tackiness. Consider this, I needed acetone to remove the residue from preparing a piece of fruit. A prediction for my future would lean toward not eating fresh jackfruit again, but the taste is tempting. My suggestion: stay away from processed jackfruit, go with the fresh cut, but always, always, always wear a pair of gloves.

I tried star fruit, dragon fruit, plantain, prickly pear, guava, persimmon and kumquats. They each were unique and although most were a great one-time experience, I'm not sure they were life changing. They might make an interesting desert salad.

In the days after mom went into the hospital I had to work twice as hard to accomplish an experience. Food challenges were an uncomplicated choice. I regret the decision I made on day 103. It was a taste bud experience that I will never forget. My mother had invasive surgery as part of her treatment. For many days after she found nourishment through a nasal feeding tube. It was horrible but mom never had to taste the Osmolite pumping through that little hose. I'm not sure why I thought it would be a great idea to drink it, perhaps it was a culmination of long days of hospital monotony, but I did it. I made a YouTube video documenting every before and after gag-worthy second of this terrible decision.

The teaching moment: "tube" food is not mouth food and I should've left it alone. The best part of the experience was the giggling joy. We didn't have enough during our days in the ICU, but mom laughed and so did my father and that was worth every drop.

Throughout my 365 days I chose to try and eat fifty-two different

s. One of the most intriguing "I ate it" experiences was on day 130 when I talked my family in to eating magic berry tablets. This was a crime against food and almost tragic in that we put together an interesting combination of items with extreme flavor differences.

What I didn't consider was how all of that would affect my stomach after it left my mouth. If you aren't familiar with the magic berry it is a fruit that changes the way food tastes. Spicy tastes sweet, sour tastes salty and everything you expect is altered when it hits your tongue. It was an experimental experience to share with my family but the burning in my stomach took most of the day to fade.

I had another opportunity to bombard my taste buds on day 172 at the local VFW's wild game night. It sounds Midwestern and I almost can't believe I attended, but I did. I was a vegetarian for fifteen years and although most people in this area fill their freezers with seasonal wild game, I was not raised in a family that did. We ate chicken and beef and pork.

Why did I go to wild game night at the VFW? I'd never done it before, and I discovered that there was wisdom in that. The wall of the banquet room was lined with tables covered with crockpots, baking dishes and plastic ware. The containers were loaded with meats I've never wanted to eat, ever. Most of it tasted like chicken or pork, which was fine, but the meats that were the most exotic left me racing for the garbage can.

What's the lesson in wild game night? Just because it is meat doesn't mean that I should eat it. I'm going to stick with what I know, vegetarianism with a sprinkle of fish, chicken and occasional beef.

When I started this challenge, it was fun and games. I was cocky enough to believe I could do this and have some fun stories to share when I turned 50. How much could a 24-hour adventure change me? I underestimated how the collection of 365 of them would redefine who I am.

On the 214th day my mother passed away. I didn't know how to continue after that morning. I was certain I should abandon this challenge and focus on mourning her.

I spent my silent moments soul-searching, contemplating walking away from what I'd already done. I couldn't shake the idea that mom would hate if I gave up, especially because of her death. Maybe it was her voice in my head reminding me that I'd come so far. I had 213 amazing encounters with self-discovery. I decided I had to finish what I'd started, for myself and for her.

The ten days after her death were beyond challenging. I was trying to eulogize this beautiful being and although it was something I'd never done before it was also extremely private, and I felt like a stone tumbling down a mountain out of control.

I ate a lot of things the week of my mother's funeral mostly because it was easy to fit into the reality I was living. My journey almost ended on day 224. It was late, family was gathered, and we were reminiscing in my father's garage when I realized I hadn't accomplished a first-time experience. In truth I was moving through most of the days one minute at a time and for some reason this day was the one that almost brought the project to an end.

I ate an ant. It was a desperate choice made at the last minute to fulfill the obligation of a first-time experience. I would never do it again and I feel like this might have been a poor decision because that little sucker came from the floor and I don't want to think about where it might have been. To make it easier to swallow I covered it in chocolate. I'm not sure how that was supposed to help and to this day I regret that cocoa covered ant.

When I started planning the edible experiences mom and I were going to do many of them, or at least research them, together. A few of my "I ate it" adventures took place in the early morning hours, sometimes before 6am.

It was a huge relief when I finished before leaving for the hospital. After completing the task, I knew there was a blog post in my future and that would loom for the rest of the day. Eating from the backyard was going to be amazing. Mom was a master gardener and playing with green stuff was going to be fun when winter turned to spring. After day 92, when mom went into the hospital I was on my own.

There's not much to eat in my backyard during winter, so the deliciousness was on hold for quite a while. I learned a bit about harvesting dandelions and discovered that this weed happens to have amazing healing elements and on day 241 I dug up the roots, minced them and drank the tea. It tasted like dirt, which ultimately many of my backyard treats would.

I ate cactus pads picked fresh in the Colorado Desert and brewed tea from the needles of three varieties of evergreen tree. The two experiences were enlightening and as much as I learned what to pick and how to clean and prepare them; both were time consuming and came with very serious concerns.

Cactus pads are delicious and as I picked them, I wondered if the flavor was connected to the freshness. They are salty and tangy and if I make guacamole, they would be a great flavor to add. The real warning comes when cleaning off the tiny stickers. They were almost impossible to see. I used a knife to peel away the larger needles but getting all the very fine hair-like bits was scary. Everything I read had a warning, sometimes in bold print and I took them seriously. I made it through without much damage to my hands.

If I learned anything on this journey, when gloves are recommended, wear them. Another warning to heed is the toxicity of evergreen needles. As I researched, I was careful to pick from trees that I could identify without doubt. I'll add that any time I chose to eat from nature I selected situations that gave me ample opportunity to investigate. The key was research and education. That is my warning about eating anything that grows in the wild.

Day 282 was anything but wild when I made the boiled combination of sweetened hops and barley, called wort. This is step one in the process of home brewed beer. Christina was an enthusiastic teacher and guide through this experiment in frothy drink making. If I'm being honest this was mostly play and a little work. Watching liquid boil and setting a timer was simple. The concoction fermented for a few weeks, and she taught me how to sterilize and bottle this brew. On day 341 we popped the top and had a sample. It was delicious and I am grateful for the shared experience.

On day 299 I landed in the mountains of Colorado. I learned throughout the 365 days that travel was stressful, unpredictable and challenging to plan. I drove with my family to a beautiful resort and along the way I remembered an ad at the airport for canned oxygen. Why? Why not!

The thing about this product is that it is literally a can of air. I paid a ridiculous amount of money to spray air into my face. I wasn't mountain climbing or exerting energy that would require the subsidy but there I was, sitting by a bubbling stream in the cleanest freshest mountain environment, breathing in canned oxygen. I made a YouTube video, and it still makes me laugh.

Canned air wasn't a high or low but If I had to pick a number one worst thing I ate in my 365 days, I would say it was acorn bread. I researched this for a few days and thought I was changing the flavor by boiling the nuts down to almost clear liquid. I was wrong in every sense of the word. I know they're edible. I know that they are high in protein and in a survival situation I could live off them but it's one of the most horrible things I've ever had in my mouth.

The lingering bitter dry cardboard flavor was ridiculous and made me leery of any more backyard treats. In fact, it was my last foraging food, and I'll admit that's a good thing because I had so many wonderful experiences experimenting with the outdoors that I'm glad I didn't miss them because of a nasty acorn.

I knew I'd have some fun food adventures throughout the year, but I'd hoped to share more of them with my mother. On my visit to Scotland, I couldn't help but think of her each time I walked through the tea section in every store. I purchased a box of Thistle tea. This is the official plant of the country of Scotland and as I followed the directions for steeping this drink, I got that earthy dirt feeling all over again. It definitely falls in the "medicinal" drink category. This was my last "I ate it" adventure and it feels perfect that tea would be the final choice.

I'll take away one thing from my fifty-two "I ate it" adventures and it's this; try it once. Mom always said," you can't judge it unless you've tried it." She was right and I did it fifty-two times. Not always a failure, not always a success. Still quite a bit like life.

Part Six

Bottom & Top

I had a few followers during the year. Some on social media, some through my website but many in my real world. As the experimental experiences piled up, questions followed. What was your favorite adventure? What would you never do again? What was the funniest and what was the worst?

The worst moment is the easiest to answer and not a surprise to anyone making it to the final pages of this book. Death is solitary but it takes everyone you love along. If I have a reflection on death from my 365 days, it is this: we don't get anything back. When the moment is gone, it's for always. Be alive right now and find just one whisper of joy. For many days this uncomplicated idea felt impossible.

One experience that I can't believe I paid for was threading my face. Yes, I said my face. It started out as an eyebrow shaping experience. Those dark hairs grow wild I'll admit but I'm also not vain and only pluck the crazy strays. I must have had a million of them because when my head rested against the beautician's chair I was relaxed.

I had no idea it was going to be the torture it was and after a few minutes on my brow the stylist asked about the rest of my hairy features. I was already crying in the chair why not thread it all. So stupid! It was not pleasant, and my eyes were tearing hours after. This was a one-time occurrence, one hundred percent. Vanity really does come at a price.

My favorite experience was also a day of complete satisfaction... after I thawed out. Doing the polar plunge, in -2 degrees, - 24 wind-chill, made anything feel possible. Standing on that frozen beach, watching and waiting, I'd almost lost the courage. I regret nothing. I feel a sense of accomplishment unmatched by the other 364 experiences, and I have no regrets.

My favorite adventure was the very last. I didn't expect it would be but when I take the time to reflect, I realized on that day how precious our minutes on this planet are.

I had already decided that Australia's Uluru wasn't possible and after discovering the Lavender fields were closed, I searched through the list of experiences I'd created the weeks before the challenge had begun. I called ahead for reservations. My 365th day ended so much like my very first, just me and the simple experience of stand-up paddle boarding.

I was sad at first. I wanted something big. How could this be it? The instructor was funny, kind and patient as he showed me every simple skill required to stay above water. I didn't want to get wet. I hate getting wet. He confiscated my phone, which also held my camera, and I worried about documenting the last adventure. He took pictures of me as I floated away, and I spent the next few hours on a lake I've only ever ice fished on.

It was quiet on this September afternoon and that was the real gift. Lake Geneva is a summer lake. It's the place for sport boating and large weekend crowds. On the 19th of September 2018 the waters were quiet, and the boats were gone from the lake. The water was crystal clear, and the action underneath was the real distraction. If I had my camera I would have flipped over in an instant. I'm happy to say that my feet got wet and my knees too, but I never went over.

I felt an overwhelming sense of gratitude floating across that lake. I giggled as I remembered the crazy year, and I cried when the reality of completion hit me. I'd done it. Up to the last day I wasn't sure that I could.

In 365 days: I wrote 365 blog posts containing 106,500 words. I read 10 books. I did 158 new things. I saw 40 new places. I made 105 new creations. I ate 52 new foods. I left behind 125 painted rockdays rocks. I did 365 minutes of yoga plank pose. I traveled 32,834 national and international miles. I spent $5,036.00. What a year.

Ready for a Challenge?

You've just made it through the summary of my year, and you think you've got what it takes? Here are a few suggestions:

1. Get organized
2. Plan your adventures- create a list of more than half of your experiences. You'll have more fun.
3. Keep a diary- write it all down, take tons of pictures because when it's over you'll be surprised at all the details you've forgotten.
4. Save those receipts
5. Take a friend along for the ride- it's impossible to do this alone and it's not as much fun.
6. Don't procrastinate- get it done in 24 hours and move on
7. Wear gloves.

Part Seven

I Never Saw It Coming

How is it possible that my intention for fun, with a side order of personal growth, would become my emotional salvation? Is it possible to love something and hate it at the same time?

I committed to this journey before sorting out how I would accomplish it. My plan was loose, super loose and cocky. Even after a few weeks I thought I'd set myself up to fail.

How is it possible for me to do 365 new things, blog about it and sometimes make a YouTube video to summarize the experience? When I stopped to think about it as a whole, panic set in. This was a commitment, and the idea of failure was frightening.

It never stopped scaring me and that was great motivation. It didn't take long to understand what one-day at a time meant. I had to be present for a single adventure every twenty-four hours. It sounds easy.

Have you ever done something every day for a year? It became a focused practice and when I reeled in the distractions and respected this idea the adventures were liberating. Not all 365 days changed my life, and I expected that, but some were significant.

The one experience I did think about while making this plan was losing someone I love. It was my biggest fear and when my mother was hospitalized on day 91 everything I knew about life, love and myself, turned upside down. I have a thousand thoughts about what came but I know with certainty that having this challenge in place saved my life.

I had an extraordinary relationship with my mother. We were kindred spirits, and I cherished our conversations over cookies and tea. For her eulogy I wrote, "To know her, was to be face to face with an angel on earth." I understand that she wasn't perfect to everyone, but she was to me. She was hospitalized late in the evening on day 91.

In a strange twist of fate, my personal first was with the Lake Geneva Fire Department. I was exhausted when my father called to tell me mom was acting strange. I rode with her in the ambulance to the Hospital. When the rest of my family arrived, we waited. This was our first night of many. We had no idea. We didn't get answers, but the initial thought was a simple infection.

They ran tests through the night and because we didn't know if she'd fallen, they did a head and neck scan. As the sun was rising, I went home to get a few hours of sleep and returned to the hospital on day 92 as the nurses were wheeling her to surgery. The scans of mom's head had shadows and the surgeon explained that a tumor was invading her brain.

The words were coming out of his mouth, but they were impossible to understand. The conversation happened in slow motion, and the memory is a split-second snapshot taken by my soul. My mother had an incredible mind, how could it be in jeopardy?

If any part of my mother was strong and fit it was her brain. She fed it with music, words, puzzles, books and media of every kind. She spent much of her senior life staying mentally sharp after watching her own mother suffer through dementia. Her greatest fear was losing herself inside her own body.

I remember standing in the hallway and hearing two words, tumor and cancer. In order to understand if this cluster of cells was malignant or benign, they had to open her skull.

Glioblastoma Multiforme (GBM), she had 22 staples to close the incision that looked wicked and tough. During surgery they removed a huge part of her brain. We didn't know if she was going to be herself when she opened her eyes and what or who she would remember.

I considered abandoning this year of firsts. It felt selfish. I wanted to spend every moment with mom, and I couldn't imagine how I might make an adventure out of being in a hospital intensive care unit. The nurses taking care of her were gentle and loving almost to the point that it hurt my heart.

On day 93 they taught me about the monitors and machines keeping my mother alive. I learned details I never wanted to know about tumors, craniotomies and rates of survival. The surgeon shared his statistics.

Mom's beautiful soul in the hospital room was reduced to a number for his medical journal. I still see these moments in my sleep. I'm not sure if they will ever go away. I was alone with mom often, listening to alarms and buzzers hoping that her ICP (intracranial pressure) numbers would stay in the single digits. Until she woke up, pressure in her skull was the focus.

My mom opened her eyes forty-eight hours after surgery, and I stayed beside her during those long days. If I was going to continue my challenge, I had to get creative to stay on track. I brought in three fuzzy fake color-changing snowballs. Standing beside my mother's ICU bed I learned how to shuffle three glowing balls from hand to hand.

Just to be very clear I'll never have a career as a juggler. The skill was gone as quick as it was discovered. Nothing lasts forever but my mother laughed and that was a win mingled in among so many losses. She was in intensive care for eleven days and being with her was a mixed blessing of medical procedures and honest tender moments.

I was aware that sitting with this inspirational human being was a privilege. I don't regret a single moment we had; only the circumstances that brought us there. Many mornings I woke up early so I could accomplish an adventure and blog about it while my mother was napping.

We had incredible conversations about the little pieces that made us who we are and most days she would ask the plan for my next adventure. I'd read the blog, and her cheerleading kept me motivated to face my fears and meet another daily goal.

We celebrated Christmas in the hospital, a first I never wanted. I put a star on the top of mom's IV stand and when I left her that evening Angel was the nurse on duty. There was comfort in that, and it felt like a gift. In all the loss and fear we still managed to find moments to make more memories.

December 28th, my 100th day and it was a long one. Most of the family was present and mom was entertaining us with crossword answers long after we'd read the clues. We sang to her and as the day came to an end I asked if I could read a story before she went to sleep.

The monitor alarms were beeping and most of the family had gone home. It was intimate and while I read, I could feel a heart-breaking change. The parent child relationship changed that night. I could feel her give way for me to take her care in my hands. When I finished the story, we were both in tears. I never loved her more than in that moment; no walls, no barriers just the perfect exchange of tenderness and understanding.

We celebrated the New Year with the faint sound of a noisemaker horn. I don't know why breathing was such a struggle for mom, but we chanted and cheered as her tiny puffs of air generated a feeble celebratory squeak.

The feeding tube came out and while mom was relearning the simple task of swallowing, I ripped an apple in half with my bare hands. Healing was slow but mom was getting stronger, and each step forward gave us hope. We were going to make it through, get out of this medical nightmare and have more adventures in the real world.

That never happened. Mom and I took turns accomplishing a daily task. Most of hers were not firsts. Her left side had deficits, so she muscled through therapy. It was depressing and the exhaustion of putting on a happy face took a toll.

My mother never went back to the home she loved. She never

walked again and only regained use of her left side for a few weeks. I worked very hard to stay hopeful and when I entered her room every morning my goal was to hear her voice and make sure she knew she was loved.

People have asked me what was my favorite, or funniest or most inspiring experience. Every day after the 92nd was the most terrible, challenging, heartbreaking and redefining of my life.

My cocky quest for personal growth, self-experimentation and adventure evolved into something bigger. Watching my mother fight cancer changed everything. We don't know what's coming tomorrow or that it even will. I witnessed my hero wither away and every evening as I crawled into my own bed I fought this new reality. I've said that having this challenge saved me; I'm not cavalier about that statement. Fighting cancer with her gave me a purpose beyond myself and then suddenly her life was over. I wasn't ready but I was never going to be.

I met a lot of professional caregivers during this time. Some offered hope and wisdom from their years of experience. In early April my mom's health started to decline. After a difficult day, I had a conversation with my mother's nurse, Liza.

We talked about loss as she moved around the room. She shared her feelings about being left behind and the void created by death. I'm a mother of two grown children. I understand how our roles change from parent to peer. That conversation, in the dim-lit room became part of me. Her time and wisdom helped me with my grief and gave me permission to mourn on my own terms.

I didn't want to watch my mother die. I wanted her to be out in the world with me conquering our fears and demolishing firsts. I cried every morning on my drive to her rehab facility. I carried two paper calendars everywhere I went. I kept detailed notes about my mother's care, at the same time tracking my 365-day progress. I wanted her to have privacy and tried not to reveal specifics about the decline in her recovery.

There was no dignity in the way she passed. Cancer is vicious and leaves scars on the souls of the family left behind. For the first few weeks after her death, I had to force myself to remember her beautiful spirit huddled over the garden flowers she loved.

On my 214th day, at 4:am I got the call that broke my soul. By voicemail I was told that mom passed away in her sleep. I sat in the darkness of my bedroom. I listened to my breath. The fight ended. As I drove to her rehab center, I wished for this to be a mistake.

I wanted that daytime drama moment where the doctors got it wrong. They didn't, I wouldn't, and it wasn't. I sat in her room staring at the lifeless body in her bed and in that moment nothing mattered. I wanted to climb in the bed beside her and die. I will fight that darkness for the rest of my life.

Until mom's hospitalization I had no idea how many of my thoughts were about her. We had thousands of things in common, and I loved being her student as much as I loved being her teacher. All of that was over. I had 151 days left in my year.

I quit on my way to the shower after boxing up my mother's nursing home room.

I quit on my way from the funeral home after kissing my mom's body for the last time.

My heart wasn't in it anymore. I was done. My body was exhausted and numb, but I could hear mom telling me not to give up. Having a purpose and focusing on the final daily adventures kept me from crawling into the tunnel of depression to hide from my life without her.

I work every single day to stay. Her nursing home room had a tall pine tree outside the window and it's the final picture I have from the place she spent her last days. I am still disoriented by her death and the void she left behind.

How could I continue this challenge and manage all the things to be done? I spent the next weeks in my parent's home putting mom's unfinished dreams into boxes. She was talented and curious, and I discovered that she had enough craft and gardening supplies to fill two lifetimes.

She sacrificed for her family. She paid attention and I never understood how much she saw. She listened but more important than anything she heard. I vowed to be more like her: to be still, not passive, and hear what people have to say. I want to honor her with love and by seeing the humanity in all of us.

Getting out of bed in the month of May was a struggle. Having 365 days of purpose motivated me to move. The darkness of depression lingered as I forced a smile on my face. I'm not sure how I did it, perhaps it was her life force guiding me from the grave, but I'd decided that finishing this year of challenges was the best way to honor mom. I missed her cheerleading. Every week, up until the last day of my adventures I would visit the cemetery and read my blogs. I'm not sure why but it felt right.

Succeeding was the real beginning. I can't dismiss all the people who helped me get to day 365, but none of them could fill the massive space. That void mingles with my success. Depression is something I've fought since I was a young woman, and it was an unexpected hitchhiker on my daily experiences. I wanted more, I still want more and reconciling the impossibility will be a one-day at a time challenge for the rest of my life.

When I say that having this quest saved me what I really mean is that purpose got me through. Learning how to juggle three balls wasn't going to change my life but watching my mom laugh with me at my failures fueled me to continue. The daily drive to the hospital was solitary and I stocked the front seat with tissues so that my sleeves would be dry when I wrapped my arms around my mother. I hugged her every chance I could, and we established a routine of body massages, manicures and pedicures.

Caring for her was a privilege. I left my job. My husband and children supported every effort to make mom feel human. I learned how to blend body butter so that I could combine it with cancer fighting essential oils. I'll never be able to use lemongrass without crying.

Caring for someone so vulnerable isn't easy but as each day turned to weeks and months, I learned how to be present when it mattered. I wish she was here for the celebration, but I know that the spirit of my biggest cheerleader is beside me and I hope that every adventure honored the woman who taught me what strength is. She is my Wonder Woman; my inspiration and I am grateful.

So, what was the point? I asked myself this question many times. Did facials and pedicures change the world? For me they didn't but the time I spent with others did. Every morning I woke up with a purpose. Sometimes it was a burden but often it was a quest. I lost my way on a few excursions and when I look back at the year, I'm grateful that this personal journey was in place to get me through the desperate moments.

I never expected to watch my mother fade from cancer. I never wanted to write a eulogy or take my mother's ashes on one final road trip. I'm also grateful that I was keeping my daily blog through all those months. I have fuzzy memories of many of my personal challenges because mother was my life.

It's difficult to look back on the year and celebrate my personal growth. I understand humility and patience on a different level. The tears come and it's unbearable to know that she didn't get to celebrate the victory with me. As I write this story the cloud of death lingers over the accomplishment, and my truth is that success came with a price. It's selfish and I won't apologize for missing my mother and feeling cheated by her absence.

Sorting through every adventure of my 365 days I know in my heart that I would change just one.

Part Eight

365 Days
365 Blog Posts

I managed to complete 365 personal firsts in 365 days while being a mother, daughter, sister and friend. I watched cancer kill and I found purpose in the darkness of depression. I did that. I believed I could, one day at a time. This is my blog. This is the personal archive of one year of my life. For better or for worse this is the diary of my 49th year on this earth.

As the challenge progressed, I learned that some adventures required details and additional formats to tell the story. My YouTube videos are linked through QR codes. Please visit my channel and watch some of my adventures. Day 261 is particularly hilarious. As a writer this is a once in a lifetime journey. As a reader I hope you feel inspired.

Day 1 of 365 – I Read It   September 20, 2017

    Day one seemed like a perfect opportunity to crack open a bottle of something I've never sipped and start my 365-day journey with a BANG! The problem is that's not the real me. I love to celebrate but I'm not turning 21.

    My life isn't about losing myself in the buzz of intoxication; it's about finding myself in the experiences around me. So, to set the tone for the next year I decided to read a book that everyone has been telling me to read. In fact, I've had the book for over a month without understanding why I put off reading it. I suppose it was the universe sending a message to my subconscious self. I'm glad I was listening even if I didn't know I was.

    As I opened the book this morning everything became clear. This was the perfect choice for day one. This "New York Times Bestseller" is spirit altering and every person who said the title to me is a perfect friend to my soul. It was as though the million-piece puzzle I've been fitting together my whole adult life, finally came to perfect fruition.

    The beautiful poetic gem, "Milk and Honey by Rupi Kaur" is the swirling breeze keeping my parachute high in the sky. If you haven't read it yet you should. Kaur opens her very soul in this brilliantly choreographed collection of poetry. She shares her darkness and her light and the long journey between the two. I know that I'm late to this show, but I'm changed. I'm enlightened and I'm also aware of the bravery it takes to tell your truth with words and pictures. Happy day 1. I hope you'll return for day 2. Love & Light

Day 2 of 365– I Ate It   September 21, 2017

Day 2 was a coffee experience. There are some things you just must do to understand how they are different from what you've tried before. It's pretty simple. Today my co-worker and friend took me for a cup of coffee. She's been going on and on for months about how amazing this coffee experience is.

Anyone who knows me has witnessed my love for coffee and especially dark delicious brews. So, I was excited to try this Nitro infused drink. I'm sure some of you will say that's old news but for, me not so much.

We went to this cool Bike shop/coffee house called Avant. Interesting enough the building has a smooth transition from cycle shop to cafe. As I was taking in the store my friend was already at the counter ordering exactly what she wanted me to drink. I was just along to consume it.

The pour was not disappointing. It's actually very similar to the way Guinness beer is dispensed in a pub. It interacts with the cup like a living being. If you haven't tried either of these drinks poured into a glass, you really must. She was right about the nitro experience. I'm so excited to have a non-alcoholic flavor that is similar to one of my favorite beers. I'm certain that I'll be back to enjoy a few more nitro-brews. This isn't a commercial for Avant, but if you're in the Lake Geneva, WI area you should stop in and check it out. Emily, you were spot on girl! Thanks for paying attention and for keeping me on the dark side when it comes to coffee. Love & Light

Day 3 of 365- I Did It   September 22, 2017

Today's adventure included ink and a very special pen. Shortly before my son left to travel for the year, he bought me a gift for my birthday, a blown glass pen. It came with love, and he picked my favorite color purple for the handle. He didn't know but I've always wanted one and I was so excited when he gave it to me. He asked me if I needed someone to teach me how to use it. I told him that it was going to be one of my 365-day adventure experiences. I was thinking that I would do this further into the year, but I've got some great plans for this writing instrument. When I came home from yoga this morning, I set myself up to experiment with this beautiful pen. I'll explain that when we home schooled we played around making pens from turkey feathers and tried writing, so the ink that we have is quite old and I was surprised the jars were so empty. I made a little video, and you can enjoy that. Hope you enjoy day 3. Love & Light

She Believed She Could

Day 4 of 365- I Did It September 23, 2017

It's only the 4th day and it feels like it went on forever. I had different plans for the 4th day. You'll find out tomorrow what they were. Instead, I spent my morning doing something I rarely ever do.

Seriously! Today I spent hours shopping for a dress. For those of you who know me well you understand how horrible the thought of this task is for me, and worse, I did it without a "wingman." I solo-shopped for a dress today and I actually found one. That was only the beginning. After wasting hours on a piece of clothing I'm probably never wearing again. (Wait till you see it, it's cute... and I can't even believe I said that.) I realized that my 4-year-old Teva sandals weren't going to match this fabulous dress.

Yep! Shoe shopping. If you're Jimmy Rogan you'll know I like my shoes but I'm a sporty gal and they usually say Teva, Merrell or Asics on the box. Not today! Today I perused the most feminine of feminine isles ever experienced and lived to tell the tale.

I'm going to pause for a minute because I know some of you are thinking about my wedding. Yes, that was a frilly, lacey and pretty puffed sleeve experience. I will remind some of you that it took a village to make that happen. I remember lunches and many delicious cappuccinos. No shoe shopping happened for me; I wore wrestling shoes and kneepads. Never forget the kneepads at a catholic wedding mass. I have pictures but the Internet doesn't get those.

Back to my fabulous adventure, after another hour testing out the wobble factor of every pair of black shoes the chick-power isle had, I found something too tight but not so terrible that I couldn't navigate about a mile and a half of walking. Yes, I calculated carefully the distance I might need to travel based on parking lot size, arrival time and two trips to the ladies room. I "mathed" my way to victory with only minor pinky toe pain. Being a chick for a formal event just isn't my thing.

I'm sure you're all wondering what the event was. My fabulous life mate and partner in mischief volunteered for us to attend a fundraising dinner. Yes, I know I'm not a newbie to those, but this event had a special guest who I've never met before.

    I'm not a sport fanatic but it was cool to meet Evander Holyfield and hear him tell his story. The event was a benefit to celebrate the 25th Anniversary of the Boys & Girls club of Kenosha. I know the picture isn't that great but there was a very big bald head bobbing back and forth in front of us all night. Mr. Holyfield spoke about his childhood and how the Boys club organization was essential to his success. His story isn't unique, but it is still important to share. His most poignant thought, when you achieve and grow it is vital to return and give back to the people and places that got you there. It sounds simple but essentially it is that voice that guides us to do good deeds and remember where you came from. Mr. Holyfield spoke about hard work, and he even quit boxing as a child because he didn't like to lose. No one really does but sportsmanship and the support of adults around you teaches us that there are more defeats than victories in life.

    I was definitely surprised by this evening. I learned a bit about myself and a lot about giving back to those who helped you on your journey. Thank you, day 4. It was wonderful. Love & Light

Day 5 of 365- I Did It September 24, 2017

Day five and the damage caused by a deer. A few weeks ago, my daughter hit a deer. We are not new to the damage of hitting them and after the incident every member of our household can now share the terror of striking an animal that can ripple steel like a sardine can. Essentially that is what my child drives, a sardine can on wheels.

That's not the 365-day adventure. After hitting the deer, we had a little damage left behind. Most of it was cosmetic and because the car was only going 40 miles per hour, we just have to repair lights. This is new for me. I can change a bulb in most cars but taking the front end apart to get to one single screw? I'm so excited. I spent a few minutes studying how all of this was going to come apart so that when it had to go back together there would not be extra pieces. Sounds easy, right?

So, with freshly painted fingernails from my adventure yesterday, I dove into this challenge at 6am this morning. Yep, I've got a 10:30 yoga class and my kid needs to drive this sucker to work today. I have to admit that I expected there to be problems. It's a repair job and there are going to be issues. I didn't have to worry about the frame. I asked a skilled person to check that. I didn't want to pay someone to fix these lights. How hard could it really be? I did a bit of shopping on the Internet and the lights arrived in time for me to get the work done on Saturday. Perfect timing because that's when my kid comes home to visit me. Love that kid!

You can watch the short video I made, and I didn't have a cameraperson, but you'll get the general idea. I was finished just before 8:00am and didn't swear one time. I'm calling this a success since everything was working when my kid drove away this morning. Day 5 challenge went well, and I really don't understand how large handed people can be mechanics. RESPECT! Love & Light

Day 6 of 365- I Made It   September 25, 2017

Growing SCOBY goo. There is this most delicious drink that I discovered on the island of Maui a few years ago. I think it's delicious, but some people think it's like drinking vinegar. Sometimes it does and that depends on how this drink is made. Kombucha is fermented black tea. When I say fermented, I mean this is tea that you make and then you add sugars and let it fester in a dark place for a few weeks. Yep, that's the deliciousness that is Kombucha.

I estimate that I've spent hundreds of dollars enjoying this beverage. Maybe that's not much to some but as tea drinking goes perhaps, I could just make it myself. Then someone says, "fungus juice" and I'm questioning the entire deliciousness factor. In order to create kombucha you mush first grow a beautiful patty of SCOBY.

This glorious living creation is <u>S</u>ymbiotic <u>C</u>ulture <u>O</u>f <u>B</u>acteria and <u>Y</u>east, SCOBY. I just love the symbiotic culture. It sounds exactly right. On day 6 of my 365 days of adventure I set out to grow my own SCOBY. How hard can it be? I sterilized my kitchen with vinegar and proceeded to boil up some super sweet black tea. It seems pretty easy, and the hardest part so far has been waiting for everything to come to room temperature so I can mix it all together.

All my research suggests that I use Kombucha to make my SCOBY. It seems like a rule breaker but as I research most people either buy their SCOBY grown or they fester their own from a warm bottle of this fermented brew. So basically, it takes a SCOBY to grow a SCOBY. This feels like a chicken/egg game and I'm not going to play. I bought the fuzziest bottle of Kombucha I could find and mixed it all at room temperature. If you stop by to see me, you can check my pantry.

I've got SCOBY brewing in there. I'll update you in a few weeks to let you know what's growing in my in the dark corners. If you want to learn more about Kombucha and SCOBY and the benefits of drinking it, use GOOGLE. I'm not going to put links to another site because I don't want to endorse any info that you might disagree with. I'm just sharing my journey. Thanks for stopping in. Day 6 seems a little gross, but this is going to be so good! Love & Light

Day 7 of 365- I Made It   September 26, 2017

Purpose in paper... Have you ever walked through the journal aisle of a bookstore? I have so many times and as terrible as I am at keeping a journal, I can't help but adore the unlimited styles and designs.

I've made a few in my days as an artist. I've hand-stitched paper to leather and created a cord to wrap around to give it that feel of ancient times. I don't know, maybe it's just me and my quirky ways. What I know with certainty is that I've always loved the look and the feel of hand pressed paper journals. Perhaps what fascinated me the most is the paper in the journal itself. I have always wanted to know how it's made.

Day 7 became my paper making day. I started out pretty early since I have a very full plate on this Tuesday. I'd call this adventure slightly messy, incredibly fun and a total success. Believe it or not I made some freaking cool pieces of paper. I'm pretty excited to share the video and a few pictures that I've taken.

It's 3pm and the pages are mostly dry and I'm in love with this process. I think it might be my new addiction. You will probably see this paper show up in a future challenge adventure. A few things I found as I was making pulp. White paper isn't always white when you pulverize it in water. My second attempt has a very blue tint to it. Also, any ink in the paper is going to come out even very subtle markings on the inside of an envelope.

I repurposed envelopes for this, and I didn't pay attention to the lines and I'm pretty sure that's where the color comes from. I'm going to shred paper bags into the next batch and see what happens. This was a great adventure. Day seven was a pretty good one. Love & Light

Day 8 of 365- I Made It September 27, 2017

  Let them eat Cheesecake. I had a couple of things planned for this day. One of them didn't happen yet so I'm saving it for another day when I know more. So far, I've had great backups and on the eighth day my plan was to bake my first cheesecake.

  I'll admit that I really don't like cheesecake, which is why I've never made one. It'll work as a challenge but not really much of an adventure. The ingredients for this were pretty basic, cheese, chocolate, eggs and sugar. I had to do chocolate because there's no other reason to have sweets. Opinion not fact but I'm saying it. The recipe came from the Internet, and I picked it because every requirement for chocolate was dark and remember that's how I roll! The recipe wasn't terribly complicated, and I've made thousands of cookies so I can follow directions when it comes to baking.

  My first problem, not finding chocolate graham crackers, so I mashed up regular and dumped cocoa powder in. I figured it would be about the same. I guess we will see. My second problem was not being able to find my round cake pan. This is why you will see parchment lining the glass pan and it's rectangle not round. Maybe I should have waited until I had the pan, but everything was at room temperature ready to go. So, you will see my amazing first cheesecake is not round. Once I made my decision to go ahead it all came together pretty easy. What you won't see in the pictures is the chocolate on my phone because the tripod fell over and made a bit of a mess.

  Nowhere in the instructions did it tell me how much this chocolate sucker was going to rise. If you look at the final pic, you will see that my parchment actually kept it all inside the glass pan. In the end it all worked. I'm waiting for it to cool. The recipe recommends overnight but it's chocolate and remember that's how I roll!

  Day eight is mostly successful. Love & Light

Day 9 of 365- I Made It September 28, 2017

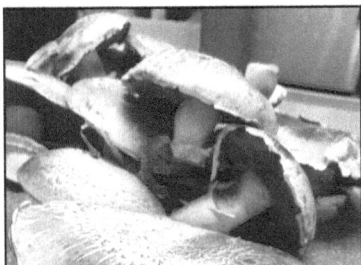

Growing 'shrooms... The other day we talked about growing accidental mushrooms. As we speak there is fungus growing in my pantry, on purpose.

Now I've got fungus growing in my basement and I'm equally as excited about that. I purchased a box of dirt and mushroom compost; the best combination of filthy ingredients for growing my delicious portabellas. As I researched this magical dirt combination, I discovered that it's important to wash your hands before handling your mushroom soil. I'll scratch my head on that later because I just washed my hands.

So, the very secret ingredient of this entire event is the "casing soil." I'm not sure what's in this bag but if I get delicious mushrooms from it I'll be happy. After I mix this magic soil over the pasteurized compost, I just have to find a warm dark place so it can fester. Thank goodness I'm in the Midwest and my house has a warm dark basement. Well, it's warm for now and since my 'shrooms should grow in a couple of weeks I don't have to worry about winter.

I know you're wondering where I got my magic dirt combination. I'm lucky enough to live very close to an actual mushroom farm. Brilliant! I was able to purchase everything that I needed to get the mushrooms that I like. I'll let you know how everything grows. Day nine is a wait and see day. Love & Light

UPDATE: We have progress on October 1st.
-October 12th we have little mushrooms.
-October 14th and my mushrooms are amazing.
-On October 19th we are busting out of the box! I'm so excited.
-On the 20th of October I cut the mushrooms because I'm really ready to devour these monsters.
-October 20th and I cooked the mushrooms with garlic and hemp oil. I topped it with fresh goat cheese and a side of crusty bread. This was delicious and a great adventure.

Day 10 of 365- I Made It   September 29, 2017

Today's adventure was to create a ZINE. If you aren't familiar with zines, they are mini handmade books, stapled or folded together.

That's a super brief summary but you can research if you want to know more. You won't be shocked to see that it's a creative adventure that I'm super excited about. When I decided to make a zine

I wanted it to be self-contained and something I could reproduce if I liked it. Well, I like it a bunch and when you see how simple it is you might want to do one too. Supplies are cheap and you probably have them around the house.

1. Paper 2. Knife 3. Pencil 4. Fine tip marker 5. Colors- I used sharpies. I have a sharpie problem; it includes almost every color of the rainbow. I support the rainbow.

The actual creation part took a bit of time as I decided to draw and write it in pencil and trace it in fine black sharpie when it was done. I made a quick video. Please enjoy. So, after ten days I have a paper making addiction and a zine creation problem. Life is good. Day 10 was a definite success. Love & Light

Day 11 0f 365- I Did It   September 30, 2017

The Light fest... Today was a late one but it was worth it. The event actually started with a short drive to a local outdoor concert venue. I'm sure it's because the location is in the middle of farmland Wisconsin and remote enough to launch thousands of fire lit floating lanterns.

I've never been to a festival like this one and as beautiful as it was in the moment, I believe I will only need to do this one time in my life. The arrival is planned in stages for parking, and they attempted to prevent traffic from backing up by staggering ticket sales every half hour. It didn't work.

We were part of the first wave of parking, and it took thirty minutes to get in the lot. We set up our chairs and enjoyed a picnic as we watched the next 3 hours of traffic flow into the parking lot. I'm glad we were a part of the first wave. I recommend this for anyone doing the event in the future.

They sell food and swag at the site, but we brought a picnic and enjoyed the live performances playing on stage. It was a very long wait and cell service was horrible so bring a deck of cards or a reclining chair so you can relax while waiting for the lanterns to fly. When we finally got to lantern lighting, it went in waves and that was fun to watch. There is a trick to filling them up and the crowd was very successful as you can see in the video.

It was a melting pot of human beings, and the lantern came with a pen so you could write whatever message you wanted to send into the world. I wrote 3 messages on mine.

1. *Love is love,* for all in the world struggling to live life without judgment.

2. *365 Let your light shine,* to light my path for the year.

3. *Just Live,* to remember that losing any life to suicide and depression needs to end. Lanterns danced across the sky, each with some message that only the writer would understand. It was beautiful. Day 11 was very good. Love & Light

Day 12 0f 365- I Ate It   October 1, 2017

Jackfruit... I decided I wanted to eat this piece of fruit long before this adventure began. I was visiting a fresh food market in Milwaukee, and I saw this ugly monster in the massive produce section. At the time I had no idea what it was, or what was inside but I'm a curious chick and put it on my "one day I'll try that" list.

Since this is the year of fulfilling those "one day" moments, today is jackfruit day. I didn't buy a whole piece of fruit because these suckers are freakin' HUGE!

Don't let the picture fool you. Getting the fruit out of this mother is like wrestling a toddler into a snowsuit and a car seat in the middle of a Wisconsin winter. If you have no idea how hard that is, consider yourself blessed. My purchased piece of fruit was a modest slice.

When I was selecting it I wasn't aware that more seeds meant more fruit. The actual fruit surrounds the seed, which is edible. I guess it makes sense but looking at it I thought it included the extremely sticky stringy crap around it, similar to the meat in an acorn squash. I was wrong, so... very... wrong. I'll discuss the stickiness later. So, if you are buying a cut piece of jackfruit make sure you see seeds, cut or whole they mean more fruit and are tasty too.

So, let's talk about the sticky bits. This jackfruit is held together by what I can only say is the spider webbing of the fruit world. HUGE warning... grease up your hands before touching the inside of this sucker; if you don't, you'll spend the next half hour going through the cabinet of

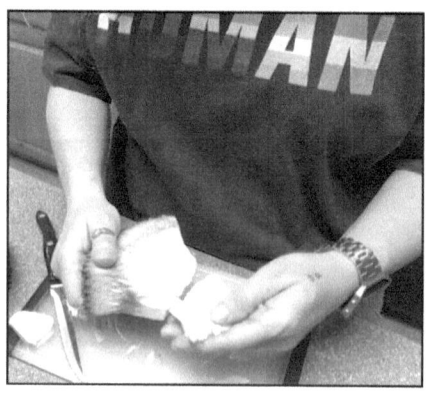

chemicals looking for something to get this crap off your skin without taking your skin off with it.

I used a combo of tea tree oil and dawn. I'm positive that the Professor on Gilligan's Island glued everything together with jackfruit glue. Not kidding, this shit is no joke. Once I dissected the slice, I was a little disappointed that I actually bought more compost than actual fruit. As I made the small pile, I was thinking maybe it tastes as horrible as it looks, and the universe was saving me from a bellyache. It was not and I'm disappointed because jackfruit is actually very tasty. The flavor is pretty unique, and I'd need to eat so much more to give you an accurate comparison.

I read that the seed is edible and can be roasted like an almond, so I tried it. It is a definite win! I was just as disappointed that my jackfruit had only a single seed in it. I pan roasted and sliced it and I'm glad I was home alone and didn't have to share. As fruit goes, I would buy a full piece, and I think most people would enjoy tasting it. Absolute WIN on my "one day" list. Day 12 was a delicious surprise. Love & Light

Day 13 of 365- I Did It   October 2, 2017

Day 13 and I'm playing some Pickle ball. I knew when I started this 365-day adventure that some of my days were going to include fitness activities. Since I work part time at a fitness center, I knew there would be opportunities for me to try some things that might make me stronger, more flexible and maybe even remind me how athletic I was before all the injuries to my body.

So, day 13, lucky 13, was all about pickle ball. If you aren't familiar with the sport, oh yes, it is a sport. The game is played very much like tennis except you use a flat solid paddle about twice the size of a ping-pong paddle. The ball is hard plastic with holes in it. It bounces on the hard surface like a tennis ball, and I was pretty surprised at how well it responded when I smashed it over the net.

I was feeling pretty hesitant because most of the people I played with today are regular members who I greet most days when I'm working. I've never had an opportunity to experience sportsmanship with them because most of our conversations focus on friendly greetings and maybe an issue with their membership.

I have to admit that the group that plays at the fitness center is a hoot! They welcomed me with open arms, and with extreme patience, taught me the ins and outs of the game. After a quick run-through on rules, scoring and how to serve we were right at it. They let me get a feel for how the racquet played against the ball and we were on. I know the first group took it very easy on me because he kept saying I was doing okay. I could tell one of the players wanted to unleash his Pickle ball beast, but he was patient enough to let me get the hang of it.

I lost the first game; in fact, I lost every game I played and felt bad for my partners. While I was beginning to catch on, I remembered my childhood dreams of tennis and playing the game like Chris Evert. I wanted to be her, and I did my best to bring that desire to the pickle ball court. Epic fail! Chris would be so disappointed.

I will say that I had a few good shots and even though I'm not playing sports the way I have in the past I did enjoy the game. In fact, I had so much fun that I decided to go back next Monday and play again. Maybe I should see how I feel tomorrow? I might have a different attitude once my muscles remind me that I don't play pickle ball on a regular basis. Day 13 was exciting and a reminder to just keep moving. Love & Light

Day 14 of 365 - I Made It   October 3, 2017

Wind chimes... I've had this pile of stuff laying around forever. Basically, I went to a garage sale and picked up a pack of glass pieces. I loved the way they sounded as they clinked and clanked in the bag, so I bought the whole lot.

I had no idea what was actually there until I pulled it out this morning to do this project. Most of the pieces were broken and chipped up so I had to modify my plan and came up with the final creation. I'll admit I HATED drilling the glass and snapped a few of the good pieces I had because of my hesitation. I've never drilled holes in glass before and I'm glad I only had to do eight pieces.

The rest was pretty simple. I used a magnolia tree branch that has been drying in my garage. My family gave me the tree as a Mother's Day gift, and it has always meant so much to me. I knew it would make the perfect base for the entire project. I have no issues with measuring and using the drill. In fact it's one of my favorite things to do.

I know when people come to visit, I've got stuff all over. They're just projects that my mind builds before my hands have had a chance. All of the materials for the project were lying around the house waiting to be assembled into something that sounds beautiful. Trash to treasure in about an hour. The video demonstrates the process and if you can get beyond drilling holes in glass the sound this set of chimes makes is amazing. I suppose if you're close to a beach this is a very simple project to reproduce with seashells or other tinkle-y items. Day 14 sounds like music to my ears. Love & Light

Day 15 of 365- I Made It   October 4, 2017

Paper beads are my arch nemesis. Today's adventure was really meant to be a light task. I decided a few days ago that I wanted to make paper beads after talking about them with a friend. I didn't really give it much thought or planning. I've watched women make them many times at fundraising shows and when you know what you're doing it looks effortless.

For me, it was anything but effortless. I got out my cutting mat and measured the strips of paper carefully. I cut them in a variety of widths and lengths. I had all of my supplies to roll the pieces of paper into beautiful beads that I could wear as a bracelet. I started with some ads from a newspaper. I figured there would be enough color to make them look interesting. I cut the strips and anchored the end to a barbecue skewer.

Easy as can be? That piece of paper wasn't square to the skewer, so it rolled lopsided. I tried a few more times and thought maybe it was the slickness of the ink preventing it from rolling up. I switched to wrapping paper in a fabulous pink cupcake pattern. Not only did the beads roll poorly but now I have lopsided pink beads. Today's adventure was not one of my greatest adventures or challenges. I have attempted to make paper beads and although I could string them and wear them, I think my standards would have to be low to be impressed. Maybe the beads will turn up in the future. I'm not sure. Day 15 is going down as a bold attempt but a real failure. Love & Light

Day 16 of 365- I Did It   October 6, 2017

     Day 16 was an interesting experience. I play a lot of games. I've gambled a fair bit but only enough so that my inevitable loss won't prevent the family from eating. I'm lucky in many things but when it comes to playing games you might want a better partner. So, today's adventure was a dice roll, literally. A coworker and very supportive 365-day adventure chick suggested today's challenge. Bunco!

     My first thought was, "isn't that the game my granny played?" I'm pretty sure it was. She has since passed but Bunco lives on. I had plans for day 16 and they did not include a dice game. I've got two super nerdy children who play miniature war games, so I've got boxes of dice in this house.

     I've never played Bunco. I've never had the desire to play Bunco. The invitation was made, and I honestly wanted to attempt my alternate plan but who could refuse a nifty night of dice with a room full of perfect strangers. If you know me, you will understand how day 16 was an official challenge and adventure.

     Getting to the host's home was a driving delight. She lives in the most twisting turning subdivision I'm glad I navigated in daylight. I love my GPS so much more on day 16. The playing area was set up like serious gaming was going to happen. Felted poker tables with place-cards and score sheets made this Bunco virgin tremble with fear. What have I gotten myself into? Over the next thirty minutes the ladies arrived. Oh, did I mention this is a lady's only game. I'm not sure why but my guess is it had to do with gender bullshit from many years ago and I don't want to wonder about the history of Bunco because I'm going to have to use math.

     Once we settled in, the rules were explained, and we sorted our foursomes around the three tables. This is where you really get to know a person. Personalities are revealed when games are played, and the true nature of competition begins.

     I'm just going to say, watch the quiet ones. Just when you get in a rhythm something called a "ghost player" shows up. Tonight, it was because a player had to bail and go be a responsible adult. Whoever plays with the ghost has to do all the dice rolling. If you're a shitty dice roller, you're gonna lose this round. Bunco is Yahtzee with less dice, partner swapping and if you play it right, gambling. Since it was our first time, we left the gambling out but everything else happened and it was entertaining.

     As a night out, Bunco is just a reason to sit around, laugh, throw things and eat snacks; pretty much all the stuff that I love to do. So go ahead and grab at least 11 of your best gals or strangers (sorry guys you'll have to find something else to do) and start rolling those dice. Day 16 was very entertaining. Love & Light

Day 17 of 365- I Did It   October 6, 2017

This 365-day journey has become an ever-evolving experiment in flexibility and adaptability. From the first day I have noticed that if I plan something the universe has a way of shifting that plan in another direction.

This morning, I woke up with early because although I wrote most of my blog for yesterday in the wee hours of the night, I fell asleep before actually publishing it. Bright and early, I posted day 16 and decided what I would do for day 17. Friday is my regular yoga day, so I wrapped myself in comfy-wear and headed to class.

There are only a few types of yoga I've never tried mostly because they don't fit into my weekly schedule. This morning my plan did not include wall yoga. The instructor today was a substitute, and it excited me to finally take her class. I've been beside her in many classes but never as her student and word on the fitness street is that she will kick your yoga butt. I prepared for the ass-whooping but when I entered the studio, she announced that we should find a place against the wall. In this situation I'm completely compliant and set up my space. Internally I'm screaming because I wanted a workout. I've got kinks to fix.

Just like my initial thought about pickle ball, wall yoga turned into something amazing and somehow the instructor and the universe lined up to work every little kink out of my aching muscles. The one thing I noticed as my butt was smashed against the wall, was that I had to really focus to do a posture and keep the right bits tight against that horizontal surface. Brain, body and breath were engaged fully, perhaps for the first time in years when it comes to yoga. This was a great lesson for me. An amazing first and a true challenge not only to my physical self but to my mental and emotional self also. Day 17 was super bendy, and I feel a renewed strength. Love & Light

Day 18 of 365- I Did It   October 7, 2017

Give just a little. Today's adventure was all about giving. I'm a fortunate adult and even though we didn't have a lot of things growing up we had a great family. I don't take them for granted. I believe in giving back. Sometimes it's by writing a check but other times that isn't enough. When I asked about helping this organization it was perfect timing as they had this event on their immediate schedule.

Today Royal Family Kids collected toys at a local Target. When I arrived, I was happy to see friendly familiar faces that gave me my assignment. I'm happy to report that my job was to smile and hand out helium balloons. I spent the next few hours doing that and receiving toys for the children who attend Royal Family Kids camp.

Last summer I was privileged to attend the talent show at the 2017 summer camp. It moved me in ways that I didn't expect and after that day I knew that I wanted to help more. This chapter of Royal Family Kids serves children in Kenosha County foster care. The men and women who give their time do it with the most love.

So, I stood outside of Target and gave away balloons and buttons and got smiles in return. A young woman stopped to talk with me and shared her experience as a volunteer and how amazing it was. I think it takes a very special person to put aside their needs to focus on children for a week. It's selfless. Something I'm not sure I could do so I showed up to this event. It's funny that it rained today. It hasn't rained for almost a month. Maybe the world needed a little wash. There's a list of things that are needed to pull off this experience.

If you want to know more, visit their website. https://kenosha.royalfamilykids.org/ If you want to make a difference, volunteer. It takes so many hands to put the camp together. If you like to serve your community locally, this is an amazing organization to support. Day 18 felt simple. Love & Light

Day 19 of 365- I Ate It   October 8, 2017

There is so much fungus among us! Today's adventure was meant to go in a different direction but don't worry I've got 346 days to make it happen. On my way to this planned adventure, I stopped to visit a friend. I want to preface this by saying I have surrounded myself with amazing women who are on this journey with me and aren't afraid to feed me new experiences. Christina asked about my adventure for the day and since it hadn't happened yet, out came a bag of fungus. You have to understand that she is the type of person who gets me. She knew I'd be all in with this. "How about a mug of mushroom tea?" I've known this woman for a while. We've bonded over many things. She knew I would drink her mushroom tea. I should share that this mushroom looks like something that burned in a fire. I'm not sure why or how anyone would see this and say, "YUM, tea!" but I trust her.

She pulls out a growler filled with the tea, pours a mugful and heats it up. It's dark like coffee and really doesn't smell like anything. I'm feeling pretty comfortable. I know you're wondering what this dream fungus is.

It's called Chaga and it grows near Birch trees. On www.chagahq.com they refer to this as the "King of medicinal mushrooms." I'm feeling privileged to have a small baggie full of this dried 'shroom. As I read through the website studies have shown that this tea is great for the immune system, reduces inflammation and is helpful in anti-aging and skin care. If you're interested in more, please check out the site. I'm planning to brew my own batch to keep ready when I'm feeling poor.

I'm not sure I'd pick this as a favorite and if you are going to drink it I suggest doing it very hot. The colder it gets the more it tastes like the dirty fungus that it is, just my personal perspective. Day 19 was interesting and if you haven't noticed it's the third experience involving mushrooms. Remember I've still got two kinds growing in a dark space right now. So much fungus. Love & Light

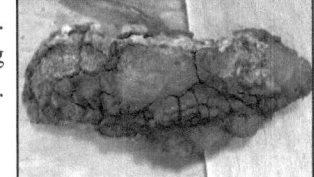

Day 20 of 365- I Did It   October 9, 2017

I just want to say I have great respect for people who do this every day. Today's adventure was operating a forklift. I did not enjoy it at all. I'm not a fan of driving equipment that can poke holes in things and drop stuff from tall spaces. Most of our equipment is old and loose around the edges and the brakes are very squishy. This doesn't help my anxiety when it comes to driving the forklift.

My plan was to pull it out of the barn, drive it around and park it back where it belongs. The guys had other plans for me. Starting this old monster wasn't complicated. I use propane when I blacksmith and this runs on the same fuel. I turned the gas on and wiggled a few handles and the engine started. The controls are reverse of how my brain actually works, so up is down and left is right and then you have to tilt and shift. Oh... and the pedals for the brake, yep, I said pedals.

So, there's *kinda stop* and *sorta stop* but not full stop even when I have one foot on each brake pedal. Thank goodness for neutral because that was my saving grace. Not really stopping but losing momentum. This forklift is not for the faint of heart. Don't let the video fool you my heart is racing a mile a minute and in my mind that's extremely fast.

I drove this beast farther then I'd planned, and I guess that's what happens when other people get involved in an adventure and want me to push myself just a little bit more. I couldn't do this all day.

I did not enjoy it at all. I guess if I had to, I would move something around and it's always good to know how equipment works. Day 20 was definitely a challenge. Love & Light

Day 21 of 365- I Did It   October 10, 2017

What is happening? Day 21 has gone out of control. I had planned to have one adventure and then another pops right up in my face. I'm going to hold one of them until tomorrow because It's big, I mean it's really big.

Now that you can't wait until tomorrow, let's talk about goats. Day 21 was my quest for goat's milk. When I posted a call for an opportunity to milk a cow I hadn't planned on a goat. It's not even close to being the same and now I'm happy it was a goat. I was the girliest girl I've been since I saw a mouse scurry across my barn floor.

The family who invited me in did so with amazing generosity. I am grateful. As we walked out to their barn their handsome stud that is currently looking for some action greeted me. Its messy business being a horny goat and it changes my mind about drinking that beer from a bottle ever again. (So many visuals)

We talked for a little while and I asked a ton of questions because I've never done this before and I'm so curious about goat farming. I'm sure Google could have answered every single question, but I would have missed out on the sights and sounds of these beautiful creatures. I really like goats. I'd say I like most animals from afar. I am not excited about getting bit by things. These beautiful creatures were wonderful. The family has two females they are milking right now so it was my chance to try it. Not a fan. Didn't like it and I suppose it was more about squeezing this poor creature's teat than anything else.

She just stood there eating her feed while I was squeamish about the rest. I suppose I'd get better over time, and the family assured me it gets easier. I tried for a while and got a thimble full, when the real pros took over there was about a half-gallon in no time.

Officially I brought this home for my cat. She just had a litter of kittens so she could use the boost. Unofficially I did try it, and it tastes exactly like goat, if you've ever been in a barn full of them, that's the flavor.

Yum! I'm not disrespecting the goat milk; it's just flavorful much like game that a hunter might shoot in the wild. It's raw and hasn't been manipulated to taste like something it's not. As adventures go, I enjoyed talking with the family. They show their animals as part of the 4H program and they love them very much. Happy goats for sure. Day 21 was pretty interesting and I'm glad I gave it a try. Love & Light

Day 22 of 365- I Did It   October 11, 2017

      Today is the 22nd day of my 365-day challenge. It's a big one for me because it's the first time most of you will get to experience another part of who I am. You know I'm a writer, an artist and an author but I'm also a super Sci-Fi fantasy nerd who gobbles up the worlds created in someone else's imagination. I've spent the last few months working on an article about how I watch television and how I feel about seeing myself in media, cinema and other forms of entertainment.

      I choose television because as far back as I can remember T.V. has had a profound influence on shaping my character. Yes, my family and friends have done that too, but I struggled to understand why I didn't see myself represented in any of them, television especially. When Netflix started their streaming service, it changed the way we watch TV. Now we can binge an entire series in the time between two first-run episodes. It's horrible but also extremely satisfying. Why is it horrible? Instant gratification and no anticipation.

      Why do you watch the things that you do? Sport is a great example. If you knew your team might never win, would you still watch? Obviously yes, because there are teams that have horrible records and yet jerseys sell and there are people spending hundreds of dollars to sit in the stadiums. Why? Anticipation.

      Sometimes it takes too long. As a young woman I looked for myself on television. Where are the people like me? I don't want the things that mainstream media is marketing to me. Where have the Wonder Women been or any woman who can fix her own life? Women do it every day. So, I got tired because anticipation turns into disappointment and I can't imagine that something good is ever going to come. That's what I'm talking about when I say representation.

      The LGBT+ community has and is living in a constant state of anticipation, looking and hoping for positive representation, and being portrayed as equally human and not just some plot device. We are all human and still governments and people in power debate whether the LGBT+ community is worthy of things the cisgender straight world takes for granted, ie. Marriage equality, shared benefits, medical care, holding hands with your lover and walking down the street, serving in the military or buying a damn wedding cake.

      The list goes on and on and exists for so many reasons but mostly because "those people" are represented as less than. Today is national coming out day. It is a day of fear and joy and every emotion in between.

The queer community has always been a part of who I am and the fight to be seen as human beings continues. For my 22nd day of this 365-day adventure I wanted to interview two women who live out and proud and do their part to represent this community. Please, take a minute and try to see what I did when I watched the videos Adrienne and Marcie made and posted on YouTube. They promote a fabulous television show that airs on the SyFy channel called Wynonna Earp.

If you haven't watched it, my article has spoilers about the series but I'm inviting you into an amazing and inclusive world. It's a manufactured place where women are strong, they make mistakes, fall in love, choose their family and the men don't take care of everything. It's magical. It's also filled with chaos, danger, demons and a sense of home reminding us that sometimes family isn't always connected by blood. Once you go to Purgatory (yes, that's the town's name) you'll want to stay.

I interviewed Adrienne and Marcie, two women who do an amazing job representing Wynona Earp. I pitched this article to my editor at Geek Girl Authority, and it is published on their site.

Today is filled with many firsts but this article is the most important because from start to finish it is a significant part of who I am and I'm proud to share it. I'm inviting you to be brave, love big and to see me and the humanity of my LGBTQI+ family. Happy day 22 of 365, October 11, 2017 National coming out day. I'm here and I'm Queer! Love & Light

Day 23 of 365- I Made It   October 12, 2017

This is ambitious. That was my thought as I looked through the directions to make cheese from the delicious milk I got the other day. I am not even going to pretend that I milked that goat long enough to get all of this, but I tried and that was the goal.

I'm not planning to become a goat farmer but after the fun I had today, I will continue to make this delicious cheese as long as I can. Before doing anything with the milk I had to strain it. I ran it through cheesecloth the other day before storing it in the fridge. I cooked the milk after adding a teaspoon of salt. It took a little time to bring the milk up to temperature and not burn it. It was an exercise in patience. Once the liquid hit 185 degrees it was time to add the curdling ingredient. I used apple cider vinegar. I like the flavor and after reading up and talking to the family who helped me with the milk, I decided not to use plain white vinegar. It was the perfect choice.

The moment the vinegar hit the milk it started to curdle up and thicken. I didn't want to stir it too much, but I really wanted the cheese! I waited and watched the curds separate from the whey. It's actually pretty interesting. After about five minutes there was a thickness at the bottom of the pan and yellow tinted whey floating on top. As it cools, I need to separate the curds from the whey. The directions suggest using cheesecloth. Well, hello, obviously.

So, I open the cabinet but there is no cheesecloth it's gone and nowhere to be found. PLAN B! I have to use a sieve, well two actually. This is where shit gets messy. Remember in science class when you talked about volume and all that crap? Yea, I didn't either and there might have been a tiny spill. I'm not really upset because it was mostly whey and the curds sloshed into the smaller sieve. According to the directions the drier you want the cheese the longer you should let the mixture drain. Cheesecloth would have been great right about now.

Nope, still couldn't find it. The sieve managed to remove enough to make a pretty tight clump of cheese. The only thing left to do is taste it. I took a sip of the whey and it's mostly just salty liquid. I was told it's great to use if you are baking bread. I might give it a try. I took a tiny taste of the cheese, and it was A-Mazing! The entire adventure took about an hour and it's so easy that I would do this again. So delicious.

Day 23 was a success, and I understand why Miss Muffet sat on that tuffet. Just sayin' Love & Light

Day 24 of 365- I Did It   October 13, 2017

Lights on! Today's adventure was a walk in the park. Well, it was a walk in the garden actually. I had a very soggy adventure at the Chinese Light show that's running at Boerner Botanical Gardens until the end of next week. I've wanted to go for a while, since my cousin had her own adventure and raved about it. My next week is pretty full so If I wanted to see this I really had to go tonight. The real dilemma was that this show is outside and when we got in the car to drive up there it was starting to rain.

I was wondering, as we drove, why would it be raining today? What was the reason? When we made it to the soggy parking lot it was clear why, the mass exodus of patrons flooding the already flooded parking lots. We put on our full-length rain jackets and popped open the giant golf umbrella.

We don't golf but it's the biggest umbrella. We were literally going against the flow as we walked to the entrance. The guard at the front gate wondered why we would choose such a rainy night, "You're going to get wet." Remember we are wearing floor length raincoats standing under an umbrella in the pouring rain... Dude, we are already wet!

We were surprised at how many people were inside and that's when I realized how crazy it would have been if it wasn't raining. I can handle the rain as long as it keeps the crowd smaller. It was really pretty beautiful, even with the terrible weather.

Each display had a lit sign explaining what the structure was and how it was significant to Chinese culture. I recommend the exhibit. I purchased tickets in advance, but the rain kept the crowds away and we could have purchased them there. One thing to mention is they sell food and souvenirs. They do a short exhibition with Chinese musicians, martial artists and dancers. It was a pretty perfect evening even with the rain. Day 24 was pretty amazing. Rain or shine it was worth it. Love & Light

Day 25 of 365- I Made It   October 14, 2017

Coffee... I know, you just read the word and now you want some. Me too. I've got a coffee problem. For the longest time I was off caffeine, but I still wanted that dark roasted flavor to drink. Tea just isn't the same.

For the adventure today I wanted to try to make my latest drink of choice, cold brewed coffee. I buy one almost every day and that adds up pretty fast. It turns out that there isn't any great mystery to cold brewing coffee. I bought my favorite dark roast and ground the whole beans with a very course grind. I used about 3/4 cup of course ground beans to 4 cups of water. I mixed it all together in a big mason jar and stirred everything together. That's it. This incredibly pricey cup of cold coffee is now brewing on my kitchen counter. It should be ready in about 12 hours. I'll taste it to see how dark it has brewed to determine if I should let it go a little longer.

Welcome to day 25. It's been a long one so I think this coffee will be a welcome wake-up on a Sunday morning. I'll update tomorrow and let you know. Love & Light 24 hours later and it was delicious with almond coconut creamer, vegan friendly.

Day 26 of 365- I Ate It   October 15, 2017

Star fruit... This has been a food experience I chose not to eat on purpose. When I'm in the grocery store and I see star fruit it always seems waxy and plastic, like those fake teeth we all got as kids on Halloween. It's cool when you're sorting through that hoard of candy, it looks good but when you actually take a bite it's freaking wax. Why?

That's how I see star fruit. So, I always said why? Last night as we were shopping, I walked through the produce section in search of my new favorite, Jackfruit. It was my day_12 adventure and I loved it and since that day I have not been able to find it... anywhere.

Back to my star fruit moment... It wasn't exciting at all. I washed it and sliced it and ate it a couple different ways. I read that the skin is edible, and this had an "ORGANIC" label, so I ate it with skin and without and I liked it with the skin better.

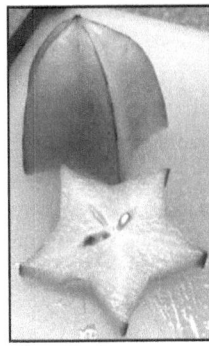

My impression? It tastes a little bit like watermelon just as you get to the white part of the rind. It's sweet but not really flavorful. That's my impression. I would definitely add it to a fruit salad to make it look cool, but I can live without it. I'm not going to chase it down like the Jackfruit. Day 26 was interesting but not really that tasty. Love & Light Update on my cold brew. YUMMY!!!

Day 27 of 365- I Did It   October 16, 2017

There's a song, maybe you've heard it, "Scars to your beautiful." I'm posting it here because it really goes with what I did today. I want you to hear the song.

I heard this a few months ago. The artist who performs it was on television singing it to a group of girl scouts. If you watch that video pay attention to the faces of the little girls as this woman performs for them. Really study the reactions and see what it means to have someone singing words that enter your soul and show you possibility. I can't help but see those little faces every time I hear that song. It reminds me that what we are on the outside is much less important than who we are on the inside.

When I got the idea for today's experience it wasn't about outward beauty so much as something I would never do because I don't really have an issue with that part of who I am. I took a drive to visit a woman who does facial threading. I know, big deal right, for me it really is. I don't care about the facial hair that started growing about ten years ago. I've never had it waxed but every once in a while, a really dark pointy one comes poking on my lip and my eyebrows just wander all over my brow.

So, I pluck the little stray hairs out and move on until it comes back in about a month. That's my entire lifetime of hair removal so today's experience was a first and a jump from how I feel about my body. The woman who ripped all my face hairs off was all business. She was funny and looked over my brow and said it's just a light cleanup. I was okay with that and thought, "sounds easy. "

HOLY SHIT! If you've ever had your brow threaded, you know what I mean. It's like having a tattoo on your face. It hurts and its horrible and I will never do it again. I had to stretch my forehead tight so she could do below the brow and that's when my eyes started to water uncontrollably.

I'm sure she didn't mean to be harsh, but she asked if I wanted my hairy lip done too. How do you answer that question when your face is on fire? I said yes. HOLY SHIT, lip tattoo! It's been four hours, and my lip still hurts and my left eye is still tearing. NEVER AGAIN!! People, this is some crazy torture.... back to the beginning of today's blog post.

This wasn't an experience about vanity, but it ended up being a lesson in self-love. This is how I'm made. Hair grows on my lip and my face and my chin and at 49 I'm really okay with it. I don't need to change that part of myself. Yes, I'll still yank out those bristle-y strays that pop out monthly, but my brows are my brows. I'm okay with myself. I've got a crazy list of experiences that I'm going to try in the next 300+ days, and some are like this because I've just never wanted to do them until now. Day 27 is a reminder to focus on the inside. Love & Light

Day 28 of 365- I Did It   October 17, 2017

    Today's adventure was HOT! I realized as I was driving to my class tonight that my 49th year is going to be really big. For as long as I can remember I have been fascinated with blacksmithing and glassblowing. I can thank my youngest child for introducing me to blacksmithing almost 6 years ago. It has become a passion and perhaps one day it'll become a lifestyle. I'm hoping time will allow for that.

    So, on the 28th day of this 365-day adventure I'm heading to my very first glassblowing class. I put on the clothes I usually wear at the forge. I know how to work with heat and hot metal so that part isn't scary, but I also understand how to move hot metal, and we don't usually move it in liquid form.

    The studio is absolutely clean, so unlike our forging area. When we heat steel, it leaves little pieces of scale, impurities in the metal, every time you hit it with a hammer. When you're working with glass there isn't anything on the floor unless you dropped your project. I didn't drop my project.

    After our mini lesson on safety, we started to discuss colors and what we were going to make. Tonight's choices were ornament or table orb. I did the orb. I wanted something that we could build a blacksmithing project around. I just love being creative, but I also wanted something for my meditation space that would be out all year round.

    I was the first person to work, which was great because I was very scared. I can't explain it other than I didn't have my creative partner there working with me. We're a great team and I didn't realize how much I'd miss him on this adventure.

    I took a deep breath and dove right in. I selected my colors purple, pink and blue with a translucent effect, I wanted to be able to see inside it. This was a guided workshop and what was most difficult was maintaining constant spinning motion on the blowpipe. The instructor was excellent at 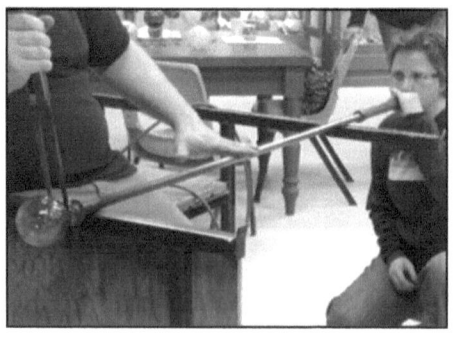 keeping my creation from becoming a blob of floppy glass and getting this project to the finish line.

The actual project took about 25 minutes, but it went very slow. Once I got over the nerves of working with a stranger this experience became a dance of blowing glass. It was completely different than what I was expecting. There is a lot of finesse and gentle skill required in this art. Aside from the temperature of the furnaces this is not at all like blacksmithing. It was a great first experience with glass blowing. I might do it again. It is so much fun to watch other people do this.

Day 28 was wonderful. Love & Light. If you're interested in visiting their shop the website is https://hotshopglass.com/

Day 29 of 365- I Made It   October 18, 2017

Take a hike? Find someplace new to explore? I had a plan to do something fun and after a little exploring was surprised to find a park restoration project practically in my back yard. Not only that, but there were hiking trails, and this would be the perfect spot to execute my plan.

When I got to work this morning there was a yellow rock outside. I'm not sure if you've ever found a painted rock from Facebook but they're all over. When my co-worker came in, she had a brilliant idea that I should take this rock on a hike and plant it somewhere. That idea grew and before I knew it I was planning to paint my own rocks and leave one behind after I have every adventure for the next 365 days.

#365rockdays is born. I really liked this idea, but the problem is that I'm on day 29 and I've had adventures all over the place. With the help of my co-worker, we hashed a plan for me to deliver my own rocks to all of the previous locations and from now on take a rock with me everywhere I go. I really like the idea.

I have no problem finding rocks, or paint or colors to decorate. I washed and prepped about 60 rocks and in assembly line fashion proceeded to splash my signature rainbow on every one. I sorted and numbered them, and the real work will be to backtrack to all the places I've been. This might take a few days, but I'll add the rocks to the pages as it happens.

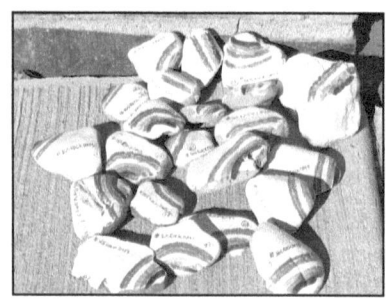

After painting and sealing them, I headed out to deliver a few. The afternoon was beautiful with the autumn sunshine, and I was enjoying the drive. I took a country road I've driven my whole life and stumbled upon a park I'd never been to. After a bit of research, I've discovered that this place is a work in progress. This was obvious when I drove up to plant my rock. I found the map for the trails. It was a little sketchy and as I drove through, the 8 cars in the three parking lots were full of guys sitting there not really doing anything. I'm not sure if they were working or just being creepers but I got the hell out of there. I did not feel safe by myself.

I planted the rock #365rockdays. Mission accomplished but day 29 was definitely weird. If you find the rock, pick it up and plant it somewhere else. Let me know by using the hashtag 365rockdays. Oh, and yes, that is a rock in my pocket. Love & Light

Day 30 of 365- I Did It   October 19, 2017

Day 30 and poetry... In May of 2017 I published my first book of poetry, "Immortal Human Truth." This was a labor of love and a very honest exploration of who I am, past and present. I've written poetry my entire life, not all of it fit to be published but revelatory, nonetheless. A friend posted about an opportunity for me to share my poetry on a nature trail. I loved the idea and although my pieces aren't about nature, I use my nature photography in most of them.

Today's adventure was a poetry walk. It was at a beautiful nature reserve very close to Racine, WI and this time it was creeper-free. I arrived with a few printed poems and set out on the trail. I planted my 30th #365rockdays rock and posted three poems at random locations along the hiking trails. I put up **"Finally"** from page 59. It's the one with the eyeball on the tree and I hope that no child gets freaked out.

I thought it looked so amazing in the forest. I also put up **"What if"** which is from page 19. I really liked the bright yellow dandelion image in the trees. The last poem I posted was **"Spine."** This is a personal favorite from page 65 in "Immortal Human Truth."

It reminds me of my youngest child who just launched himself out into the world.

It was a beautiful day, and I stopped to enjoy a few poems that had been planted by other authors. It's a fabulous way to share written work, tangled among the branches and fallen leaves. If you get a chance, go take a hike and plant a poem in the trees. If you don't write just read them. Your heart might just get a boost. Day 30 was good for my heart. Love & Light

Day 31 of 365- I Made It   October 20, 2017

Day 31 was filled with all kinds of updates and one new experience. I'll get the updates out of the way. I grew the most delicious mushrooms and if you haven't checked that blog post it happened on day 9.

I grew a pretty good SCOBY and have now advanced to brewing my first batch of Kombucha. I started to plant rocks for my #365rockdays experience. If you find one, follow me on twitter or instagram @edgyartist and let me know if you replant it. I've made paper about ten times and I'm pretty sure it's going to be a problem for me. You might find that popping up in a future adventure.

On to day 31! As a parent we sometimes make terrible decisions that lead us down a horrible road. We've done this a few times in our house. Once was when my husband didn't change the channel on PBS before Barney the dinosaur came on. The next 4 years were filled with "I love you, you love me." It was cute once, just once.

Another incredibly unfortunate incident occurred before our children hit their teen years. I raise my hand. It's my fault. I led them down the fantasy filled path to miniature war gaming. It happened by accident. I saw the lure on the sidewalk and walked right into it. It was so bad for me because all those thousands of dollars could have been spent on practical things, instead… our children GAME.

Today's adventure was all about confronting what I have avoided for over 8 years, building miniatures. My delighted and enthusiastic daughter helped me select the perfect team of Warhammer Space Marine Terminators. They come in a box, attached to a sprue (it's the plastic frame crap that gets recycled) with tons of tiny pieces. Remember that my eyes turned 49 too and they're kinda shitty. I put on my super adorable magnifying glasses and proceeded to cut these tiny little pieces from the plastic frame.

I built five model figures. Each one had about ten parts. The most fun and joy inducing task was sanding the cut edges from all those tiny bits. YEP! They are called bits and after you pick the bits you want there are left over bits. Where do these go? In a bits box. This shit is real people; there are conventions and trade shows and gaming groups that will blow your mind.

After I spend about an hour sanding off the seams from the molding process I'm pretty over this adventure, but I look beside me, and my kid is smiling because I'm finally here building minis. How can I be anything but happy because most people wish for the kind of relationship I have with my adult children. I get all of this sanded and assembly begins. You know from previous adventures that I'm not a patient person. It turns out that miniature builders understand my pain and invented a spray that accelerates the speed at which super glue dries. I'm serious. It's like an alternate world where bits go in boxes and glue dries so fast it keeps you interested in the building process. Magic!

It's adorable as I glue the guys together that I'm singing "Heads, shoulders knees & toes," in my head. I'm having a great time all the while my super happy daughter is smiling beside me checking my work. I'm getting the thumbs up and even more exciting is I haven't glued myself to anything yet. Once assembly is complete, we need to wait for all the glue and accelerant to dry. Time to complete a few side tasks.

Flash forward a few hours and it's time to move on and prime these guys. I take my adorable killing machines outside and spray them with a flat black primer, so all the tiny cracks are filled, and it creates a base for future color. I've been inside of gaming shops plenty of times and I know that these minis need to be painted with tiny detail. That won't happen today. That's a future challenge and I hope you can all wait for that because getting time with my kids is very limited these days. That's the magic of day 31. I've got an army of guys, and I can't wait to use them. Love & Light

Day 32 of 365- I Did It   October 21, 2017

On the 32nd day I had a full plate. I decided to take my very first solo blacksmithing class. This is pretty big for me. I got a chance to work an entire project alone. Some of you know that my youngest child is my partner in creation when it comes to blacksmithing. The kid is my muscle, my second brain and quite often has the solution to whatever problem might pop up. It's amazing to be able to think backwards and deconstruct a project and make it work. That is not a strength that I have and today I was on my own.

The blacksmithing group had some returning students and quite a few new ones. The best part was that there were plenty of seasoned blacksmiths to help everyone attending. The plan for today was to create hook & eye latches from 5/8" metal round stock. This shit is pretty thick and on a good day it's tough to move. On a good day, I mean when my muscly kid is around.

Most of the techniques involved with this project weren't terribly complicated and I was able to work through. I had to heat it extra hot to move this metal on my own. The problem with this is twofold. One, getting the metal extra hot in a coal forge is tricky because the heat isn't consistent which leads to burning the metal. Oh yes, you can burn metal. I'll confess, I burned my metal a few times today. The second issue, and I'm still working on this, is waiting for the metal to get hot.

I've discovered this about myself. I think I might need to address my inability to be patient in the next 333 days. Patience and paying attention to a coal forge are crucial and most of the time I'm not on my own for this. I really missed my partner. Something else I've never had to worry about at these events is getting hit on. Today I was hit on and you should have seen how filthy I was. Never gonna happen dude. This dynamic did affect the way I work. I just want to enjoy building the project without any bullshit. I will remember to bring my kid next time.

I was fortunate to work with another woman who was there for her first time. It was exciting to share my experience with her. The event was a full exhausting day and by the end I was so ready for a shower and a nap but blacksmithing wasn't the only plan for the day.

For Day 32 I also took my family on a torchlight Halloween hike. Yes, after all of us had a full day of work we went on a hike in the dark. It was wonderful. The weather was perfect, and the night air was so cool that it made an intriguing setting. We were the last group to arrive and had the final tour on the trail.

The guide led us through the hike intended for families. As adults it was humorous to hear the performances given my grown men and women in animal costumes. We made our way through and picked up an adventurer, a snapping turtle, a frog, a bee and a crow. It was like some crazy joke, but we enjoyed every bit of it. With stars twinkling and shooting across the sky we hiked through the evening. It was the perfect way to end the day. Day 32 was full but amazing. Love & Light

Day 33 of 365 - I Ate It   October 22, 2017

Today's experience was an interesting one. I played with aloe vera. Don't shake your head. It's not just for skin irritation. I've been reading quite a bit about the leaves of this plant. I've always had one in my house for burns but never thought to use it for anything else.

The leaf that I bought weighed about a pound before peeling it. Taking the skin off is pretty cool unless slime triggers your gag reflex. It's the slimiest thing I've ever had in my kitchen. My intention is to eat this slimy plant. I've read that it's full of vitamins and minerals and that it's as hydrating as coconut water.

After I cut this into slimy little chunks, I had to take a taste. It's not very flavorful and is similar to cucumber without the seeds. I added it to a smoothie, and it didn't change the flavor. I kept the peelings and put them in the freezer to use on skin rashes and burns. I've purchased gel for sunburns and have had the plant in my kitchen for years, but I've never eaten it. I guess we will see what happens tomorrow. Love & Light

Day 34 of 365- I Did It   October 23, 2017

Day 34 and Celtic knots... I have always had a fascination with Celtic and Egyptian art. I've spent a ton of time playing with ancient Egypt and making cartouche symbols with many kids, but I've never tried to draw Celtic knots and especially the triquetra. It's got all different names but I'm settling for this one.

I'm not sure if you've ever tried to draw this symbol but it's not for the faint of heart. My first attempt was really a mess. It's important to start with a perfect equilateral triangle. Have you ever tried to freehand draw one? Yep, nearly impossible and if your triangle is wonky the rest is all crap. I downloaded a few eBooks and as I read through them the diagrams were impossible to follow. I think it's the math. I really don't do math. Once I figured out 60-degree angles and found the old protractor a triangle was established.

Don't let my video fool you, I've got a pile of crumpled mistakes going to the shredder. It's a good thing I've still got a paper making problem caused by day 7. I worked through two pencil erasers and finally had to break out the old grade school pink eraser to finish this job. I'd say it was a success, and I will try my hand at a few different styles. I'll update if I figure them out. Day 34 was another test of patience and erasers. Love & Light

Day 35 of 365- I Did It   October 24, 2017

Day 35 was wild! My 35th day included Bison, alpaca, llamas and bucket loads of other wild beasts. Believe it or not there is a Safari almost in my own backyard. I got a ticket for a rainy-day adventure, and little did I know it was going to be more amazing than I ever expected.

If you haven't heard of the Safari, Lake Geneva, you have now. It's a very cool drive through safari. On a busy day you'd be in an open trailer having the most amazing time filling the bellies of very eager wild animals. I happened to be the only one for the 1:00pm time slot so I got a VIP experience.

We hopped in the massive 4WD pickup truck and sloshed through the gooey trails. I was totally spoiled in the front seat of the truck where it was very warm. Once we entered the gates of the protected area the creatures came running. If you've ever watched a movie where big beasty animals step in front of a car you might have thought, just honk or keep driving. Totally impossible! These big animals control the roads.

As we drove through the safari it felt like the world faded away and I was there with these amazing animals. I felt so small. When you book your safari, it comes with a can of food to give to the animals. In the open wagon they will come right up to the sides. Your kids will have the best time.

The Safari Lake Geneva is dressed up with huts and exotic animals you will love to see. I'm so glad I journeyed out into the wild of Wisconsin to experience this adventure. I'm sure all of you who have had true African safari experiences will find it a little less exciting, but I was happy to have huge horned yak and Ankole-Watusi cattle come charging at the truck. The animals are pretty cool when they are bumping up against the vehicle. The park is open for visits until October 31st and will open again in the spring of 2018. Go have an adventure. It's pretty wonderful. Love & Light

Day 36 of 365- I Ate It   October 25, 2017

Day 36 and I'm eating the fruit of a Dragon.

Okay, it's not the fruit of a dragon but it is the fruit that looks like something a dragon might cough up if it was choking. I decided I needed to eat this fruit at some point in the experience. If you go back over the last 36 days, I've got quite the delicious fruit salad going. When I cut this fruit open, I was surprised it was white on the inside. It's such a contrast to the fiery magenta on the outside. It looks like a kiwi but its firm and not as slimy.

It tastes amazing. It's sweet and the tiny seeds add a crunch to it. If you see this fruit in the grocery store pick one up. They are super delicious. A tiny side note: the dragon fruit is full of vitamins but it's also light and super refreshing. I wonder what it would be like frozen. I'll let you know. Day 36 was yummy and my new favorite fruit. Love & Light.

Day 37 of 365- I Made It   October 26, 2017

Bowyer, I know you're probably trying to figure out what the hell that is. Today I got a chance to sand and help build a 64" hickory longbow. My son is learning to be a bowyer and as much as we value people with four-year degrees, he is a tradesman and a very talented one.

On day 37 he and the shop owner decided I should help build a bow. You already know I like creating things, but this involved power tools that I wasn't prepared to use. I'm impressed by the creations hanging in the shop. There are some beautiful bows and if you visit the Bristol Renaissance fair next summer stop in and see them.

I didn't plan to make anything. I was there to watch but I guess the shop owner must be following my adventures because he was ready to teach. For the first time since I started this adventure someone else had an idea for me and made it happen.

Hickory longbows were the project of choice, and I had great fun shaping and sanding it. In the process I decided that I'd rather be a blacksmith. I enjoy moving metal more than I like working with wood. All the edges of the stave (unshaped bow) need to be sanded and shaped. I did this and there might be video of me squealing as I ran my bow against the sander.

The second part of my job was tillering the face of the bow. This is a delicate operation because it will ultimately determine the draw weight. My finished bow had a 37-pound draw. I learned so much about bows today. Thanks go out to the amazing guys. Day 37 was right on target. Love & Light

Day 38 of 365- I Made It   October 27, 2017

    Flight and arrows... My 37th adventure was all about building a bow. I had the best time but that seems like only half of a project. On the 38th day I made three arrows to accompany that bow.

    The best part about making custom arrows was being able to pick the color and style of fletching. It might not sound very exciting to you, but I was out of her mind with joy. I haven't been able to draw a bow for a few years because of a shoulder injury but I was able to draw the bow I made using my left hand. I guess it's time to learn how to shoot as a lefty. The process is pretty simple but includes a few steps. After the colors are chosen, the fletching is cut to whatever length you choose. I wanted longer fletching.

    I chose white as the cock feather; this is different from the others to make it easier to nock the arrow. The purple feathers fade to white out to the edges, so the combination looks pretty slick. The fletching is glued to the shaft using a pretty cool jig that theoretically keeps everything in line. I did my best, but it was off a little bit. I wanted to finish the arrow by wrapping the shaft just ahead of the fletching. It looks so great I'm not sure I'll ever want to shoot them.

    The finishing touch will be tips, and I haven't decided what I want to use. I guess since winter is coming, I've got time to make that decision. Day 38 was another success. Love & Light

Day 39 of 365- I Did It   October 28, 2017

Busting it up- Stones are the bones of the Earth. My 39th day is an adventure through the Ohio renaissance festival. I was pretty sure I was going to experience something new, but I had no idea there was going to be snow on the way to the Faire.

When we went to bed last night the weather said cold and rainy. In Wisconsin there is very little chance of snow before Labor Day weekend, so I've never worried about that when I'm lacing up that corset. Ha, as if!

When we woke up this morning the rain was turning into snow. The back window of the car had a nice cover of flakes. I'm sure that this is not Ren Faire weather and I'm only going because my adorable youngest kid works there. As we walked through the venue, I was excited to see a very welcoming sign that read, "Stones are the bones of the earth. " I knew this was where my adventure had to take place. The store was a rock shop, but it was unique. They sell unopened geodes. Oh yes, I went to Ohio Renaissance Faire, and I got a rock.

This is some absolutely amazing adventuring going on here. I have never opened a geode before. I sorted through the tables of round stones looking for the perfect one. The shop owner came over to school me in the ways of stone selection. Since I knew what my price range was, I let him explain what might be on the inside based on the color and markings on the outside. His disclaimer: I'm not always right but I guarantee you'll like it.

I had a choice on how we cracked this rock, either the jaws of a dragon or the guillotine. I chose the second because who wouldn't want to see a rock cut that way. Since I'm using pressure to split the geode the whole operation is slightly dangerous, and they wrap the mechanism in a towel to keep us all from getting ripped apart by flying geode shrapnel. It only takes a few seconds and the rock pops open.

The funniest part is the shop owner shows my geode to all the people standing in the crowd before he shows it to me. It was cute and totally worth the wait. Day 39 was certainly an experience. Love & Light

Day 40 of 365- I Read It   October 29, 2017

The numbers game... Today was an adventure in numbers. Have you ever looked at the clock and 11:11 comes up? It seems to happen all the time, and I've wanted to understand if there's a higher meaning to it.

My plan of attack was to sit down and read the mysterious ancient secret of numerology. Don't laugh, it's a thing and science and math are involved. The part that surprises me most is the religious connection to numerology. The Hebraic Kabbalah teaches a very simple system and that's what I read about.

It turns out I've been doing the number calculating my entire life and never knew it. There's this thing called fortunate numbers, which come up for some of us often, like 11:11. If you're looking for something in 1111 you could do a couple of things. Obviously two 11's or you could add the 1's to make 4. You could add 1+1 twice to come up with 22 so your fortunate numbers might be 11, 4, 22. Just as an example. Why do I care? Numbers fascinate me. I just wanted to know if there's a deeper meaning. I'll be honest, this shit is complicated and more than I can absorb in one day.

What I learned is that the alphabet has single numbers 1-9 associated with each letter. If you sort through all of it you can find the numeric equivalent to your written name. It's Math people! My name number calculates to a 9. In the summary of significance, it is a number of dominance, efficiency, consciousness and humanitarianism. I suppose it's time to honor those parts of myself.

There is so much more, and I won't bore you but if you can't find me it's because my math got tangled up in my alphabet and I couldn't escape. Day 40 is a 4+0=4 which is a great destiny number. How appropriate! Love & Light

Day 41 of 365- I Made It_____October 30, 2017

It's been days but we have kombucha! Back on the 6th day of this adventure I started growing a SCOBY so that I could brew my own kombucha. I waited a few weeks for the SCOBY to grow.

It was pretty thick and ready to move on to fermenting the actual drink. I transferred the initial liquid in to jars and added some fruit juice. I actually used fresh purple grapes and disintegrated them in the NINJA blender. I strained out all of the clumps and set it in a dark place to grow some more. It's been 10 days since the transfer, and I opened up my grape Kombucha and it wasn't horrible!! I'll be totally honest it's just like vinegar but grape-ish. That's what it tastes like when I spend $4 for an 8-ounce bottle. I consider this a win!!

I strained each jar to keep out any chucks that might have settled during fermentation. This is not a drink you should guzzle, and it certainly tastes like it should be good for you. Since my little jars created some beautiful mini SCOBY, I am brewing up another batch. It should be ready in about a week, and anyone interested in a taste should let me know. Here's to your gut health. Day 41 was tangy. Love & Light

Day 42 of 365- I Did It   October 31, 2017

      Day 42 was a special experience. I had the privilege of attending Gateway Tech 25 years ago. I graduated from their Police Science program and picked up a few essential tools for life in the process. It wasn't all related to law enforcement, it was also lessons in perseverance and the dedication involved in reaching those goals. I did receive a scholarship. It was a small one but at the time it allowed me to pay for books and materials necessary to complete my classwork.

      Why does this matter? It matters because I worked full time in the summer and part time during the school year and I still needed financial aid. I wasn't lazy. I was a middle-class kid who happened to be the last child to attend school. The system didn't give me anything. I had to earn it all, even the scholarship.

      After I graduated, I went back a few times to visit the campus, and it seemed like that experience was so far removed from my current reality. I know... what the heck does this have to do with my 42nd day experience? I'm getting there.

      Today I went back again but this time it was for an anniversary party. The Gateway Foundation is celebrating 40 years of making ends come together for students like me. My in-laws are part of this organization, and I was proud to stand in the culinary school that they and the foundation made happen.

      It's how all of us can give opportunities to students who might not be able to make it all come together on their own. It's not a handout; it's a hand up and we should be doing this more. You don't have to travel out of your own county to help people. The need is right in your own back yard. Day 42 was another unexpected lesson in charity and responsibility. Love & Light

Day 43 of 365- I Made It   November 1, 2017

Monkey fists... I'm just going to admit right now that my house looks like someone had a bad case of craft store and vomited all over. I've also determined that I love doing the projects that come with all these new experiences.

I've got the biggest stack of homemade paper you can imagine. I had intended to do about a dozen sheets, but I really like making it and might just have to turn this into another adventure. I've got a second batch of mushrooms growing in my basement and I'm so excited to cook those with some delicious goat cheese that I've preserved in my freezer. It feels like I've become a "prepper" for the apocalypse but that's not what I intended. I can, however, build a bow and make arrows. There might be something to this.

Today's challenge and experience was to tie a Monkey Fist knot. Maybe you know what it is but some of you might not. HA! see what I did there? Why a monkey fist? I wanted to make a useful knot that would also work for a future adventure. The origin of this knot is a self-defense. When you see ninja's throw that cord with the balls on the end, those are monkey fists.

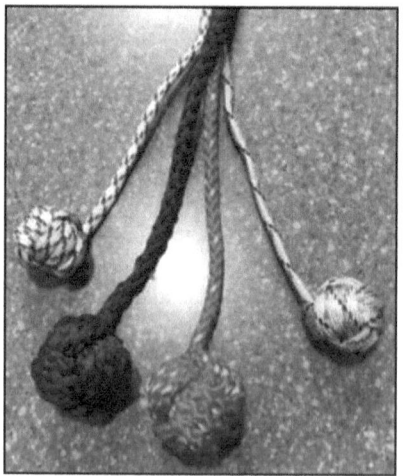

The process for tying them isn't complicated and since I didn't have any marbles or ball bearings, I used a simple knot of cord as my core. You can use your fingers as a jig to wrap and tie this knot. Three passes in three directions and a little cinching and you've got a Monkey fist. I might have had a great time making these and there may or may not be monkey fists all over my kitchen counter. I have a variety of colors too. Lucky, I caught the craft-fluenza. Day 43 was another success. Love & Light

Day 44 of 365- I Made It   November 2, 2017

Bombing a bath... NO, this was not some weird adventure in a hot tub. Today I made a little treat for my feet and other parts of me. I've had quite the first 44 days. I've eaten things I've always wanted to and tried a few adventures that I would not have made the time for. I think it's giving me a unique perspective that'll launch me into an adventurous second half of my life.

The next couple of days are going to be filled with unknowns and tense experiences. I'm not feeding the anxiety caused by the unpredictability, but I do respect the space we all need when it comes to processing it. I'm surrounded by all kinds of human beings and some of them handle change well and others need extra love and hugs. I decided that today might be the day to make some bombs for the bath that are filled with fizz, calming essential oils and a little bit of love. These little fizzy balls are made of a few very basic ingredients.

You probably have them around the house. I used baking soda, Epsom salts, corn starch and a little bit of coconut oil. I don't know the science, but these little bombs react like the baking soda and vinegar volcanoes you made in the second grade. (you might have made some more recently if you are me and you like that kind of thing) I used some food color to tint. I suppose you could buy some dyes at a craft store, but I used what I had.

I mixed up all the dry ingredients and found all the tiniest little cuts on my hands. Not kidding, all my wounds are clean now. After the dry was blended I added coconut oil and my essential oils and mixed it all together. The kitchen of my house is so cold that I had to warm the oil to keep it from clumping. Winter is definitely coming.

I added a 1/2-teaspoon of water and a little fizz happened until I stirred it all up. This mix hardens quick, so I mashed it all into a mold and let it set for a minute. I'm storing them in little mason jars. They turned out pretty amazing and I can't wait to share them. I might even use one myself just to give it an official thumbs up. Day 44 was tons of fun and this would make a great activity for kids to do for a parent or grandparent as a holiday gift. Love & Light

Day 45 of 365- I Did It <u>November 3, 2017</u>

    Floors… Day 45 was all about putting down a floor. We've been doing all kinds of repairs to our house and today we had to put down a new floor. I chose a product called Lifeproof Rigid core vinyl plank flooring. When I asked my brother in law to help me with this experience, I said, "We should have it done in a few hours." NOPE! That's why I'm posting this blog at 11:15 pm on Friday night. I did not take a few hours. It took about 5.

    Setting the first pieces required a bit of cutting and planning. Once that was done it was just a matter of laying it out so that the boards looked random and rustic. The style we chose has an appearance of old barn wood. It's really beautiful and works well in the small space.

    Most of the cutting was done with a Dremel multitool and was so simple. The thing is, I wanted to get the ceiling painted before the floor went in. I ran out of paint for the walls and had to get more so I could do the ceiling. It turned in to a drive around the countryside buying what I should have and rushing to get it done on time. The paint isn't finished. It feels like everything is half finished so I had to make this floor happen! I think it turned out beautiful. Day 45 was an adventure I can enjoy for a very long time. Love & Light

Day 46 of 365- I Did It   November 4, 2017

Coming out of the darkness. What if you could wear a string of beads that demonstrated to the people around you your grief and loss? Would you put them on? Would you invite strangers and loved ones to ask about the colors you were wearing? What if the person beside you had on the same color, and finally you saw someone who's been where you are?

Today I attended the Out of Darkness Walk for suicide awareness. This is the first time I've ever participated in a walk for survivors and their families. Every person in the crowd had been touched by suicide and the emotions that come from it. Every community was represented, as suicide and depression know no boundaries. It doesn't care if you are young or old, queer or conforming, Christian or Jewish or any human being on the planet.

Why did I walk? I walked for you and for me. I walked because when I was young, I was in a dark place, and no one should ever have to be there alone. You are not alone. As I sat in the warm and dry pavilion waiting for the walk to start, I heard a little boy ask his mother about the beads around her neck. She explained and when she told this child in his dinosaur raincoat what suicide was his expression changed to one of sadness. The purity in his reaction stopped me cold.

The next thing he did was reach forward to touch her string of beads. She was wearing purple and blue. He took the blue beads and put them around his neck. It was beautiful and so innocent. I've been to a lot of Suicide and Depression awareness programs and events since writing "Dear Kane; what I wish we would have said." I've listened to so many stories and sometimes all I had to do was hear them. I've learned to be quiet a let someone tell me their story.

Today was rainy and wet and so cold but it didn't matter. We have to start asking questions and take the time to listen to the answers. Day 46 was humbling. Love & Light

Day 47 of 365- I Made It   November 5, 2017

Soft Tack... Sunday morning of daylight savings, when you roll back the clock and gain that ever-elusive extra hour of sleep.

Not this Sunday! Because my days are unpredictable and I'll do a 365-day experience whenever possible, this beautiful morning shouldn't be any different. My daughter is a quirky one and focused on navigating an ever-evolving life path, the trip so far has had some turns that involve interesting choices.

This morning at 0500 we baked bread. Not fluffy crusty bread. That would have been amazing with my cup of coffee and maybe a bit of blackberry jam. No, we didn't bake crusty delicious bread, we made soft tack. I'll preface this by saying that I'd bake mud pies with either of my kids at any time. I love them that way and if you know me at all you'll remember that any time you came to visit when my kids were young, we were making messes, exploring and being creative all the time. No apologies, just seizing every moment.

Back to the delicious soft tack bread that we baked. It's a little bit better than those bits of paper I used to chew on in grade school before the lunch bell rang. Yes, I was that hungry in second grade. At zero dark thirty we mixed up very basic ingredients and in military fashion pounded out a thick layer of dough.

The recipe isn't complex, but it does require security clearance and since the internet is not secure, you'll have to contact a veteran and see if they're willing to cough it up. Really. Or, I'm told a History professor brought this during a lecture and my daughter asked for the recipe, but I like my story better. She might give it up if tortured with Starbucks. Just sayin'

The dough is rolled out pretty thick and then we cut it in to rectangles a little bigger that a slice of crusty bread. The important features of soft tack are the tiny holes poked in the surface to help vent the dough during the baking process. A tiny side note: I use parchment when baking so I never have to worry about food sticking. I asked my kid to line the pan, something that's been done every time we bake anything together. Instead, I find waxed paper on top of the baking sheet. I explain all the things that will go wrong here.

I'll pause, you imagine. We have a great laugh and I'm happy to share this morning together. I really love this kid. So, we've cut and poked our soft tack and pop the tray in at 400 degrees for about 20 minutes. I drink coffee and the kid gets ready for work. For once I fight the urge to peek in the oven because I'm very curious and impatient.

The timer dings and I open the oven door, and I'm not impressed. I don't eat a lot of bread these days so when I do, I really want something tasty. That's not soft tack. I'm happy to say that my kid will be eating this all week for breakfast and it went out the door this morning.

I don't have to worry about consuming it again. If we had the time we might have made hard tack, which is twice baked soft tack. It's a freakin' cracker people. I will note that hard tack was meant to be a military ration and that explains why my kid eats it. Thank you, Parkside History department. Best part of day 47... My daughter, in my kitchen, being amazing and quirky and baking bread. Love & Light

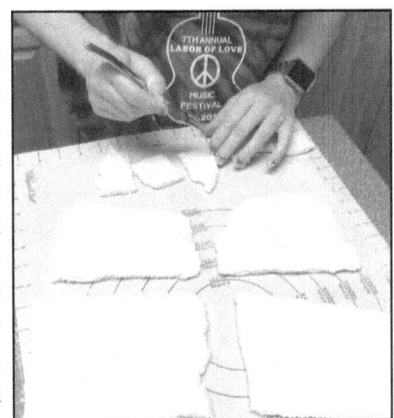

Day 48 of 365- I Saw It   November 6, 2017

Cats and dogs and little bitty animals... Today I visited a no-kill animal shelter for the first time. I believe that I've avoided this because I didn't want the emotions that come with watching so many animals living without a home. The shelter I visited is newly renovated and still there were cats filling two rooms. The smaller dogs were in cage kennels, and I wanted to take them all home.

I understand how cat ladies are born. My goal for this 365-day experience was to make a donation in the memory of our sweet Jake. He was the best dog, and I miss that big hairy beast every day. If you've ever looked at no-kill animal shelters you understand that resources are dependent on public support. The shelter website has quite a long list of needs. It brings up the issue of private breeders and people who are willing to pay thousands of dollars instead of rescuing an animal from a shelter. There are some beautiful creatures there.

Our Jake was a rescue and one of the greatest gifts and a member of our family. He had a Kitten named Jon Snow. I'm not going to roll out the Sarah Mclaughlin music, but you probably know what I'm talking about. Day 48 was mostly sad. Love & Light

Day 49 of 365- I Ate It   November 7, 2017

Day 49 started pretty early. I woke up with no idea for the day. My plate is a little full and as I started this 365-day adventure I found all these amazing opportunities have also happened. I have to keep them quiet, but you'll find out soon enough, I have so many new experiences.

As I rolled out of bed and stumbled to the life force that nourishes my brain, i.e.. the coffee pot, I walked around wondering what my adventure might be today. Then I saw it... an amazing piece of rotting fruit. I once wrote a poetry piece about rotten fruit as a metaphor for life. No idea where it ended up.

Anyway, sitting on my counter is a beautiful ripening plantain. No one will ask why. In the next 316 days I imagine I'll have all sorts of festering things in my house. I guess I already do so I'll keep piling them on.

The plantain was purchased last week with the idea that I would bake it or fry it but if felt boring as heck so every day I looked at that piece of fruit as a challenge. I'm not being dramatic, but I wanted this to really be great.

I went back to the coffee pot (it has a starring role) poured a big Wonder Woman mug and went to the refrigerator to get my coconut milk creamer. I opened the door, and I saw it. Maple Syrup. What goes best with that? PANCAKES!!! Yep, this morning on day 49 I made plantain cakes. One ingredient blended plantain. I did a Google search on the nutritional value of this fruit. It's pretty high in sugar so I'm drinking water for the rest of the day. 100grams is about 100 calories.

The sugar to calorie balance is off the charts so if you're getting ready for a workout this monster cake will hook you up. I made one single 6-inch cake. I prepared the fruit by blending it in the ninja. Yep, that's the same one I use for making paper, don't worry, it's clean. I took this thick liquid and poured it right in the small saucepan and on medium heat let it brown. It took a long time to become solid enough to hold form but once it did it was easy to do a one hand flip to turn it over.

I cooked it until it had a nice crisp edge. My house smells like caramelized sugar. This sucker is dense as hell, and I had a very difficult time finishing it. If I made them again, I'd do small silver dollar size and maybe top it with some fresh goat cheese to cut the sweetness. Super delicious day 49, Love & Light

Day 50 of 365- I Did ItNovember 8, 2017

Geocaching… I have to confess that I regret doing this adventure today. Geocaching would have been so much better with a full 12 hours of time but more important I think I would have felt safer with a companion.

All of that aside this is one of the coolest ideas that I can't believe I've never done. All over America people have hidden little containers and it's my job to find them. I downloaded the app to my phone and the GPS built into the program leads you to all these hidden treasures. My first one was in a little plastic tube, and the information told me to bring a pencil so I could write my info on the card inside. I'll admit I had to search around, but it was amazing when I finally did locate it. I could get hooked on this and when my 365-day adventure is over I might go again to keep the adventure alive. I did blur the contents just in case it's private. I didn't read the disclaimers.

I might try to incorporate this on another day and hide my own for someone to find. I had no idea this would be so much fun. Day 50 was an exciting adventure. Love & Light

Day 51 of 365- I Read ItNovember 9, 2017

Reading the lines. Today started out as an adventure in forgetting things. Even though I wasn't working today, I was still required to be on the go early in the morning. The worst part is I was hurrying around with the ultimate goal of sitting and waiting. I can't explain the reasons for all the down time, but you'll understand soon enough.

Today I spent time exploring the world of palmistry. This is where the reading between the lines comes in. Like so many other experiences this one has been on my mind for ages. I've never had my fortune told, been to a psychic or a tarot card reading but I've always wanted to. I'm just curious that way.

I've owned this book on palm reading for a very long time. I bought it with the idea that one day I would figure it out. Welcome to experience number 51. I cracked open the book and in the quiet space I read through the first four chapters, the entire time looking back and forth from the pages to the palm of my hand. There is a science to this. I'm actually pretty surprised as I continue to read. The author says, "If it's large on your hand, it's large in your life." I've never looked so closely at my palm before.

I'm not saying I'm an expert, but according to the shape of my hand, reading the lines and looking at my unique features, I'm creative, like to communicate and really enjoy spending time alone. I'm thinking my palm knows a few things. To be honest I've summed up this reading a lot. It's pretty involved and there are so many aspects to consider all while I'm actually staring at my palm in public. The lighting in the room is horrible so I can't actually look at all my fingerprints, but the ones I can see just confirm my courageous and creative self. Busy hand or Peaceful hand, Day 51 was educational and self-affirming. Love & Light

Day 52 of 365- I Saw It   November 10, 2017

Today I ate a Wendy's cheeseburger for the first time. It was pretty horrible. I also watched someone I love wrongly convicted of a crime.
There's not really anything else I can say. I'm shaken
Love & Light

Day 53 of 365- I Did It   November 11, 2017

Sweet Send Aways... Losing a child, no matter what age is devastating. Losing a sibling leaves a hole in your soul. The day after it happens can bring darkness you don't understand. How do you find a light?

Today I found that light by listening to that voice inside. I knew what I was going to do would be emotional, but I also believed that it might be healing. A few weeks ago, my cousin invited me to volunteer with an organization called Sweet Send Aways. The group does something quite extraordinary. They give the gift of memories after the loss of a child and sibling. These volunteers create garments for babies born sleeping or who pass away shortly after birth.

When I arrived this morning, I was so impressed by the group. Women of all ages and some men were moving around like a well-oiled machine. For the last few weeks, packages filled with old wedding dresses arrived from all over America. Today they were unpacking them and turning old bridal gowns into burial garments.

Throughout the room we all worked cutting, ironing and sewing. After unboxing the dresses, they are cut apart and the fabric is ironed and packed with a label of the name of the donor. The amazing women behind this organization have patterns of all shapes and sizes in hopes to never turn away a family in need.

After cutting out a few pieces for tiny dresses I worked on making bracelets. I made one for an adult and another tiny version for the child. This group of volunteers is something special. I've been so fortunate to have such amazing opportunities this year. If you want to get involved, follow them on Facebook. If you've been touched by a loss like this and need help, contact the group. They are so willing to be there for families in need. Day 53 was very healing. Love & Light

Day 54 of 365- I Saw It   November 12, 2017

I'll be honest; today is still pretty dark emotionally. I was struggling to come up with an idea for today, but I really just wanted to stay in bed and pretend that the last few days hadn't happened.

My morning routine is pretty simple. Wake up, write down any weirdness from my dreams and hit social media before I crawl out of bed. This is all done while wearing my super awesome cheater readers. I broke the cycle this morning and messaged my kid for coffee.

Sundays are for coffee and tea at Starbucks. We sit together and share the craziness of our week, and this week had a bunch of crazy in it. Instead, we looked at memes, laughed and enjoyed each other's company. One of the best parts was when my husband showed up and we had some time together. This set the stage for day 54 as we went on a pretty cool adventure.

Today we went to visit Northpoint Lighthouse in Milwaukee Wisconsin. This was my very first climb to the top and it was pretty amazing. This particular lighthouse was built in 1887 when Milwaukee was a booming trade port. Who Knew?

The lighthouse has a tiny museum in the space that once housed the families who kept the lamp signals burning. The docent on staff gave us the most detailed tour. After all the stories we climbed to the top of the tower. One of the most unique features of this place is that the tower itself has been built and rebuilt a few times, each retaining original parts of the previous structures. As you step up to each level you travel back in time. The first part was built in the 1900's, as you reach the third flight the tower is part of the original piece moved from the eroding shoreline. Every time the lighthouse was rebuilt, they placed the wrought iron lantern room on top. We climbed that today and my heart was racing, and it wasn't from all the steps.

This lighthouse closed in the late 1990's when everyone switched to satellite navigation. We can thank a small group for rescuing the abandoned structure and restoring it into a museum. It's worth a visit and if you want to spend $8 you can climb to the top. It's worth every penny. Day 54 was illuminating. Love & Light

Day 55 of 365- I Made It November 13, 2017

100's & 1000's… Today's experience happened by accident. I was walking through the grocery store when I passed the aisle with ingredients to bake and decorate cookies for the holidays.

Yep, I haven't put away my Halloween pumpkin yet and the Christmas trees are already spinning at Wal-Mart. When I looked through the shelves of ingredients, I picked up a container of sprinkles. Do you know what those tiny gems are made from? It's not natural and I think I could use them to start a fire in the fireplace.

Maybe I'll try it. That's when I decided to make my own sprinkles. I must admit this is a complete leap of faith as I searched for a way to mix them up. When you make them at home it's sugar mostly and patience. Not a great combo for me. I can handle sugar but being patient, as you should know by now, is not my thing.

I mixed sugar with water and cocoa powder in an attempt to make the yummy sprinkles I like on ice cream. Once it was blended together, I piped it out on to waxed paper. I used blue and purple food coloring to make the other colors. You can buy food dyes that are all natural, but I don't have them anymore.

This next step is the actual patience part because those stripes have to dry out to become solid, but I really want to know if it worked. Once all of those sugar stripes harden, I can chop them up and make those tiny sprinkle-y bits. I got impatient and instead of cutting them I wrinkled the waxed paper and got a nice little dish of sprinkles. I'm not sure how they taste because I got the brilliant idea to make sprinkles, but I didn't have the brilliant idea to buy any ice cream to put them on. I'll have to update you tomorrow. Day 55 is still up in the air. Love & Light and maybe some yummy sprinkles.

Day 56 of 365- I Made It November 14, 2017

    I want to start out by saying that although I'm continuing to do this challenge/adventure it doesn't mean that I'm not struggling with the emotions of last Friday. I'd like to mention a few things that have helped me in the last couple of days.

    First and always is my husband. He is a rock and when I'm at my very worst he somehow manages to be there. Secondly, I have to mention a few resources, although I don't think about suicide the darkness of depression is looming and not just for me. I have been solid for so very long but last week really shook me. I reached out to people and places that would talk me through. National hotlines like 1-800-273-8255 and Hopeline a 24/7-texting hotline text "HOPELINE " to 741741 are always available and free. It is very humbling and as proud as I am, I'm not so proud to admit that I'm struggling. Being brave.

    If you ask me, I'm not okay but I'm also not pretending to be either. I'm not going to be there for you. I'm not sorry because I need to care for myself today. The people who have emailed and messaged me, thank you. I love you for listening and for being heard.

    Now that I've explained where I am today. Somehow in my hustle to accomplish a lot on my day off I hardly accomplished a thing. I was cleaning up a mess that I made and that gave me a brilliant idea. I was mowing the grass, trying to occupy my mind. As I parked the mower in the barn, I knocked over a box and found a bunch of parts for a light that I wanted to repurpose. I'm amazed at the way the universe is working for me right now. Even as I write this, I'll admit that I thought day 55 was my last adventure. Knocking over that box of crap gave me another day.

    Originally, I got the idea online when I was putting together the 365-day idea list. There's a ton of mason jars in my basement and I've had an old blue ball jar filled with buttons that are just as old. I want to use them for something.

    Lightbulb!! Literally. So, I brought in the pieces I needed and dumped the rest of that box. I took the top of a jar and painted it black and drilled a hole large enough for the lamp base to fit through. This cord and assembly were from a hanging light, so the switch is built into the bulb base. I connected it all together and was happy that the weight of the buttons created a pretty stable base for the light. Embracing the antique feel of the jar and buttons I splurged and got one of those really cool Edison bulbs. This one happens to be LED, and it looks pretty cool lit and unlit. I was going to try and make a shade for it but I'm not going too.

What's really cool about this, and I thought of it after the fact, if you make it from a two-part lid & jar ring you could paint them different colors to change it up. Not only that if you want them for a party of for camping then entire assembly could be flipped around and stored inside the jar. I might have to go to the goodwill and grab a couple more lamps to repurpose this repurpose idea. Day 56 turned itself around Love & Lots of Light

Day 57 of 365- I Made It   November 15, 2017

A national day of Bundt... Happy Wednesday. If you didn't know it is also national Bundt cake day. I'm not usually one to get on board with national anything day but I've never baked a Bundt cake before and since my darling friend and Bundt cake pan owner messaged me this morning, I thought I'd join in the fun.

National Bundt cake day isn't a celebration of cake, it's an opportunity for bakeries to sell cake. Since that would have been a total cheat for the day, I busted out the Kitchen-aid mixer and went to town.

Since I keep dark cocoa powder on hand for baking emergencies that helped me decide what kind to make. Remember it's a day to sell cake, and not bake it, so if I didn't bake the quintessential Bundt cake recipe, I don't care. It's all about dark chocolate in my kitchen.

My dear friend Becky was kind enough to share her pan with me so all I really had to do was purchase some dairy products to make this delicious cake. Finding this recipe required a simple web search and then I was off. I know how to bake. I'm not sure what the big deal is about this particular cake, but it's got a ton of dairy products in it.

The mixing process was slow because everything was blended on low speed. Since my kitchen is like a freezer it was a challenge to whip up that butter. All combined the batter was a bit thick. I was worried that it wouldn't rise up when it baked. It actually took about 15 minutes extra because of the stoneware pan. My kitchen smells like chocolate, and I can't think of anything better. Once it cools down, I will add the dark chocolate glaze.

Everything came together. The cake itself cracked coming out of the pan, but you can't really see it. I made the glaze from MORE chocolate, whipping cream and butter. Each slice comes in at a whopping 315 calories if I cut it in 12 pieces. Please notice the use of the home-made sprinkles. Day 57 takes the cake. Love & Light

Day 58 of 365- I Did It   November 16, 2017

Tap & die… Today's experience was absolutely a first and a chance to share this adventure with my father. He's an amazing human being and taught me so much about being independent and resourceful. For as long as I can remember he has made time to be a mentor.

As a child he never limited me based on my small size or on my gender. What a gift it was to have limitless guidance built on a foundation of love. It's truly inspiring and was a huge part in how I raised my own children. The holidays are coming, and I've had a few requests for chainmail jewelry. If you didn't know, I make bracelets by hand. I use copper wire and turn it into rings and hand weave them to make each piece.

What does this have to do with my 365-day experience? I cracked the most important tool I use to turn the rings. Instead of spending a bunch of money to replace the broken part, I decided I could make it. This idea generated my day 58 adventure.

I needed to drill a hole in a piece of steel. Not a big deal but the finished result needed to be threaded so I could attach the mandrel rod used to turn the rings. This is where my brilliant idea of tap & die comes in.

I was pretty sure my dad had a set so I asked him if he would teach me how to use it. He was happy to help, and we spent the rest of the afternoon making a 8/32 threaded hole in a piece of bar stock metal.

My dad taught me how to check the threads to determine which tap to use. After confirming the measurement on my mandrel, we drilled a starter hole in the bar stock. The tap was pretty simple and after a few turns I was through the hole, and the mandrel screwed right in.

Perfect on the first try. I was surprised how simple the process was, and this will definitely come in handy on future blacksmithing projects. Thanks Pop! Day 58 was an excellent experience. Love & Light

Day 59 of 365- I Did It   November 17, 2017

Getting a weave... It's Thursday and I was supposed to do something really cool today. When other people are part of the plan the day can get unpredictable. The teacher didn't show up so instead I had to get my weave on. This plan to have one new thing to do every day often turns in to having a stockpile of things just in case things go screwy. Today was such an occasion. I bought a weaving frame a few weeks ago because I knew I had to try this as an experience. I've always wanted to do a huge blanket or rug but to be practical I decided to start with a tiny little coaster sized project.

I'm glad I started small because as easy as this weaving thing is to do it's also really monotonous and a tiny bit boring. The skein of yarn that I bought was multicolored and my plan was to weave a continuous line of rainbow color. Not today! The colors were about three times the length of the sections I was stitching so instead I had to cut every color apart. Once the weaving was finished, I had to tie all the loose ends together. The task of tucking and knotting the ends together was messy for my first attempt. I like how this project turned out. I might do it again with different yarn.

Coasting through day 59 Love & Light

Day 60 of 365- I Did It   November 18, 2017

HOLY SHAZAM! Today's adventure has been an experience. This is my very first time hanging Durock cement board. I know it's hard to believe but over the next few days I'm about to do work that I've never done before and I'm solidly STOKED!

Today, working with great teachers, we laid the foundation for doing the tile in my new shower. I didn't get to use the exciting power tools that have taken residence in my garage but it's coming. You're about to experience awesome. Setting the foundation included putting down the rubber floor for the shower. We also cut and placed and the cement board. Some of you might find this adventure dull but I've been waiting weeks to do this.

I'll admit I wasn't part of the supply-gettin' but that seems less important right now. My new shower has a very basic layout, and all of the cuts are on the same wall. We managed to get it all in place so that tomorrow's experience will happen. Just wait, it's going to be amazing.

What a great 60th day. Love & Light.

Day 61 of 365- I Did It   November 19, 2017

  A minister of marriage... There is a ton of back-story to today's experience that is just too much to share, so I'll summarize. A few months ago, I was asked to perform a wedding for two people who are very special to me. I was honored to be asked and am just as honored today as I complete the process of becoming an ordained marriage minister.

  If you know me, you also know that I left being a part of organized religion when my faith leader told me to turn my back on the LGBTQ community. You'll also know from reading any of my published works that this would be impossible because I'm queer. I love my LGBTQ family as much as my conforming family. I also happen to love myself enough to never let any person or organization dictate how to care for the person I am and the people I'm surrounded by.

  It seems appropriate for a Sunday afternoon to read and complete the paperwork process making me a legal administer of marital vows. That's legally married for all people in the U.S. since June of 2015. Yes, this is a ceremony for two women who love one another. They are extraordinary beings of love & light who have had their fair share of hardships when it comes to getting married. You can read an amazing article Roz recently published.

  I don't want to be part of any religious organization any longer. It doesn't mean I don't believe in a higher power; it just means that I don't support organizations that make money and collect shiny things in the name of one.

  All of that said, I am becoming a marriage minister for these extraordinary women because I believe in love, and I believe in the joy that comes with being loved in return. It's rare and it's delicate and love is love.

Today I learned so much about the ceremonies and what's important and what is not. I'm lucky. I've had the incredibly good fortune to be married to an amazing person who loves beyond imagination. If you find it, you should never let it go. On day 61 I embrace my new ministry.

  Yes, I really do! Love & Light

Day 62 of 365- I Did It   November 20, 2017

Concrete floors… Today I made more progress on the exciting adventure that is my bathroom shower. The experience of the day involved water, concrete mix and a trowel.

As much as I wanted to jump in there and make a mess, I was mostly an observer with a fair amount of instruction. At the same time, I was making a concrete pie I was also watching the finishing touches hit my tub, toilet and sink basin. The room is actually starting to look and function like a bathroom again. Every part of this adventure brings new opportunities for me to learn and get messy. I've also had to do a few things that I dislike and that's mostly painting. What's been the most exciting part?

The tools! I love to learn about new tools and this project has had many. Today as we mixed up the concrete, I used a massive Milwaukee drill. I talked with my teacher/ tile person, and we discussed this treasure of a tool and how nothing is made to last like this anymore. We mixed about eight buckets full of concrete and that drill made me very happy.

Building up the floor of a shower wasn't as difficult as I thought it would be. Most of the real work went in to marking the high edge and working the mix toward the drain. The real skill is in sloping the floor just enough to make the water run toward the center without having a dramatic grade to the floor. We totally nailed it!

Day 62 was amazing! Love & Light

Day 63 of 365- I Did It   November 21, 2017

Tile...today, for the first time in the history of me, I cut and set my own bullnose tile. I've been looking forward to this for so very long. I know at 49 I should have had this experience by now, but I've been super busy and needed an actual project to tile.

For the past few weeks, we have been chasing a leak in our bathroom. Once we found that little sucker, we had quite a mess to clean up. In doing all of this I had to rebuild my shower. The process of fixing the mistakes of others can be time consuming and frustrating. I really want my bathroom back.

As of this morning I have a working sink and toilet. I'll get my jet tub back in a few days. Now that my tile is set in place all it needs is grout. That was my experience for the day. I got a pile of mud and used it to stick my tile to the wall. I'll admit that I've been hesitant to do this because I thought it would be very complicated. It really wasn't. I just blew the mystery out of tiling.

This didn't require a lot of spacing or intricate measuring and I'm okay with the simplicity on this first-time project. The best part of all of this was the tile saw. Making those cuts with that saw was COOL! I'm totally serious people. The bathtub's tile is done, and the shower is 30% complete. The complicated cuts are coming but I'm woman and I'm ready to roar. NO MERCY! I can see the light at the end of the tunnel and it's so bright. Day 63 was magic and I'm so proud of myself for this one. Love & Light

Day 64 of 365- I Made It   November 22, 2017

    Mini painting… I've waited quite a few years to paint miniature war game figures. My kids have gamed for a while now and it's fair to say that I've avoided this on purpose.

    Why? I just don't enjoy miniature war gaming. What I do enjoy is spending time with my kids and if this adventure brings us together, I'm doing it.

    This hobby isn't a cheap one so I'm borrowing many elements from their paint set to get this job done. I selected purple from the palette as the base color of my mini killing machines. Don't worry this is all make believe. The process is tedious, and my eyes aren't great with the tiny close-up painting.

    The figures are less than 3 inches tall. I used about a dozen colors and the skinniest paintbrushes ever. I'm so glad that my army only had 5 guys in it because this is not my thing at all. Day 64 got me one step closer to gaming. Love & Light

Day 65 of 365- I Did It November 23, 2017

Thanksgiving 2017 and it's the 65th day of this adventure. Our family of four is back in the same house and I've got a sense of gratitude, also I hear the sounds of grown people behaving like children and it's music to my ears.

My youngest man-child is home from traveling with the Renaissance faire and he brought new toys with him. If you know my kids, you are aware of their obsession with Star Wars and light saber dueling. My youngest kid brought home man-child Light sabers, and the battles haven't stopped, neither have the whooshing sounds these electronic swords make.

When my kids were in Karate, they learned 10 step. It's a stick fighting technique that I've watched 1000's of times but never tried because sticks and stones break bones. I'm smart that way. Today's adventure was learning all 10 steps but with a twist; we are using lightsabers instead of sticks. Something you should know… just minutes before teaching me, the two kids dueled. It was epic and there were ice packs involved. I decided I should wear gloves and a helmet.

You should enjoy the pictures and the video. I love my family and the support they are giving me through this 365-day adventure. Day 65 was amazing. Watch the video. At 4:25 the kids show you how it's done. Love & Light

Day 66 of 365- I Made It   November 24, 2017

I survived black Friday shopping by spending time with my kids again. They are masters of so many things, and I can't imagine where they got that. Today I got to add some pretty cool features to my miniature killing machines. In my head I was just finishing up an experience, but my daughter assured me that this was going to be pretty involved and that it's a separate skill all together. I was a tiny bit skeptical but I'm all in now.

If you've been following my miniature building adventures, you'll know that I built them on day 31 and I painted them on day 64. So, on day 66 they will finally be complete and ready to use as imaginary killing machines to devastate my opponents. I know you can't wait to read about that adventure!

Today's process included sand and grass. Not the fun kind of grass. This is micro green itchy stuff that you might have slipped down the back of an enemy in the 4th grade, If you had any. I started by gluing the base of the figure and dipping it into the very fine sand. When you think of the scale of these guys, you'll understand why the fine sand looks like rock under their feet. It's pretty wonderful and I love the process.

It did take the better half of the morning doing the gravel and grass but to finish them off we added decals to the shoulders. I really don't know why. My kid tried to explain it but for some reason it went in and went out. I'm not sure I'll be very good at the actual gaming part of the war gaming experience.

Once all the glue and water dried, I had to spray my mini guys with a spray that makes them not shiny. Fighting machines aren't shiny. Day 66 makes things complete. Love & Light

Day 67 of 365- I Did It   November 25, 2017

It's a Jeep thing! I've heard this from a few people and the itsajeepthing hashtag has popped up a couple of times on my Instagram and twitter feeds. I've never driven a Jeep so today I attacked the experience with vigor.

We visited a local dealership and walked through rows of Jeep vehicles. They had some amazing beefy choices and colors. I met up with our favorite salesman. Yes, I have a favorite.

I chose the new Renegade for the test drive. I like the vehicle, but this new style is a bit boxy. It's 4-wheel drive and it felt like it as I drove down the highway. I did find that it wanted to go fast. I should have used the cruise control. The salesman confirmed that yes you can get a ticket during a test drive. I had a difficult time keeping it under 60. Apparently, in a Jeep, I can't drive 55.

When we drove on the recently surfaced roads the ride was pretty good for a truck but once we hit the bumpy side streets it was like being a stone in a rock tumbler. Not exactly a cross-country road trip vehicle.

I've decided that the test drive was good enough for me. I don't plan to do any off-road mudding, and I probably wouldn't do it in a $30,000+ vehicle. Just sayin' Day 67 was a Jeep thing and once was just enough. Love & Light

Day 68 of 365- I Did It   November 26, 2017

    Grout… When you start a really big project there are milestones that you can't wait to hit and once you experience them a sense of relief comes from accomplishing your goals. In my bathroom, it all started with a drip in the kitchen ceiling. When this happened, we had no idea how much fun was ahead for us.

    Today we hit a big milestone. We finally have the tile in place and are ready for grout. Most stages up to this point have been enjoyable but none have made me as happy as smushing grout into the cracks and crevices of my wall and floor. This means we are only days away from actually taking a shower or using the jet tub again.

    You've been on this journey with me as what was broken is now fixed. I'm wrinkled and pruned from endless hand washing. I think the paint and the dust, and the cement and grout have taken their toll on my skin. It's been worth it.

    I've learned so much about things that I've always held back from doing. None of them are incredibly complicated but the techniques involved have been intimidating. As much as I am excited to hit the grout stage of this bathroom repair, I've decided that I'm not ever going to become a tile woman. It's just not for me. I'm a technology person and I'm happy there.

    Although there will not be pictures of me christening the tub or shower, I'm sure I'll let you know when it happens. I think this newfound admiration for cement and grout has motivated me to try making a mosaic. Maybe you'll get to experience that one with me. Day 68 was rough on the hands, but we've almost made it to the finish line. Love & Light

Day 69 of 365- I Made It   November 27, 2017

Kama Sutra, Ha! Did I get your attention? Day 69 did not include the Hindu book of love, but it did involve twisting, spinning and winding around and around.

Today I turned a big pile of wool and fur into yarn.

This time last year we said goodbye to our sweet dog Jake. He was the most beautiful beast of a Siberian Husky and an important part of our family. I still miss him very much.

He was a rescue and came to us eighteen years ago. He had one blue eye and one brown and was frightening at first glance. That night he came to us I was afraid, but it only took one day, and we knew he was home.

He didn't play fetch or catch a frisbee, but he did one thing very well. He shed like a monster. Our youngest kid was Jake's best friend. They were constant companions and every change of season when Jake's winter coat fell out, our youngest would collect that fur with the intention of making something from it.

Today I decided to accomplish his goal. I purchased a drop spindle which is a device used to spin fiber material into yarn. It's a tiny bit more complicated than I thought it would be and after about three hours of focused spinning I might have about 5 yards of yarn.

I'm calling it yarn because as I wrapped it around the spindle it did appear to look like something you could make a itty bitty scarf from. I had hoped it might make a hat, so this could take a while. Once I figured out the technique, I felt like I was making good progress. The problem is that the fur doesn't mix in well. I bought the smallest carding combs on the planet mostly because they were very inexpensive.

I'm pretty sure this isn't the hobby of my dreams and I'm going to retire my drop spindle once I run out of fur. Day 69 had a few twists. Love & Light

Day 70 of 365- I Did It   November 28, 2017

Day 70, One dead tree and a few sharp axes. Today's adventure was not without a tiny bit of excitement. I've never chopped down a tree before and I'll be honest when I say I'd still be out there if I didn't have a bit of muscle helping me swing those axes.

On day 70 we attacked a very tall and very dead pine tree. I'm guessing it was about 30 feet tall. I had plenty of space with no danger of dropping it in the wrong direction, but I was pretty sure it was going to hit in the way it finally did.

There's an old story about George Washington chopping down the tree; it must have been a small one, or he had an accomplice, because it is a ton of work. My kid and I have been splitting firewood by hand for years. Swinging the axe vertically is so different and we very rarely have bounce-back that places our shins in danger.

From start to finish it took about 90 minutes and that's after cracking the handle of our better tool. I swing a hammer as a blacksmith but after 30 minutes of chopping, this axe felt like it weighed 1000 pounds.

The tree was a real sucker to drop. We made it all around the base and I was sure it would fall over but it didn't. I'm no expert but for a dead one this tree was pretty solid. As we stripped away the bark and chopped deeper toward the center we uncovered all kinds of crawly things. It was like a mini wildlife adventure, super gross and extra icky but that habitat of a tree is still there because I don't have a chainsaw, and I've never used one. Can you see a future adventure?

Day 70 was so much fun but next time I'll use more power. Enjoy the video. Love & Light

Day 71 of 365- I Did It   November 29, 2017

Metal on metal action... On day 71 I wanted to do something that wasn't terribly physical. My tree chopping adventure on day 70 was exhausting. Today I needed to use more brain and less brawn.

What did I choose? Welding... You might be surprised that a person who enjoys blacksmithing as a hobby has never used a welder. I've had tons of opportunities since we own a MIG welder, but I have just never tried it. Now that my metal magician is home from his travels we are back in our happy workspace.

My instruction started with a few explanations about materials and types of welds. Since I'm not the most patient person I just wanted to spark things up and melt some metal. That's why my kid and I work so well together, when I want to go wild, he reels me in, and I do the same when he's excited for a new experience.

Once I slowed down, and listened to his instruction, sparks were flying, and I was melting metal in horribly disfigured ways. My lines were bumpy, and nothing was actually sticking together. That's the learning process. We stacked up more scrap and I started again.

My teacher was very patient, and I wanted to get it right. We spent the next few hours working and decided to attempt to build a project. I've been thinking about this since I made that cheesecake on day 8.

That's when my tripod fell over and dumped my phone/camera into the chocolate batter. It was messy and since that mishap I've wanted to counterweight the tripod with a solid base. That's what we made today.

We cleaned up a few pieces of scrap metal on the grinder and I set a tack weld to hold them as I moved around the edges. As I worked each of the four sides my welds improved and by the last one, I was very happy.

I'm not going to become a welder, but I might be able to put some unique accents on future blacksmithing projects. Sparks are flying on day 71. Love & Light

Day 72 of 365- I Made It November 30, 2017

Yarn and a niddy noddy... When I bought my drop spindle a few weeks ago I knew exactly what I was going to do. I wanted to make yarn, and I wanted to incorporate the fur from our beautiful dog Jake. He was the most amazing Siberian husky, and I loved him very much.

Jake became sick very suddenly. My kid started collecting fur every time he brushed the dog and saved up quite a pile. I used as much as I could in this first adventure in spinning. What I didn't know at the time was that spinning was just the first part of the experience. Today I built a niddy noddy, which is a contraption for finishing this yarn. With about $3.00 worth of PVC pipe, I constructed the niddy noddy and started winding my material around it. With the yarn secured to the device I soaked the entire thing in warm water for about ten minutes.

The idea is to lock it all in place and keep it from unwinding. For the next half hour, I beat the twisted skein against a dry towel to get all of the excess water out. It would have been more fun if my arms didn't still hurt from chopping down that tree.

Don't get excited yet because that pile of wet yarn needs to dry so everything locks together. I added weight to the wet skein and hung it up to dry. This is the patience part.

Something very interesting happened once that yarn got wet. Our oldest cat, Jakes good animal buddy, started sniffing at the material.

I'm not sure if the dog's scent was suddenly stronger but our cat was intrigued, and it was a little bit sad. As adventures go this one was fun. I liked the idea that adding Jake's fur will make the yarn and whatever I use it for something special. Day 72 was another success Love & Light

Day 73 of 365- I Ate It   December 1, 2017

Chicken and doughnuts… When the suggestion was made to go to this restaurant, I was a little skeptical. Chicken and doughnuts, who does that?

A few friends wanted to be my co-adventurers today, so we all took a chance at Mike's Chicken & donuts. It was a first for all three of us, which made it so much better. From the outside the place looks like a bar but when you enter it has an old-time diner feel. The first thing you see is the display case filled with amazing, sweet treats. We chose a seat at the counter, and it was perfect for friends to enjoy the full experience of this restaurant.

At first glance the menu seems ordinary, but it was anything but. When we chose this place as my experience for day 73, I knew I was going to get a chicken and doughnut combo. That's exactly what I did. Our waitress was someone pretty special.

Her suggestions were spot on and the attention she gave us was the best. I have absolutely no regrets about putting this combination of food into my body. It was the perfect pairing of sweet and salty. There aren't enough words to describe the heavenly flavors and satisfaction I walked away with. If you're ever in Kenosha, WI this place is worth a stop. Next time I think I should take a few doughnuts home with me. Day 73 was worth every calorie. Love & Light

Day 74 of 365- I Saw It December 2, 2017

Trains for Christmas... It wasn't so very long ago that my oldest kid professed a profound love for trains as we rode through the zoo with the "toot toot" whistle blowing. We've ridden trains all over the country, visited old wrecks and museum antiques. I think both of my kids at some point had piles of "choo choos" in the playroom. In our home they were the definitive toys.

Today's adventure was a real step back in time for me. We went to watch the Christmas train roll into Wisconsin. It was pretty wonderful and the only thing missing was that kid who loved trains the most.

We spent an hour in the car driving to the station. When we were about a half mile away the traffic was heavy. Apparently, I wasn't the only person who saw the advertisement on Facebook. There was a massive crowd of people walking through the darkness toward a railroad track that wasn't visible.

I was surprised to see such a huge crowd. This was the first stop on the way to Milwaukee, and I can only imagine how many people were waiting at that station in the city. It didn't take long to hear that whistle blow and see all of the Christmas lights shining. If you've never seen it, watch my video. In the darkness it was pretty cool to see all the lights as the train pulled in. There were so many families waiting in the cold, and I imagine some kids were wild with excitement. The weather really was perfect for this experience. As adventures go day 74 was a great one. Love & Light

Day 75 of 365- I Did It   December 3, 2017

Losing fear and cutting up. It's the third of December and 55 degrees here in Wisconsin. Five days ago, I chopped down a pretty huge tree. On day 75 I need to clean this mess up. One tool essential to getting the job done is a chainsaw.

I'll admit that I've put off using one for so long because they scare the crap out of me. I've watched videos of crazy people who cut more than trees or branches when using this powerful tool. The set-up for the day was pretty simple. Check oil, gas it up and let's go. I've been using a gas weed trimmer for years, so I understand the process of starting the machine. With some help I get this beast running and it's time to lose the fear and cut it up.

From the moment I touch the downed tree I don't like the power of this saw. It pulls me toward my cut, and I feel like I'm fighting as I move it up. I know to cut from the bottom first so that when I make the top cut the log will fall away and not pinch the blade. This works perfectly and, in a few minutes, I've got a small pile of logs at my feet.

I think this is where I should mention steel toe shoes. I bought myself a pair about eight years ago and I won't even cut grass without wearing them. Fortunately, nothing hit my foot during this adventure.

I had a nice little pile of logs before my arms were too tired to continue safely. Maybe it's fear or just a healthy respect for the power this saw has to take my body apart, but when I was tired, I was also done. My youngest kid was happy to have a chance to rip this tree apart. We made a pile of the logs and felt pretty satisfied with a job well done. Day 75 and another fear falls away. Love & Light

Day 76 of 365- I Ate ItDecember 4, 2017

I learned today that a prickly pear is only prickly on the plant and tastes nothing like a pear. So, I get the prickly part but not the pear. As you might have noticed I'm eating things that I've avoided for 49 years. Many of my experiences with food during this 365-day adventure have been with items that either look horrible, or I've heard they might be a bit nasty.

This prickly pear thing brings me back to the Jungle book full-length animation movie. Baloo, that fun clueless bear, sings about the prickly pear as he plucks them from the cactus.

Then he just pops a pile in his mouth. You don't have to point out that this is a cartoon. I know that. It doesn't make it any easier for me because as I cut up this piece of fruit, I loved the color but actually eating it was not great as experiences go. First, half of what you get with this little gem is skin or rind. Second, the actual amount of edible fruit inside was as disappointing as my jackfruit from day 12.

Third and finally, who put the buckshot is these suckers? I'm not kidding. The seeds inside this fruit are hard enough to crack a tooth. I had an extremely difficult time chewing any of it. If you are like me and you eat the seeds in watermelon, it's not so bad. If you try to bite down on the prickly pear seed, you're going directly to the dentist. I'm really not sure how this became a person food at all. Let the animals have this one.

I ended up mushing the fruit around and just swallowing it. It's hard to get a true taste eating it this way and there are so many seeds that it's impossible to eat around them. As a whole I would give the prickly pear a thumbs down. It was my absolute least favorite new edible adventure. If for some reason this post inspires you to run out and devour a prickly pear, mush... don't chew. Day 76 could have been a tooth emergency. Love & Light

Day 77 of 365- I Made It   December 5, 2017

Today was a rather sticky experience. My youngest kid and I are blacksmiths and as much as he likes to make knives, I prefer to create candleholders or hummingbirds. I've never made a knife with a handle for or by myself. Day 77 was the start of this adventure. When we forge knives, shaping the steel is just the first part. It's a process to decide what you plan to use the knife for and to shape your blade so you can accomplish that objective.

Today our focus was on the second step of knife making, the handle material. This takes time and patience. On day 77 I made a super sticky mess in an attempt to glue up micarta handle scales. If you aren't familiar with the process, when you put a handle on a blade you can either hide the knife tang (the part you hold in your hand) or you can sandwich it. When making micarta we intend to sandwich the pieces together so that you can see the tang.

The process for making micarta isn't complex but it can be time consuming. We decided to do two types, cotton layering and yarn filling. When layering the first pieces we used cotton fabric cut in strips. Each layer is slathered in epoxy and stacked together. We used about 30 strips of fabric for this project. When it was soaked through completely, we put wood covered with waxed paper on the top and bottom. We clamped the entire project together and left it to dry.

When doing the yarn filling, we used a plastic container with a skein of string leftover from day 59. We mixed our epoxy and poured it over the top of the material and pressed it together so it would soak up the resin. Once we were sure it was coated, we compressed it using a heavy weight. We made a video of the process. I hope to share it once we edit it down. I'm sure you don't want to see 45 minutes of gluing and clamping. Day 77 was the start of something good. Love & Light

Day 78 of 365- I Did It December 6, 2017

First Person Shooter... When I was a kid the first video game that we had was called pong. It was literally a square that bounced back and forth on the screen and each opponent tried to deflect it at the other. It was ping-pong but it was on the television. I remember feeling like nothing would be greater than this.

A few years later my family got the Atari 2600, and we had Pac Man and Space Invaders, and I was beyond excited when I got a chance to play. My father built tables for the joystick controllers to mount to, and he became the Pac Man champ of the house. It was the next level of technology that felt like the top of the heap.

Not too long after Atari the Commodore Vic 20 entered my home and suddenly I was making characters fly across our TV screen. I was the luckiest kid alive and when I think back on it, I wonder how my parents could afford these high tech toys on our very limited family income. I never wondered as a child, somehow, we always had enough.

Fast forward to December 6, 2017, and my wristwatch has more technology than that 1980's TV and gaming system combined. It's something to think about as I turn on the PlayStation 4 to try my very first "First Person" shooter game.

I've held off playing this for so long because I hate shooting games. I've always thought the purpose was to use the other team players as targets. On day 78 I tried to play one of these games. Rainbow Six Siege is the name of this one and my goal was to eliminate 9 enemies. This was a training level. I didn't even make it into the actual game part of the game. I spent well over an hour trying to steer my gun so it would follow my body.

The blood spatter from my virtual flesh kept spraying all over the obstacle course. I hadn't even made it inside the room of the training level. I seriously could not steer my guy. As video games go, for me this is ZERO fun. Back in the days of Pac Man we had four directions and a trigger button. In the age of PlayStation 4 you have two joysticks moving in 8 directions, eight buttons and four triggers. It's no wonder I can't get my character to walk in a straight line.

After being shot, blowing up and dying in so many ways I decided I'd had enough of this one. I'm a Tetris kind of gal, four directions and a button. I don't really need much more. Day 78 was definitely a one and done experience. Love & so very much light.

Day 79 of 365- I Did It   December 7, 2017

Since as far back as I can remember I have loved fishing. My maternal grandparents were amazing fishermen, and I loved spending that time with them. I was fortunate to grow up with a pond in my back yard and property with a channel that led to the lake. For a girl who loved fishing it was perfection.

In the summer I spent a lot of time digging for worms. I didn't have fancy poles, and my father was always patient when I'd turn my reel into a tangled mess of line. I really really love to go fishing. Tonight, I learned how to tie my own flies for fly-fishing. I knew this was one thing I absolutely had to do during this 365-day experience. I have always wanted to do this ever since I opened the tin box that my father kept his flies in. I don't remember going fly-fishing with any of my family. I'm not sure why.

My first thought when putting this adventure together, was to get a kit and watch some videos. I went online to do my research and what I found was a ton of ideas, but the materials were outrageously expensive.

With the recent closing of Gander Mountain, I was forced to visit the Bass Pro shop to look for ideas. I guess this was the universe sending me in the right direction because they offer free classes every Thursday night from 6-8pm.

Today we did a very basic fly but depending on the hair color I chose my creation would attract a variety of little and potentially big fish. I didn't learn much about flies as we snipped and wrapped our tiny parts to the hook. It really is a very involved experience and the materials that can be used are endless.

The odds are that I will lose this creation when I use it. There's something really soulful about creating these flies when you may only ever fish one time with them. By the end of the class, I'd completed two pieces, and I was very happy with the results. The instructor did a great job of introducing me to this new skill and it was actually very relaxing. Day 79 was another long awaited experience that I'm so happy to have accomplished. Love & Light

Day 80 of 365- I Did It   December 8, 2017

That's a knife... It's my 80th day and so far, this experience feels like a chance to prep for an apocalyptic moment. I'm pretty sure I could hunt and fish and if today's project works out, I'll be able to cut up whatever I might get with my archery skills or my fishing moments.

Today was my first encounter with an angle grinder as I accomplished my first stock removal knife blank. I was cleaning out a cabinet the other day. I was really looking for a paddle drill bit and in the leaning tower of tools I found a very old very well used meat cleaver.

This monster belonged to my grandfather. I'm sure these four pounds of steel carved a fair amount of meat in its day. Since I don't have many occasions to cleaver animals, I decided today would be another repurpose experience. I will confess that I'm not a fan of the angle grinder. My youngest kid told me, "Be careful, hold it straight or it'll shred and rip your flesh off."

How could this possibly freak me out? Since this is the year of challenging fears and trying new things, I revved up that grinder and cut myself a knife blank. It wasn't as easy as that, but my kid is a great teacher and in about an hour I had what resembles the shape of a knife. The next step was using the belt sander to remove the extra material.

My kid built this machine. I call it the knuckle grinder because it turns so fast it bounces on the floor. I'm not a big fan of this piece of equipment but here I am again, crushing all my fears one day at a time. I'm happy to say no blood was shed during the creation of today's experience. I'm actually pretty happy with the outcome and I was able to keep the original company marks on the steel. I think my grandfather would really like what we created. Day 80 makes the cut. Love & Light

Day 81 of 365- I Made It   December 9, 2017

It finally snowed in Wisconsin last night. I had plans to do a new project today but instead I broke out the materials to make myself a no-sew blanket. I will admit that the reason I've never made one of these before is that I don't really like them.

I was shopping the other day, and I saw these little throw blankets. I felt the material and although it was soft there wasn't much substance to them. Ding! Ding! Brilliant idea. I bought two of them and cut off the edging with the idea that I could tie this all together and have an adorable blanket for when my feet get cold. Anyone who has visited my house will know that I keep it as close to 60 degrees as possible. I find that it weeds out the weak and keeps away the riff raff.

Back to the blanket... how hard could this no-sew project be? I mean really, NO SEWING! It's not complicated at all but because the fabric is so stretchy it didn't come out perfect when I hit those corners. My first one bubbled up and I fought the material for a while until I decided that first times aren't always perfect. I just let it go and tied an endless number of knots.

As much as that angle grinder scared me yesterday, I enjoyed it more than making this blanket. Working with fabric just isn't my thing. KUDOS to all of you who can sew and quilt. It's day 81 and you know by now patience is just not my thing. As adventures go this one falls short. I finished tying it all together, but its child sized now and maybe only large enough for my feet. Day 81... it's a wrap. Love & Light

Day 82 of 365- I Made I   December 10, 2017

Beveling an edge... Today's adventure was one of the best moments I've had working with metal. This experience wasn't about being a blacksmith; it was about taking a bunch of new skills and using them to make a tool.

On day 82 I built a beveling jig. It's a tool for grinding the edge of a knife blank into a blade. I cut all the pieces for this project using the angle grinder and welded the entire thing together.

The purpose of the jig is to stabilize the knife blank so that both sides of the knife are even and balanced. I've never built a tool before. I've never welded a tool together and used it like I did today, and it was pretty amazing. Day 82 opens the door to so many possibilities. Love & Light

## Day 83 of 365- I Ate It	December 11, 2017

    Why would you eat this? I've sampled a few horribly nasty things in the last 83 days, but this one is right up there with the prickly pear. Today I sampled the guava. Much like the scent of a urinal in a national park, this piece of fruit just lingers, and I could just not get that flavor off my tongue.

    I knew I was going to eat guava for a few days as I bought it very green and let it ripen to this lovely golden color. I'm sure many people would have thrown this away, perhaps I should have too, but everything I've read about this fruit suggested it would be delicious when it got to this outward ripeness.

    NOPE!! I cut this little gem open to find some serious seeds happening on the inside. These looked like the buckshot seeds I found in that prickly pear on day 76. I read that people eat this fruit, skin and all. I chose not to and just bit into the flesh of the guava. The texture was so much like Elmer's glue pockets we made in grade school.

    Remember pouring glue in the palm of your hand and letting it dry? Well, I did that but once it dried it made a cool film, and I'd squirt more glue in that. Why did I bite it? I have no idea, but it squished in my teeth and felt gross. That's what my guava experience was like too.

    I've discovered over the last few weeks that many of the fruits I've tried haven't been very good. Maybe my fruit instincts are telling me something. Do we have fruit instincts? I don't know but I'm going with it. Day 83 was not so tasty. Love & Light

Day 84 of 365- I Made It   December 12, 2017

CUT! It's more of a chop. Day 84 was something very special. In the last week I've spent a lot of time learning to make and use new tools. My inability to overcome fear has kept me from making a knife. Fear doesn't just go away; it fades as mystery becomes knowledge, and apprehension turns into experience.

I had no idea when I started this personal challenge that I would come to discover I had so many fears. It is humbling.

Today I spent most of my time assembling and using parts from previous challenges. My micarta experience turned into knife handles. My angle grinder skills helped me to cut and shape the beautiful blade that I'm chopping apples with tonight.

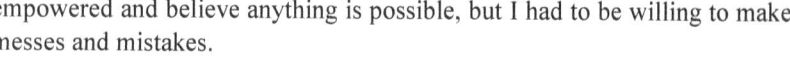

I learned so much about power tools I never thought I'd be comfortable with. I do feel empowered and believe anything is possible, but I had to be willing to make messes and mistakes.

I made one tiny mistake today. I forgot that the edge of my knife was sharp when I was doing the finish polish on my handle. Super glue was created to close wounds on the battlefield. My kitchen isn't a war zone but today that miracle adhesive stopped the bleeding.

When all was said and done this blade has the weight of a small cleaver but the edge of a carving knife. I'm proud of this experience and I was so happy to keep all the maker's markings from the original piece we started with. I hope you like it grandpa. Day 84 was one I'd do a thousand times. Love & Light

 Day 85 of 365- I Ate It   December 13, 2017

Christmas is 12 days away. Hanukkah started yesterday. The holidays are upon us. What's the first song that comes to your mind when you think about this time of year? I'm not sure why but The Christmas song; Chestnuts roasting on an open fire has been stuck in my brain for a few weeks. I'm generally annoyed by Christmas music before we hit December. This holiday season I can't seem to escape dogs barking to the tune of jingle bells. What does this really have to do with the holiday? I'll never know.

Chestnuts roasting on an open fire brings up beautiful visuals. Today I wanted to experience the sight, sound and scent of this part of that song. I pulled out the patio fire-pit and started a beautiful fire. It's a little cold today and some snowflakes were falling. It was the perfect setup for this experience. I put my cast iron griddle over the flames and in a few minutes, it was smoky, and the olive oil was dancing across the top. Everything I'd read suggested putting foil down, so I did that and I'm so glad because when the heat hit those nuts, they started to crackle and pop like breakfast cereal. I think your kids would love doing this.

It took longer to build the fire than it did to roast the chestnuts, but it was worth it. Once the shells started to split, I just rolled up the edges of the foil and pulled the whole pile off the flame. Chestnuts roasting on an open fire... top notch holiday cheer. Day 85 was a song come to life. Love & Light

Day 86 of 365- I Did It   December 14, 2017

     Staracle… When I was putting together the list of experiences I might attempt to do during this year, quite a few people suggested todays. You should name a star. I wasn't sure that it would be legitimate but the more I thought about this experience the more I realized that the stars have always been a huge part of my dreams so I should make sure they are a part of the 365 days of new experiences.

     When I was a child, I wanted to be an astronaut more than anything in the world. As I grew up, I came to realize that motion sickness might prevent me from accomplishing this dream but that didn't change the passion that I had to understand the stars. My senior year of high school I took my first astronomy class and connected with the constellation Orion. For day 86 Shazz Angelici became the name of a star in Orion's belt.

     You can find it here:

          Right ascension: 5 ° 34024.3500
          Declination: −0.9325°
          Magnitude: 11.79mag
          UCAC3-Identifier: 77482283

     I'm pretty excited that my star is part of this constellation. Right now, Orion is visible in the southern horizon at about 9 pm in the Midwestern sky. It's easy to find because the three stars of his belt are some of the brightest. Tonight, on my 86th evening, just look up and "Shazz Angelici" will be a part of your starry night. Love & Light

Day 87 of 365- I Did It   December 15, 2017

Feet... I know quite a few people who hate feet. They're glad to have them but are pretty grossed out by the idea of touching them let alone grooming them as a profession. Day 87 is all about feet; mine to be specific. With the help of some enthusiastic friends and one pretty talented pedicurist my feet enjoyed a fabulous spa morning.

u·to·pi·a yoo͞ˈtōpēə/
noun: an imagined place or state of things in which everything is perfect.

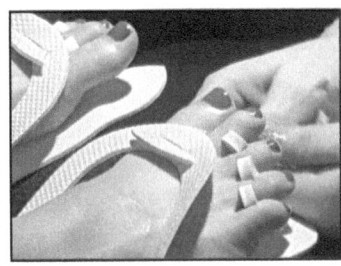

YES, I'd say this was my experience. We went to a place called Utopia. The name is fitting. I've never had such a pampering for my twinkling toes. The pedicure area is hidden behind a sliding door creating a dark space of mystery. Everywhere you look the signs are posted for quiet. That was a little intimidating and made me feel like a child in church.

I received a strange pair of disposable flip-flops. They got me from the coat hooks to the chair in the secret mystery room. Remember this is my first time and I have no idea what to expect. The chairs are shiatsu massagers and as soon as I sit down the rollers flow across my back. I like this already.

There's a blue pool of water at my feet and all I can think is Windex. I know this is nuts but the entire time my feet are submerged I can't think of anything else. I'm sure it wasn't glass cleaner, but I was too busy being quiet to ask. The rest of my experience included a bunch of clippers, metal tools and buffing pads. It was all I could do to keep silent. My feet are sensitive and once Maggie started to care for them, I couldn't stop the giggles. Let me remind you again that this is all new. I had no idea that so much clipping and scraping was involved. It was interesting when the massage part came. Warm oil is poured across my shins and rubbed in to the skin. A hot towel is wrapped around each leg and I'm feeling what a defining moment is like. UTOPIA, it was perfect.

I'm a simple person. I don't need a lot of fancy clothes or makeup to feel good. Since I don't have another experience to compare it to, I'd say this foot spa was top notch and I would like them every Friday forever! Day 87 was worth every tickle. Love & Light

Day 88 of 365- I Saw It   December 16, 2017

Face to face it's a new day. When I was 3 years old, I met a girl. Her name was Michelle. We played together every chance we got and lived through 100's of firsts, until the day she moved away. I don't think I ever got over the loss of her. As friendships go, we were the best even when we grew to become teenage girls. We had no control over the physical distance between us, but we tried hard to prevent the emotional space.

As teens we spent our summers together. I don't know how my parents did it, but they flew me halfway across the country. She and I camped out watching movies, playing air guitars, laying in the hot sun and just being together.

On the 88th day of my 365 adventures I finally got to meet the mini version of my best childhood friend. She's about the age that Michelle and I were when we started our mischievous adventures. As we sat around the table, I couldn't help but remember growing up with someone who knew me so well. I also felt a deep sadness for the passing of time and the changes that came between us.

I'm not too proud to admit that a long time ago hurt feelings got in the way of this amazing relationship, I'm human. I am also not too proud to ask for forgiveness. There has always been a very deep love, even through the hard times. I can't undo, or go back and even if I could, I wouldn't. We have both become amazing human beings in our time apart.

I'm a very firm believer in the power of forgiveness. I also believe that if it wasn't for the journey of the last 87 days my heart might not have reached out. We had an amazing time and the extraordinary child she is raising reminded me to be in the moment and to value right now. I'm very grateful for this 88th day. Love & Light

Day 89 of 365- I Saw It December 17, 2017

Barn... I've been to quite a few weddings, celebrated in a variety of places but I've never been to a barn wedding in the back country of Montgomery, Texas.

Today was an interesting first. I knew that we would be attending these nuptials, but I had no idea the unique space we would be in. The ceremony itself was a typical non-church experience with gorgeous flowers and rows of benches filled with family and guests.

Essentially everything I was already expecting. When we drove up to the property it felt like it was going to be just another outdoor wedding. It really wasn't. At first sight the space was unique and the covered bridge leading us to the parking lot set an uncomplicated yet elegant tone.

The location where the ceremony was held felt special, like any vows could be made from any faith, any commitment could happen, and it would be sacred. The walls were covered with rough cut repurposed wood. Vows were said and hands clapped in celebration. It all happened quickly, and after, we were able to explore the reception barn and the property surrounding it.

It is a magical place in the daylight but after the sun set it came alive. A misty fog set in and highlighted the miniature lights hanging in the trees and surrounding structures. That covered bridge was even more amazing with the lights inside. This was a beautiful place, and I was happy to be in it. The 89th day was certainly special. Love & Light

Day 90 of 365- I Did It   December 18, 2017

Bang & Boom... Today's adventure was twofold. I'm not even going to pretend that these two adventures weren't out of my box but completely amazing. The first adventure involved a trek through the woods riding on a four-wheeler. I've ridden motorcycles before, but I've never driven a quad and certainly not through the amazing property we were on today. I had such a fun time.

Don't make fun because I'm pretty sure I didn't go over 15 mph. It didn't really matter because the ground was muddy, and I had a flight to catch home from Texas. I didn't have time to take a shower, so mud baths were not on the menu.

My kid and I rode for about an hour, following my brother-in-law through the trails. Nature in "somewhere Texas" was stunning and the little river flowing through made me want to drop a hook and go fishing. If I had one more day I'd still be there.

I will admit that I was content to bask in the joy of overcoming my fear of the four-wheeler. Then the big gun came out. Some of you might know that I spent a bit of time training for law enforcement.

I've handled firearms before but when I chose to become a mom, I chose not to have guns. I'm not against them I just didn't want them around. It's really the first thing we learned in the academy, as a cop you're bringing a gun to the scene. I didn't want them around the "scene" of my home. That said, it doesn't mean that I don't know how to handle a gun, and I think I surprised the people I was shooting with today. I fired that AR-15 like a pro and had a smile on my face when I was done. When I was in school, we trained with 12-gauge shotguns and 38's.

I chose not to have anything else. When I was a child, we shot at clay birds. I remember my first time and how the recoil knocked me on my ass. That was not the case today. I hit my targets and one of them launched into the air. Day 90 was a score! I'd like to do both again. Love & Light

Day 91 of 365- I Did It   December 19, 2017

When you call 911 you have expectations that people are going to come. That's why they are there. I've had personal experience being in the back of an ambulance but until today it was never as a caregiver, only as a person in need. I hadn't realized what it took to be the person who arrives on the scene.

Today's adventure started at 7:00 am. To say I was nervous would be the understatement of this 365-day adventure. I have a huge respect for human beings who face the complete uncertainty of working emergency services.

I spent the day shadowing the guys of the Lake Geneva Fire Department. It happened that all the people working today were men. I settled in as breakfast became the first order of business. We met around the table and after introductions we hit the ground running. In emergency services they work with constant uncertainty. They spend their non-rescue moments preparing for the rescue ones. It didn't take long for the alarm to sound, and we were in the ambulance and out the door. As an untrained observer, so many things were going through my mind; I can only imagine how it is for the full-time team.

In a few minutes the jovial crew transformed into a streamlined team of caregivers. I watched in awe. I'll admit that I didn't expect to be so surprised. Their ambulance is a rolling ER, minus some drugs. They're trained to react. You don't have time to think you just listen, observe and respond.

After that call we returned to the station to finish checking every emergency vehicle in the department. Readiness is the key. They know a call is coming but there is never an idea of what, so every scenario is possible. I don't think I could have that much uncertainty in my daily life. I think that's why I appreciate this crew so much.

I was welcomed with open arms, and it was humbling. I didn't expect this to impact me the way it did. I'm not sure I have it in me to become a regular part of this team but I'm proud to have spent the day learning about the sacrifices made in this profession. Day 91 brought new awareness. Huge thanks to the L.G.F.D. You're an amazing group, Love & Light

Day 92 of 365- I Saw It December 20, 2017

    You're probably going to want to get a tissue. I've been writing today's experience in my mind since 2am this morning. It was at that moment when my father whispered in my mother's ear, "You're the love of my life, don't forget me."

    I've been crying off and on since witnessing that exchange. My mother, my inspiration my mentor and biggest cheerleader in this adventure went to the hospital today. I don't know why parts of the body start to turn on each other. After the last 24 hours I have a thousand more questions than answers. If I am strong, it is because this woman has inspired me to be so.

    She hasn't only been a mother to me; she is a mother to every stray I've ever brought home. She's amazing that way. If you've come for a visit, you've probably been fed and taken a nap after because she loves you with food and comfort. That's who she is.

    On this 92nd day I didn't know how to turn one of the scariest days of my life into something that anyone reading could understand. When I arrived back at the hospital this afternoon, I followed the red dots on the floor that led to my mother's room.

    Thank goodness for those red dots because I might still be wandering the halls of that huge place. I didn't know what to expect when I returned after going home to sleep because the call came, and I heard two words, emergency and surgery. I don't remember much about the drive back to the hospital, but I made it with just enough time to tell her that I love her.

    She wanted me to call and send an edible arrangement to the staff that took care of her. Even as they rolled her out the door for surgery, she wanted to bring comfort and food to others. I love her for that. When I left the hospital tonight, she was in a very deep sleep. She was covered in blankets with tubes and wires running in every direction. She looked beautiful and her extraordinary strength of spirit was lighting the room.

    I want her to wake up and ask me what my adventure was. She told me it's one of the first things that she looks at in the morning. I want her to remind me to send that edible arrangement, but most of all I want her eyes to open. I want her to look at my father and see the love of her life reflected back in the gleam in her eyes. Day 92 was long, exhausting but I love my mother & father and am filled with gratitude. Love & Light

Day 93 of 365- I Saw It   December 21, 2017

Life and monitors... As of 2017 we all arrive on this planet in the same way, through the womb of a woman. For many of us that woman becomes our mother, our mentor and teacher. I've spent the last day and a half watching and waiting. If you've been following this 365-day experience from the beginning, you'll remember that patience is not my strongest attribute. So, it seems appropriate that my mom would be the one to exercise this weakness in me.

I'm not too proud to admit that this is a part of who I am and I'm working on it. I'm honestly impatient about my patience. On this 93rd day I'm surrounded by technology that I've never experienced before. The beeping and pulsing of equipment in the corner of the room is telling us everything that is going on inside her. It's like that gadget my mechanic uses to check my car. I don't understand that either, but I want all the readings to be good.

What this can't tell me is what's happening to her spirit. There isn't a machine on this planet that can manage this. What I want doesn't matter and when I want it isn't even a consideration. The powerhouse of love, who I call mother, is in charge for the moment but I really don't enjoy this patience thing.

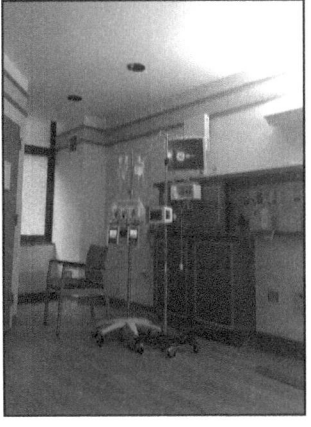

There aren't requests for miracles here, only faith. I have faith that whatever comes to us we will find the love and light to get us through. That means I've invited every entity to bring her the strength she needs to be a fighter. She's a wicked good fighter.

On this 93rd day I'm grateful for the new technology surrounding us. Love & Light

Day 94 of 365- I Saw It December 22, 2017

I didn't get it. It's supposed to be the most wonderful time of the year. Thousands of movies have been made to celebrate the holiday season. I've seen a few and today I watched one that I've never seen before.

I've mentioned a few times that I'd never watched "A Christmas Story." I'm discovering through these adventures that there are reasons I haven't done so many of these firsts. As movies go, this one did not impress me. A friend told me that this is a quintessential Christmas movie, so my expectations were high. I really didn't make the connection. Most of the film was about silly pranks and family dysfunction. Yay, holidays.

Show me how the piggies eat... really?? I think I'm going to stick with the Grinch and The Little Drummer Boy. Happy day 94 Love & Light

Day 95 of 365- I Made It   December 23, 2017

Pincushion... Today's adventure involved a ton of needle pokes and a moose. I've wanted to try felting for a while. I watched a woman create a felt dragon when I was at the renaissance festival a few years ago.

I bought this kit with the idea it would have teaching instructions. It did not. In fact, this particular experience was a medium skill level purchase, and I'd never picked up a felting needle in my life. I didn't realize that I should also get a surface to felt my projects on, so I had to do this all in my hand. This is where the pincushion part comes in. The first time I stabbed myself with the felting needle I adjusted the material so it wouldn't happen again.

This worked well for quite a while because forming the body of my project required making an egg shape for the torso of my felt moose. The rest of this adorable little creature was made with love and uncountable curse words. I poked my hands dozens of times all day long. I did not enjoy this part of the experience.

The right tools make all the difference. If I created another felting project, I would buy that darn surface. When I finished this experience, I was happy with the adorable creature I made from a pile of multicolored wool. As adventures go this one was good, but I don't really need to do it again.

Day 95 I made a felt Christmoose to give to my amazing mother. I can't wait to see if she likes it. Love & Light

Day 96 of 365- I Read It   December 24, 2017

My experience today was meant to be about feminism. I've got this book that I've been trying to read for over a year. I've carried it with me from Scotland to Colorado and back to Wisconsin. The original purchase receipt is still tucked in the middle of the book where I placed it after I paid for it.

It's not that I don't understand feminism it's just that I want to hear perspectives from other people. Then I got sidetracked. I witnessed something very special and also something that reminded me about how I was raised. I grew up in a house with both of my parents. They adore each other but also live very independent lives. I never realized what a gift that was. I was a pretty wild child and didn't adhere to gender roles at all.

At the time no one cared. I had success and I had failures, but I explored all of the possibilities of being. For the last week I have been holding vigil over my mom. It's extremely difficult to leave her every day. She and my father loved me so much they planted seeds of curiosity and watched me bloom. It wasn't perfect but I've never felt limited by my gender, and no one ever held me back because I was a woman.

What I realized is that I could study all I want but my reality is I don't need to draw lines and check boxes about my ability to be a feminist. I have to live without boundaries and reject the limits society prescribes. If only the world had been raised by my mom & dad. Day 96 took a turn. Love & Light

Day 97 of 365- I Did It   December 25, 2017

I've celebrated the holidays in a lot of places and with many different people, but I've never had Christmas in an Intensive care unit. Today's celebration was hardly what we had planned. This day is usually filled with food, stories, games and maybe a few quarrels.

Christmas 2017 did have moments of joy. The medical equipment supplied blinking lights and beeping noises. Our carols came from a tiny CD player propped on the corner of the bed. We didn't celebrate with many of our food traditions, but we made an attempt. We nourished ourselves to strengthen resolve no time for gluttony this year.

I'd never choose a Christmas like this, I'm not sure anyone would but I also see the joy happening in this place. An angel spent the evening in our presence. Healing is happening around us followed by moments of strength and peace. The nursing staff created calm and comfort that the presence of a higher power might invoke.

There is good work happening here, but it will never replace what we know as Home. To all of you who follow Merry Christmas, while I'm sitting here holding my mother's hand I wish for a sense of love and light to all who spend these days in the care of others. I wish kindness and patience for the caregivers we depend on; their desire to help and serve is selfless and I admire it very much.

If you are home tonight send love and light to those who can't be. Day 97 was a Christmas first. Love & Light

Day 98 of 365- I Did It   December 26, 2017

Motion sickness... If you are one of those people who can ride a roller coaster, I envy you. On day 98 I took a spin in the world of VR, and it spiraled out of control. I was pretty sure when this experience was discussed that I was going to get sick. I have a difficult time riding in a bumpy car. I've ridden one roller coaster in my life, and I ended up with my face in the garbage can. It ruined the entire day.

So, when I hopped in my virtual spaceship and flew, I could tell this was a bad decision. If you've been following, you'll remember that I have a very hard time with first person shooter controls on the PlayStation 4.

The VR experience just enhances that because I can't look down at my hands to see the shapes on the buttons. I am completely in the dark. It just comes down to getting lost in space and having no sense of where my body is. The technology is very realistic but it's also a one-way ticket to puking in the garbage can.

I've determined that VR PlayStation games are not my thing. I guess if I'm going to make myself sick, I should do it in the real world but after laying down for 30 minutes I think I'll skip all of it and just stick with non-vomit-y experiences. Day 98 was SICK! Love & Light

Day 99 of 365- I Did It   December 27, 2017

Flying balls… It's the 99th day and officially the last double digit one of my 365-day adventure. It has been a super huge challenge to keep vigil in the hospital and come up with an idea that I can complete without getting kicked out of this place.

Today was pretty good as far as things go. I decided to take a try at juggling. I'll confess that I made a feeble attempt as this was taking place in an ICU hospital room filled with extended family members who managed to cross paths at the same time.

With humorous instruction my fuzzy artificial snowballs were flying all over the hospital room. The best part was the encouraging words from the peanut gallery, AKA Nana. She was very entertained.

I will say that in the end my focus was more on my mother than on the juggle, but I was successful at making one loop of threes tosses. I will have to continue this experience as we progress through the next 266 days. Day 99 was another good one. Love & Light

Day 100 of 365- I Read It December 28, 2017

This might be a tissue day. I know it was for me. When I woke up this morning, I was exhausted, as I've been for the last 9 days. I had no plan for an adventure, and I will confess it's a struggle to continue this experience, but something happened at the end of the day.

My mother, and biggest cheerleader was also my adventure today. The idea came from my youngest kid and once he made the suggestion, I loved it. I asked mom if she wanted to be part of day 100 and her reply was, "why not."

Exactly... why not? On my first triple digit day mom handed off the parenting torch and allowed me to read a bedtime story to her. My mother, aka Nana, is an avid reader. As far back as I can remember books have been a part of my life. As a child, in the summer we would go to the public library and borrow books.

I would pick the pocket-sized hard covers and take them home to read. I will confess I liked to read but my retention isn't impressive. As I made myself comfortable beside my mother I started to read from "The tales of Beedle the Bard," a Harry Potter book.

The stories I read were touching and my mother sat there occasionally closing her eyes. I hoped she was listening and when we got to the end I could tell from the tears that she heard every word. Day 100 was a gift. Love & Light

Day 101 of 365- I Did It   December 29, 2017

Pop... It's the 29th of December in southeast Wisconsin. That means construction has stopped and winter is here. It's pretty damn cold and today I thought I'd try freezing a bubble.

The idea isn't terribly complicated. It's just soapy solution and a bubble wand, but the execution had a few bumps. First thing, have you ever tried to find a bottle of bubbles in the middle of a Midwestern winter? Not a lot to be found. I mixed up a batch using Dawn dish soap and water.

Here's the fun part I didn't consider, freezing cold winter and liquid. In my head this was going to be so cool. The execution took some time and a little bit of solution down my sleeve. Freezing cold wet hands and sleeves made for a fun challenge. It felt like the wind picked up and the snowflakes managed to pop the first bubbles I blew.

I really wanted one large one so it would be easy to see. I finally got one using the bubble pipe. It's a good thing I kept all our bubble blowing supplies from when the kids were little. Once that bubble froze it was like a plastic bag popping. It's pretty cool. I think I'll try it again on a colder day. Check back and see. Day 101 was another success. Enjoy the video. Love & Light

Day 102 of 365- I Did It   December 30, 2017

Playing the hand I was dealt. Today I found myself in a waiting room with my family. It's becoming kinda normal. Finding new things to do can be a little challenging and maybe a bit stress inducing at a time that's already unpredictable.

My kid and my father have been passing time by playing cards, today I grabbed that deck and searched for a new game to learn. As I searched through Google, I found a few YouTube videos describing a game called Egyptian Rat Screw.

The name intrigued me, and I decided this was going to be the game. My sister and my niece were up to the challenge, so we watched the instructional clips, and I dealt the cards.

Here's the entertaining part. The two of them beat me in only a few rounds. This game plays a little bit like slap jack but with some more complex rules. Even after winning a huge part of the deck, I was eliminated from the game. I sat for the next twenty minutes while the two of them battled it out. It was actually pretty funny.

As experiences go this one was great, and I was happy for the opportunity to include a few more of my family members. Day 102 was a great escape. Love & Light

Day 103 of 365- I Ate It   December 31, 2017

It's the last day of 2017 and we are celebrating in the driest location possible, a hospital. When I say it's dry, I'm not talking about a lack of moisture, I'm talking about a lack of alcohol or more specifically a lack of champagne to toast the New Year.

We don't always celebrate with the bubbly and sometimes I go to bed way before the clock strikes midnight. On day 103 we found a new beverage to ring in the New Year.

Let me set the stage for today's experience. My mother has been in the hospital for the last eleven days and her time here includes a feeding tube until she's strong enough to eat. I've been watching the light brown liquid flow through her nose and down into her body. I will admit I've been curious to know what this concoction tastes like.

Here's the gift that mom gets that I didn't. When she's fed through the tube it bypasses the taste buds and actual swallowing. This is some kind of nasty stuff. I had the Osmolite in a syringe and squirted it into my mouth. Once that crap ran across my tongue that gag reflex hit. I didn't puke but I will never drink this again. Day 103 was gag-worthy. Enjoy the video. Love & Light

Day 104 of 365- I Did It   January 1, 2018

Baby it's cold outside. Happy first day of 2018. I wanted to start this year out with a big adventure. I knew I wanted to do a polar plunge but in my head, it was going to be a sunny 32 degree day. What are the chances that the coldest day in 40 years would fall on January first?

100%! I turned the news on this morning to see an announcement that the Kenosha Polar Plunge was cancelled due to weather. I also noticed the -25-degree wind chill as the current temperature in Milwaukee. This did not sit well with my ideal plunge experience, but I was still determined to do it on the first day of 2018. Remember my patience thing? It isn't getting better.

I read through my list of necessities:
    1. towels
    2. warm robe
    3. dry clothes
    4. hand warmers - I forgot these
    5. gloves - my selection not warm enough, it should have been mittens

What was the most important thing to bring? People who are crazy enough to be your team who will help you strip out of your clothes at -25 degrees. I was fortunate to have four, Kathy, Jim, David and Davie, and they were spectacular.

Here's how this experience went down. We arrived 45 minutes early and still had to park about a half mile away. I'm sure that distance isn't so bad when it's 32 degrees, but today, after my dunk, it felt like miles. I found a spot close to shore but the water along the edge was frozen into a steep shelf. Some amazing person created steps down to the water and I eyed the location. Just before the twelve o'clock horn I dashed to the lake.

I really wanted to have this experience in Lake Michigan. I felt like it would be the perfect "one and only" time to have this adventure. It felt exactly right.

Once my feet hit the lake the entire experience happened fast. I wanted to go under the water, so I just let myself fall back. It was COLD! No, I really mean it was cold like I've never felt. My next mission was to get out and get dry. This is where the team comes in because it was all I could do to stay warm. They bundled me up and dried me off and it was all a blur.

Some brilliant experienced polar plungers had a fire going and I had enough brainpower to ask if I could steal some heat. This was right about the time that I couldn't feel my fingers. Please refer to #5 on the list of necessities.

When it was over, I was invigorated and felt pretty good. The crotch of my pants froze on the long walk back. I should have stripped off my swimsuit. Live & Learn. Day 104 was Brrrrr. Enjoy the video. Love & Light

Day 105 of 365- I Did It   January 2, 2018

Feeling strong. So, I'm not a songwriter. That was made very clear today. Mom has a bunch of words she is using as therapy, and my original idea was to write a song using them. It turned into a country frolic with candy and cocoa. You really had to be there to understand how horrible it was.

Instead of promoting the epic fail that my song lyrics were, I decided to rip an apple in half. Yep, with my bare hands I took a whole apple and made it two.

My son gave me a few instructions, and we discussed leverage. I was impatient and because that kid is quick with the camera, he caught it on tape. It went pretty fast, and I even felt it was too easy, so I ripped another one. The second one took a bit longer but I'm 100% confident that if I need an apple halved in the future it will not be a problem. I know this is pretty tame compared to the jump in the lake yesterday but take a minute and try to rip an apple. It's not that easy. Happy apple adventure on day 105. Love & Light

Day 106 of 365- I Read It   January 3, 2018

Mysteries of the unknown... If you sit in a hospital long enough you wonder about the unknown. There are so many right now and answers come slow. Patience is a continuous lesson. It's crap! Today I took another trip into the world of the mysterious unknown by learning a little bit about ancient runes. I say ancient because they've been around for ages. Some people use runes to see their future and some just use the ancient symbols artistically. For this experience I'm interested in both.

I spent a few hours reading through the meaning of the symbols. My set happens to be on gemstones, but you can purchase them in many shapes and sizes. I poured out my stones and started to put together what could come from the pile in front of me. Some stones landed with the markings up and others were turned over. You can only read the runes with the symbols up, so I separated them.

I'm not going to go into detail about what I found as I sorted through, but it was beyond interesting, and it made me think about what's going on for me right now. Day 106 was enlightening. Love & Light

Day 107 of 365- I Did It   January 4, 2018

Pop goes the Asti. Today's experience has been a topic of conversation in my house for quite a while. My son is a YouTube person, and he has watched a few videos about today's challenge.

If you do a web search, you'll find tons of people who've attempted to open a bottle of champagne using a sword or saber. Most of my mornings start pretty early and day 107 was no exception. At the break of dawn, we ventured out in the cold to uncork a bottle of champagne with flair.

Remember I've been studying the technique for hours.
With my camera-kid at the ready I removed all the labeling and wire ties from the bottle of bubbly. Remembering to start strong and follow through, I knocked the top off that bottle. It is all about technique and I really wanted it to work on the first try. Success! Day 107 made a real celebratory POP! Enjoy the video. Love & Light

Day 108 of 365- I Ate It   January 5, 2018

    Silence, I've been writing this post all evening. I've typed half the page and deleted it a few times. I've got so much to write about that isn't related to this adventure and I keep getting thrown off track. The last few weeks have been a struggle. Being a member of a big family looks like it should be simple. Are we ever honest enough to share how horribly things are going?

    On the 108th day of my journey I'm intrigued by science, and I hate the justice system. The question of remorse and the concept of forgiveness have been running through my mind. Should I forgive someone who chooses harm? Should you show remorse for something you didn't do?

    Many of you have been following my 365-day challenge since the beginning. I've pushed myself to do things that I fear, and this has been very good for me. I feel different. I see things with new eyes. I had hoped that doing this challenge every day for a year would make me a better human being. In many ways it has, but life has once again reminded me that the world keeps moving even as I watch it through the hospital window. Many things happened today that were firsts, but I don't want any of them to be a part of this challenge. I really don't even want them to be a part of who I am.

    All of that said I'm sure you're wondering what my experience was for the day. A magic cup of ice cream, that is neither magic nor ice cream. You should be laughing. I've never had a cup of ice cream that didn't melt.

    This little Styrofoam cup is sitting in the window. I know it's below zero outside, and I can still turn this sucker over with the cover removed. I think that's the magic part. As I inspected the cup a bit more, I realized it's actually a dessert. I guess I can relax because the chemistry involved in this delightful dish is loaded with calories and protein.

    I guess we can compromise our standards because any food is better than none at all. Do you get where this is going? Back to the magic. When we uncovered this little delight it looked like yoghurt, acted like Jell-O but tasted like Pepto-Bismol. Mom called it something else. Whatever the case this is some medicinal hospital crap food, and they use the word MAGIC so that you'll take that first bite. Day 108 happened. Thanks for reading. Love & Light

Day 109 of 365- I Did It   January 6, 2018

I am not Houdini but given enough time I could escape. Today was an interesting experience. The goal was to open a lock without using a key. I've watched my son do this many times. After today I can say that I've done it myself.

My youngest kid was a very patient teacher. With him as a guide I unlocked a file cabinet drawer. This might come in handy someday. My teacher wanted to capture it on video, but I didn't think it would be good to show you how it works.

I'm not sure I want to know how he learned to do this himself, but it was fun, and I will continue to improve this skill. I'll admit that this was a bit tricky and if I wasn't so inspired, I might have given up after failing quite a few times. Locked up day 109. Love & Light

Day 110 of 365- I Did It   January 7, 2018

Cut… It's no surprise that I like to play with fire. I'm not a danger girl but I do enjoy pushing boundaries. Today I decided to take the empty champagne bottle from day 107 and cut it using a little bit rope and hand sanitizer. When my youngest kid suggested this experience, I was excited to use that Asti bottle. It seemed like a perfect pairing.

The process was so simple that this could be used to make fun candleholders or other things to use around the picnic table. I'm not sure the technique is precise enough to make drinking glasses, but it would be fun to try. Maybe I'll attempt it with a factory-inked bottle.

The experience went off without a cut or a burn, which most of my family will be shocked to hear. As experiences go, I enjoyed this about as much as making paper. I'm going to have so many hobbies in the years to come. Day 110 was another success. Enjoy the video. Love & Light

Day 111 of 365- I Did It   January 8, 2018

I've had 19 days of interesting experiences. Some I would have done even if I wasn't spending all day in a hospital. Today's experience was accidental.

In the last few weeks, I've probably witnessed 100 games of cribbage. The game really doesn't appeal to me, but the good guys huddled together have found comfort in the rhythm of the game.

Since I am a curious being, I decided to see what this game is all about. I played three-person cribbage and although I didn't win, I also didn't get skunked. That's an actual thing that I kinda understand. As card games go this one can go on for someone else to play. Happy day 111. Love & Light

Day 112 of 365- I Made It   January 9, 2018

Eat This... One hundred and twelve days in and this is really becoming the challenge I thought it would be. It's been an intense few weeks and after all the serious I needed to find something fun to do. It's not always easy to assemble and execute an experience that works and do it all again the next day. Today was a long one but I finally have it together.

On day 112 I built a simple structure for spinning bubbly liquid sugar into cotton candy. The assembly was hot glued together and I scavenged a can lid and arrow shaft to make a spinning base for the molten mixture to fly through.

This is where the shit gets messy. The liquid was at 180 degrees and ready to go but for some reason it was too wet. I think when I added the raspberry flavoring it changed the thickness. I did get a handful of cotton candy so I'm calling it a success. Don't plan on coming over to get some because this will definitely not be on any future menu.

Day 112 was sticky and sweet. Love & Light

Day 113 of 365- I Ate It   January 10, 2018

It's day 113 and my mouth needs a good washing. Today I ate my very first piece of Nigiri, which should be pronounced NO-WAY-EEE!

I've had a lot of maki rolls made many different ways. I love the flavor of the Nori seaweed paper and I especially love the pop of the tiny fish eggs covering the sticky rice. I use the wasabi paste and the heat of that is like a beer chaser after a shot of whiskey. I love my wasabi. I'll eat most sushi, but I've never had any raw fish and that's why I've avoided the Nigiri.

Going against tradition I took a bite of the salmon piece first. I decided to try it without wasabi. To be honest I wanted to spit it out. It's just not tasty to me. I put wasabi on the other half and finished that piece and it just didn't help. NOPE, I'm sticking to my favorite… NOT raw maki rolls. I'll be having the spicy crab roll, Thank you very much. Day 113 I stepped out of my comfort zone and it tasted NO-WAY-EE!! Love & Light

Day 114 of 365- I Did ItJanuary 11, 2018

Space Hulk and the Warhammer... If you've been following my last 100+ days, you'll remember that I spent a few of them in preparation for today's experience. On the 114th day I crushed it with a game of Space Hulk.

This Warhammer experience involves imaginary creatures that look like something from the Alien movies. My goal is to defeat the creepy things as they get in the way. Look, this involves some imagination and since I spent all of that time painting my little army I wanted to get the full experience. My oldest kid belongs to a group of people who gather together to game and socialize.

They invited me to be a part of their family tonight. They really are a family. The group made a meal, and it was the perfect start to the experience. I felt a bit spoiled. My kid and I set up the game. It's a maze of cutout boards that can be used over and over. Tonight, my mission was to make it from one end to the other and firebomb the last chamber on the board.

It sounds easy but there are tiny cards and numbers and so much dice rolling. It's not complex but it is a little intense as the battle begins. I had a great time. I think it was more about being invited into this world where my kid has always felt at home.

On the 114th day I'd like to say thanks to my kid and her other family. You're a great group of human beings. Love & Light

Day 115 of 365- I Made It   January 12, 2018

Ring the bell... I have not given up. Ringing the bell was my experience for the day but first I had to make it. It's been a few weeks since I've been out to the forge, and it's been months since I decided that I wanted to make this old school dinner bell.

The design wasn't a problem I knew this would be three pieces and I planned to forge them all at the same time. That plan went to crap as I discovered my 1/2-inch square stock required more attention and a large amount of muscle. In my head this was an hour and a half build. Execution actually took about 3 and a half.

I tried to clang the metal to determine if the sound would be good, but that triangle shape really makes the steel sing. As experiences go this was music to my ears. Day 115 is a dinner bell. Love & Light

Day 116 of 365- I Did It   January 13, 2018

Chess on ice... That's how the introductory video describes this game. Rocks and sweeping and booties all while you target the rings and stones of your opponent. I didn't actually play chess on ice. I attempted to learn the sport of Curling.

I've watched this Winter Olympic event many times on TV. According to club members this sport originated in Scotland and is a gentleman's game. The emphasis is on sportsmanship and although it plays a little bit like bocce it really is unique and a stand-alone game all on its own.

The club had an invitation open to the public, so I showed up to give it a try. The first trick to this game is that you are playing on a frozen surface that you can't scrape of scuff. No blades on this ice and if you look very closely the surface isn't smooth. I found this interesting because we spent a lot of energy rubbing the ice so that the stones could slide.

Curling is about balance and just to prove that to you the first thing you learn is to step on the ice with your non-dominant foot. Why? Because your dominant side is the one wearing the slippery booty for gliding on the ice.

To launch your stone, you have to squat and balance on one foot while pushing off in a lunge. It's a little bit of a dance, which is why I sucked so terribly. Did I mention the slippery ice and balancing on one foot?

Once you send that stone toward the target it's up to your teammates to sweep a slippery path so that rock lands in the center target. It's a workout no matter what position you're in. This open house event was all about teaching technique and I'm sure if I had a desire to play, any of the volunteers would have been excited to teach me more. As experiences go this was fun but I won't be investing in slippers, rocks or a fancy synthetic broom that really doesn't sweep. Day 116 was cold, slippery and fun. Love & Light

Day 117 of 365- I Did ItJanuary 14, 2018

Show me... I had an interesting experience today. The morning started out calm and the afternoon ended in a sports bar. Neither of these experiences are new for me. My first-time adventure happened sometime in between.

For my 117th adventure I attended my very first gun show. In general, I'm not for or against guns. I've been around them my entire life. I spent my childhood watching my father and his friends shoot skeet in the back yard. I was reloading his shotgun shells way before I ever learned to drive.

I'll be honest and confess I don't know much about guns. I don't have a deep desire to shoot but that doesn't mean that I don't know how. When I made the decision to be an at home mom, I also decided to put the guns away. If you haven't been to a show like this, there's a shitload of weapons being sold. There are also grips and clips and ammo and so many collectibles that it's as much about history and it is about the second amendment right to bear arms. It's intimidating to walk through an event like this.

As experiences go this was outside my comfort zone and I won't be trading weapons any time soon. I would suggest you bring a gun-nut with you if you ever attend. They might help answer questions if you have as many as I did. Day 117 was eye opening. Love & Light

Day 118 of 365- I Made It   January 15, 2018

Snow... I live in the Midwest, and my least favorite days of the year are when the snowflakes are flying. I hate to drive in it. Shoveling also scores a zero on the fun meter. When the kids were little, we spent a lot of time playing in the snow. Truth is we were mostly shoveling and when my youngest kid wandered off, we would eventually play and build in that fluffy white fun.

I think the innocence of childhood makes snow an adventure because I haven't found it fun for years. Since the storm that rolled in last night has pinned me in my house, I've decided to make lemonade from the icy lemons. On day 118 I turned a pot of snow into a lovely pile of ice cream. Here's the scoop. <-- see what I did there.

It's a pretty simple process. I used evaporated milk, a bit of sugar and some vanilla extract. I mixed that deliciousness together to build my flavor base. I collected a huge pile of pristine white snow. Don't worry I was careful to avoid anything yellow.

When I put all the ingredients together it made a delicious vanilla ice cream. When I mixed the snow in, I was a little surprised by how thick it became. If you haven't tried this, you should. I ate more than I expected to. The best part was adding some day 55 sprinkles on top. Day 118 was a real treat. Love & Light

Day 119 of 365- I Made It   January 16, 2018

Soap… On my 119th day I decided it was time to make my own scented soap. I've probably washed my hands a thousand times while visiting my mother the last few weeks and the soap there smells horrible and has made my hands beyond dry.

I buy most of my soap at farmer's markets and vendor fairs. I do this because I love patchouli, and I've never been able to find that scent at my local grocery store.

This process was easier than I thought. I found meltable cubes containing the base ingredients. I'm not going to list them all, but I chopped it into tiny chunks, mixed in my patchouli essential oil and cooked it all together. I used some Celtic knot molds, which were so perfect.

The hot soap took about an hour to set and I'm very happy with the final result. I made an exfoliating bar by adding ground apricot pit to the base. Day 119 was another experience that could become a habit. Love & Light

Day 120 of 365- I Saw It   January 17, 2018

Service… For months I've been reading about a film titled "Served like a girl." I'm pretty passionate about bringing awareness to depression and suicide, which cannot be addressed without changing the state of our mental health care system.

Every day precious resources are sent to help people in foreign countries. During that same 24-hour period American veterans sleep on the streets. Depression, PTSD and so many other physical and mental health issues prevent those same men and women from seeking the help they need. The suicide rates for our American Veteran sisters and brothers are frightening. I follow many groups on Facebook, and some happen to be dedicated to US veterans. I grew up in a Navy household. As the youngest child I don't remember relocating as many military families do. I've never been homeless.

On day 120 I watched the film "Served Like a Girl" on Amazon Prime. This film is an eye opener and a call to action. In the current state of the #metoo & #timesup world, it is no surprise that women veterans are horribly underserved. Watch this film. Let it change you. Love & Light

Day 121 of 365- I Did It January 18, 2018

White teeth... Today you are going to hear about my teeth. If that grosses you out, you might not want to read on. Why is my 121st day about teeth?

I've always had issues with my pearly whites. In recent years the fact that they weren't white was a big problem for me. I hate having my picture taken because time and circumstances have made them brown. Here's the real problem. As a child my teeth were damaged. In the early 1980's my four front teeth were bonded with a tooth-like material. After 30 years of coffee, tea and whatever else stains teeth, mine were looking extra icky.

This is a vanity thing. I'm not ashamed to admit it. I visited my dentist and had my bonding replaced with a modern material. I think they look better, but they will never be white. Today's experience involved a less chemical way of whitening. For the next 30 days I'm brushing my teeth with activated charcoal. I'm going to take pictures and time lapse them together. Stay tuned for the video. Love & Light

Day 122 of 365- I Made It   January 19, 2018

Let there be light. Well, let there be lamplight. Today I made a candle. It was not a typical candle. Today I took an orange and made it into an adorable flickering light. Here's the deal. I've been away from my refrigerator a LOT in the last 30 days. Being present with someone I love has become my focus and although these days have added another angle to this 365-day challenge, it has also brought some joy at the same time. Somehow these crazy shenanigans keep me balanced.

Back to the orange that's burning in my kitchen. I saw this on the internet and thought I'd give it a go. First step was to take that fuzzy forgotten orange from my neglected fridge and chop it in half. Next step was a cautious gutting of each half being careful to keep the center pith so I could use it as the wick. See the genius in the design? The other half of the orange had a clump of pulp so I created a star shape cutout so I could cover the bottom bowl.

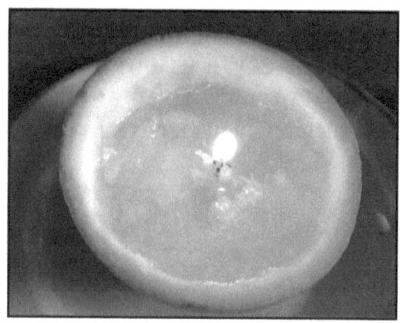

The final step was actual fuel for the flame. I tried olive oil. It wouldn't light so I dumped that and switched to coconut oil. I actually liked this change because when the whole thing cools down the liquid oil becomes solid until I light it again.

This worked so well. Why would you ever need an orange peel candle? I have no clue. I can't even say a doomsday prepper would make this. I guess it doesn't matter because the sucker actually lights and burned for about a half hour before I snuffed it out. Day 122 gave me a moment of chill. Love & so much LIGHT.

Day 123 of 365- I Did It   January 20, 2018

People power… This morning, I marched in the rally for women. We started at the courthouse in Milwaukee with an inspirational crowd and some empowering speakers. I've never marched for or against anything. I've never felt so unrepresented as a woman. It's impossible to be a part of an event like this and not get political. The women who spoke this morning are tired of being less than. I'm tired of being less than.

I stood in that park with my husband and my youngest kid. I'm proud to have a spouse who values me not just for gratification. I've raised my kids to be respectful gentle human beings. I'm proud they are mine. What I saw today invoked a range of emotions. Each speaker addressed human rights issues that women continue to face even after years and years of resistance. I don't understand why we are still fighting all of this.

On my 123rd day I chanted, cheered and clapped for all women of every color. I don't care what makes us different, but I do care that our body configurations make us less than. We are not less than! Love & Light

Day 124 of 365- I Did It   January 21, 2018

    Stained Glass… I have wanted to learn how to make a stained-glass window since I was a child. I'm not sure why I've never done it before. The process of making this piece of art will take more than one day and I had no idea that each step is so time consuming. On day 124 I learned the first step and perhaps the answer to why I've hesitated for so long, cutting glass at On a Whim.

    Cutting glass seems simple enough, right? It really should be, but I have so much hesitation even after a few hours of doing it. The glass-cutting tool is very basic and as I roll it across the glass the crunchy grinding sound is extremely unsettling. After tracing and scoring the glass, I have to snap it and cross my fingers with hope that it actually separates where I want it to. I had a 75% success rate but was pretty good at placing my pieces so that I had enough material for every piece.

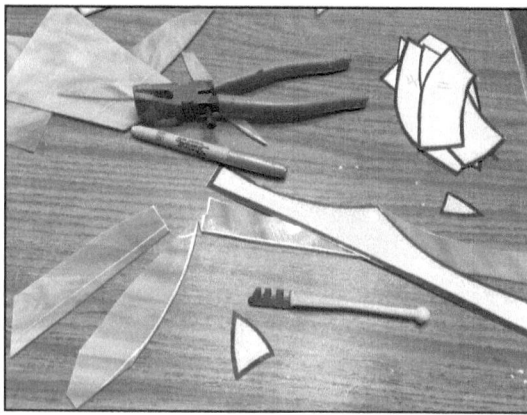

I'm not going to give away what the final project will look like, but you get to see the blue colors that I chose. On day 124 I had the best time overcoming another fear. Love & Light

Day 125 of 365- I Made It   January 22, 2018

Noodles... It's a cool rainy January afternoon. I live in the Midwest where we should have a few feet of snow but instead we have about that same measurement of rain. What the heck?

So instead of the adventure I had planned I decided on day 125 I should hand make some egg noodles. What I should have done was make soup and add the noodles but that would have required a bit more planning. I really love noodles, and I especially love egg noodles, but I've never mixed, rolled and hand cut my own. The recipe is so very simple and mixing this took no time at all. The real work came in kneading the dough and rolling it about 1/8th inch thick. It took a bit of time and a lot of muscle.

I wanted to use my cookie cutter to put a rippled edge on the noodles, but the old, tired tool just made a mess. I used the pizza cutter and rolled out a delicious pile of fresh goodness.

The recipe calls for a lot of waiting and you'll remember that patience is just not a thing I have but today I actually rested the dough for ten minutes and let the noodles hang dry for a few hours. I didn't want all that hard work to go to waste with a gloppy noodle mess. I grilled some chicken and added cheese sauce. The real experience here was the rich chewy texture and flavor of the noodles. They were amazing. Day 125 was delicious. Love & Light

Day 126 of 365- I Made It   January 23, 2018

Whip it! Remember a few days ago when I called out the weather in Wisconsin? Well, the universe was listening and now I'm trapped by 7 inches of snow. Yesterday I made some amazing noodles and the recipe called for only egg yolks.

When I separated the eggs, I kept the whites with the idea I would use them for something. I figured I had a few days to make that mess, so I put them in the fridge. It turns out that being trapped in my house by 7 inches of snow gave me the perfect opportunity to have another kitchen adventure.

My son and I enjoy meringue cookies and I've spent a few dollars at the grocery store purchasing them. As I searched the web for a recipe, I was happy to discover that I already had all the ingredients. What was the warning that came up during my YouTube recipe search? Make sure your mixer is clean and dry. Heeding this warning I prepared my equipment with vinegar. Since growing that SCOBY on day 6, I started using white vinegar to clean my jars and continued when making kombucha. Yep, I've still got that growing in the pantry.

I cleaned all my tools for whipping and beating those egg whites and got started. I set the oven to preheat at 200 degrees. As the eggs made a foamy mix, I added the sugar one tablespoon at a time. I thought this process would require more patience, but it went pretty quick and looked shiny and a bit like frosting.

The problem is that raw egg whites that look like frosting could also cause a problem if I licked it from my fingers. To test the proper consistency, you need to feel the meringue to make sure the fine sugar granules have been beaten out. Just don't lick your fingers. That was my chant the entire time it was mixing. I added some almond extract to the mix just as my liquids turned to shiny solids.

I was going to spoon the meringue out on the baking paper but decided to pipe it using a Ziploc bag. It didn't go as planned so I made some lopsided cookies. They baked for about two hours on that low heat and made a beautiful, finished result. Day 126 was another delicious adventure. Love & Light

Day 127 of 365- I Did ItJanuary 24, 2018

Get Out! I've heard so many people talk about escape rooms and using logic to get out of a locked environment.

Tonight, I took my three loving family members with me to escape the room. Since it's an experience meant to challenge your wits, I was certain that each of my people would bring a different skill to this challenge.

I was so very right! The four of us worked that puzzle and relied on each other to find the right clue and combination in the right order. It was so amazing and a bit of an adrenaline rush. I don't want to be specific because any info might spoil it for future endeavors. I will say that BR8KOUT Escape Rooms did an amazing job creating the challenge.

If you haven't tried an escape room, you absolutely should. Just remember to bring your gifted and talented people with you. Day 127 was liberating. Love & Light

Day 128 of 365- I Did ItJanuary 25, 2018

Bump and a lot of grind. A few days ago I learned how to cut glass. I should share that I made it through that experience without hurting myself. I think that in itself is quite an accomplishment.

Cutting glass was the first step in my stained-glass project. On day 128 I moved on to the very treacherous glass grinding.

My instructions were quick and a bit unsettling:
1. Make sure the grinding wheel is wet.
2. Move your glass along that grinder in the opposite direction of rotation.
3. You will get covered in minute particles of glass, DON'T RUB ANY OF YOUR SKIN!
4. The edges are shiny, grind the shiny away.

She did a short demonstration so I could see what to do. I put on my safety eyewear. As she left me there with my project glass and grinder she also warned of cuts and not to worry she had Band-Aids. As I explained earlier, I didn't need the Band-Aid, but it did make me more aware of how I was working.

The process took about 90 minutes, and I was indeed covered with a fine wet film of something itchy. I used my extra water to wash my arms off when I finished. I'm hoping this part of the stained-glass adventure is complete because it was easy enough but not my favorite. Love & Light

Day 129 of 365- I Made It   January 26, 2018

Great Balls of Fire!! A few years ago, a family friend showed this to me, and my son reminded me about it. I'd watched the YouTube hijinks and thought it might be a tiny bit nuts, which made it perfect for day 129. Flaming balls that you hold in your hand might sound a little kooky but after 128 days I'm ready to go way out of my comfort zone.

The preparation was pretty simple. Cut some cotton fabric. Shape and tie it into a ball. I made two because I wanted to hold one in each hand. It's very important that all the material is 100% cotton, so it'll hold the alcohol fuel and not melt from the heat. Polyester fabric and string will melt.

The balls were dropped into the bowl of alcohol and swished around so all sides are coated in the liquid. The alcohol burns off pretty fast. When the flame died, I did keep dunking it. Using tweezers, I picked up the balls and lit them on fire.

Here's the thing, those flaming balls need to be moving because the longer you hold them in the palm of your hand the hotter they get. Don't worry, I didn't get burned and my house is still standing. I'm pretty sure that my mother would disapprove of this challenge if I had performed it in her kitchen. I can't wait to show her the video. This was one of the COOLEST experiences. Day 129 was a hot one. Love & Flaming Light

Day 130 of 365- I Ate It   January 27, 2018

Mmm Mmm not so good... Let's talk about the Miracle fruit AKA Magic Berry. This little red gem is in fact a bit magical. Here's how my adventure went. The little red tablet is meant to change the way that foods taste. I saw a video of people using this magic fruit and having an interesting reaction to some extreme food flavors.

Let's start with what was on the menu. Each of these items have distinct flavors. I invited my people to join this experience, and we started with the apple. We found that apple tasted like nothing at all. It was all texture and no flavor. This tricked us into thinking that the tablet didn't work so we moved on to the hot sauce.

On a normal taco-eating day this sauce has some zip. I like the kick it adds to just about anything, but this is where we start to take a taste bud turn. That hot sauce was like the sweet syrup. I had to take a second little spoonful because I couldn't get over the difference. We confirmed hot status when my sweetheart felt it on the tender lip zone. It was indeed HOT! We chased that deliciousness with cottage cheese. I'm not huge on dairy and this tasted like eating butter. It was so rich I didn't need any more. I know you're wondering what could possibly be next.

How about kosher dill pickles? This was almost an experience ender. I LOVE pickles... well most pickles. My grandmother, bless her, made the worst pickles and she made a lot of them. When she passed, we inherited more than anyone could ever eat. Thanks, Granny. My magic berry flavored pickles tasted like the worst thing I've ever had in my mouth. I did not spit it out, but I really wanted to. Calling it sour like festering milk would be an understatement. There should be a Bertie Bot Bean and it should be called "magic berry pickle" because it's almost as bad as skunk or dog food. If you don't understand the reference, please Google it.

Moving on from the trauma, we sampled lemon, lime and pomegranate. All three had the reverse taste than you would expect. Lemonade and limeade came to mind immediately, and I was surprised by the sweetness. The pomegranate was pretty neutral. It wasn't great or horrible.

In the middle of all this someone had the brilliant idea to taste brandy. Sometimes too much is exactly that. The brandy didn't exist in my mouth as a flavor until it burned from my throat down to my stomach. Yep, none of the flavor and all the burn. This would also be exactly how the final treat of apple cider vinegar felt. I'm not sure if there is an opposite of taste but this might be it. What's the takeaway for day 130?

Antacids! My stomach is still burning, and it's been hours. Just because you can't taste it doesn't mean it's a good combination to eat. On the other side of things, if you want to have fun tasting food in an interesting way this might be it. Forget family game night, this 30-minute pill will entertain the whole crowd. Love & Light

Day 131 of 365- I Did It   January 28, 2018

Ice Ice Baby! Today's adventure was exciting. I had my first ice fishing experience on Lake Geneva. The morning started pretty early and involved a minimum amount of coffee. There's no ladies room on the lake.

When I arrived at the home of my fishing host family, the Wingers, they brought me out on the lake. The sidesaddle quad ride was pretty chilly as we towed the portable ice shack out.

As fishing goes the Jack and Eric had the super special spot where the little fish were biting the day before. Setup was fast and efficient. I think Eric and Jack might have done this a few times. We used a few augers to make two different sized holes. Fishing gadgets are set up in one 5" hole and we jig our tiny poles in the second 8" opening. The ice was about 8 inches thick, and I felt pretty safe until some crazy fool drove his pickup truck out to his shack. You could hear the thunder of the ice crack. NOT COOL!

Once we sat down it didn't take long for the fish to swim in. The guys have a video camera dropped down to the bottom of the lake and I watched the fish swim in and snatch the bait. It was an occasional distraction from actually catching a fish, but it made the first-time experience something special.

We spent about 6 hours on this fishing trip, and I could have stayed out there 6 more. As hosts go these guys are amazing and I should thank Di for setting it all up. I really needed an experience that disconnected me for a few hours. I'm sure you're wondering how it went. We got a few. Day 131 was a perfect catch. Love & Light

Day 132 of 365- I Made It   January 29, 2018

The pen-cil is mighty. Today's experience started early. I woke up with the pencil making idea in my head. That's how it works sometimes. I knew this would be something to do because I've always wanted to buy one of those tree branch pencils from the cracker barrel gift shop. If you've been there, you know what I'm talking about.

On day 132 I hand crafted a stick pencil. The materials are so quick. I went out in the back yard and snipped a few branches from my favorite trees. One magnolia, one lilac and another mystery bush because the limb was so perfectly straight.

I used drafting pencil leads for the writing part of this little project. I happened to get HB which is pretty hard and that was smart because it did require a lot of pressure to insert the lead. I trimmed away most of the twisted and gnarly twigs to create the shafts. The next part was easier than I thought it would be. I drilled the center hole for the lead to fit into. I was worried I might split the pieces, so I took my time. I drilled out four just in case.

The final part was gluing it all together. Sticky good fun happened, and I slathered the lead and globbed a bunch on the top on the sticks. Everything came together but the depth of my drilled hole limited the length of the lead.

As experiences go this was so fun. I'm waiting for the project to dry so I can sharpen and use them. If you're a scout mom this might be a great activity once your kid can handle a pocketknife and a drill, or you could go old-school and use a hand drill for the pioneer affect. On day 132 I enjoyed this mighty experience. Love & Light

Day 133 of 365- I Made It   January 30, 2018

    Fire… Today I wanted to do something that is completely reckless and a little stupid. I made and shot a flaming arrow instead. I've watched many movies and TV shows with a fiery arrow used for dramatic affect. That was not my goal today. On Day 133 I just wanted to build and launch an arrow that would hold flame, fly and hit a target... ON FIRE.

    I used a coconut oil soaked cotton cloth. I decided on this fuel because it turns to a solid when it gets cold. This way it wouldn't drip while I was lighting it. I knew it would stay lit because it made amazing fuel for my candle on day 122. I tied the cloth to the shaft of an arrow. It was really that simple and here's where all the fabulous fun happened. We built a quick target, and I took a few test shots. I was using the bow that I helped build on day 37. This is the first time I actually fired it and I love this Hickory bow.

    From beginning to end this experience was a success. I might have been a tiny bit off target but when the arrow hit the ground it was still on fire. As experiences go, day 133 was extra-flamey. Love & Light

## Day 134 of 365- I Saw It	January 31, 2018

  The moon was neither blue, nor bloody and only a tiny bit super. This morning, I woke up early to go outside and catch a glimpse of that once in a lifetime moon. I read on NPR that it was a perfect trifecta of a lunar experience. Why? I got to see a blue moon, a lunar eclipse and super moon all at the same time. This hasn't happened since 1866.

  We get to see a blue moon when two full moons appear in the same month. A lunar eclipse happens when the moon moves into the shadow of the earth. A super moon occurs when the moon is closer to earth's orbit and more than 10% brighter.

  And if this wasn't amazing enough, while that moon is in eclipse it will take on a reddish color creating the blood part of this equation.

  When I stepped out into the tropical 32-degree air I was excited to actually see this moon. I wasn't sure if the clouds would be in the way. I went in the house to grab my DSLR and attached the monopod for stability. Low light and high speed need a steadier hand than I have. The top picture was the first one that I took. I was pretty pleased to experience the eclipsing before the clouds rolled in.

  My problem came as the transition started to set behind my barn. I got the brilliant idea to hop in my car and drive to a location where I could see the entire moon set and eclipse in all its glory.

  That's when it all went to hell. Those clouds rolled in and just as I put my car in to park the moon disappeared. I'm not disappointed because what I saw was beautiful and I managed to take a few pictures that I'm extremely happy with. Day 134 was worth the cold and the drive. Love & Light

Day 135 of 365- I Saw It   February 1, 2018

Hands... This was an interesting day. There are so many new things and experiences swirling around inside this hospital space. If I'm honest, I could give you a new medical experience for the last 40+ days that would probably cover the entirety of the 365.

My focus on day 135 was on breathing and the comfort given by hands. Illness and disease create stress for everyone, those in crisis and those who support the person in crisis. An observation over the last weeks has been the constant touching that goes on out of necessity that does not involve tenderness. It gets lost in the realities of hospitalization.

My role has been one of support and today was like starting out all over again but something pretty wonderful happened. On this 135th day my mother let me massage her hands and share calm breathing techniques. This might have been more therapeutic for me than it was for her. I've been waiting for permission to give her care. Outstanding nurses and their assistants have surrounded her; all foreign hands taking care of needs. Until now she only wanted their care.

Today she finally asked for help from my untrained hands, and I felt joy. I am certain she has no idea the strength it has given me. She has the ability to bring out the 10-year-old child still lurking in my heart. Mom's hands have been in a hospital for a while.

Today they were so dry and with minimal words she asked for lotion. We talked about a hand massage I had a long time ago and how the therapist worked on every joint of each finger until my hands were soft and happy from the experience. Mom closed her eyes and let me work. We held hands for the longest time.

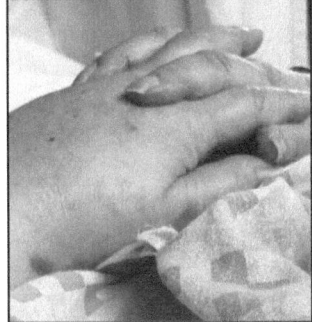

I love you mom. Day 135 was something I never imagined would be a part of my journey. Love & Light

Day 136 of 365- I Made It   February 2, 2018

Spring... I heard that Punxsutawney Phil saw his shadow this morning. I'm not sure why we take weather advice from a giant rodent that burrows through the yard, but it got me thinking about spring and all the beautiful flowers that pop up every year. The thing is that those treasures were planted in my yard. Many of them came from my mother.

My incredible mother is a master gardener. She has spent years learning about flowers and plants. She has beautiful gardens and every spring she plans what she will do next. Spring of 2018 will have some slight modifications for now. On day 136 I had the idea to bring one of her favorite spring flowers inside to her. Since tulips were a topic of conversation with her on day 135, I decided to learn how to make them from paper and plant them in her window at the hospital.

The plan wasn't complex, but execution had to happen in stages. Shopping for supplies at 7:00am was sketchy but I found everything I needed before her breakfast meal was served. I explained my plan and her little half grin was all I needed to see.

Mom watched as I made all the parts and assembled the first flower. I asked if she wanted to help and I got the little wave that she makes when she's Okay to be an observer. I continued. Before long I'd created two more flowers. She asked me to go get her some water and when I returned, she had taken over part of the task. This really was a moment of joy. I know it's not the same as digging in the dirt but for that moment we were gardening in our paper field.

I think I could have spent the entire day making those flowers with her, but reality set in and we had to tend to the business of healing. When I came home this afternoon my youngest kid and I finished filling her tiny steel bucket with tulips, this time in her favorite color yellow. I think mom would be delighted to know another generation of flower making was born, even if we grew paper tulips. Day 136 was another hands-on day filled with hope.

Day 137 of 365- I Did It   February 3, 2018

Pets... We have two cats. They are exactly the cats that you see in comics and cartoons. Two females and they are the worst. Affectionate on their own terms, they rarely need humans unless we bring food and water. Today I thought I'd take a break from my sassy cats and see what was out there in the world of pets.

On day 137 we attended a huge pet expo. Remember how I went to a gun show a few weekends back. I've decided these make terrible experiences because they are not what I expect them to be. I wanted puppies and baby animals. I thought it would be more like an adoption fair but instead it was all the crap that people buy to try to humanize their animal friends. Some people I know would have LOVED this experience.

We walked the massive pavilion, and I did enjoy the Husky rescue groups that were there. It made me miss my dog, but it was also very clear that this space is catering to the canine crowd. Since we lost Jake in December of 2016 it wasn't as interesting to navigate. The occasional roofing booths and the Cutco knife table reminded me that this is a vendor fair as much as it is a pet event. I really don't need to attend this one again. There was an area with reptiles and tarantulas. I did walk through the snakes and decided I didn't need any of that anxiety, so I scooted out of there. Creepy crawly things are a no-go with me. Day 137 was for the dogs. Love & Light

## Day 138 of 365- I Made It	February 4, 2018

Pizza… It's super bowl Sunday in the USA. If I told you that I really don't care much about football unless the Packers are playing it might express how little I actually care about the game itself. Back in the day we would celebrate the many January and February birthdays on game day just so we had a wonderful gathering. We haven't done it for a few years, and it isn't happening today. In fact, it'll be a quiet evening at home, so I thought I'd take advantage of the captive audience and experiment on them.

On day 138 I decided to make cauliflower crust pizza. Pizza for a football game sounds exactly perfect so to make it an experience I decided to get all the ingredients to do it with cauliflower. I worked at a pizza parlor when I was a college student, and I tossed a few crusts in that time. Today there would be a ton of squeezing and zero tossing. I'll admit right off that I didn't rice the cauliflower myself.

I spent the morning with mom and time forced me to purchase it already prepared. I cooked it up and pressed out as much of the liquid as I could. It's a lot like doing the goat cheese on day 23; the drier the better. Once the riced cauliflower was dry, I added and egg and some feta cheese. I mixed it all as if it was dough but extremely squishy and slightly gross. I added an herb blend of garlic, oregano and pepper just before pressing in into a pizza pan lined with parchment paper.

I baked it for 40 minutes to set it and start that crunchy crust that I love so much. So, it wasn't exactly crunchy. If you ever try this, you need to use cheesecloth and squeeze every drop of fluid out of that cauliflower. My crust didn't dry out, so we had to eat it with a fork. It was delicious and amazing, and I'd do it again. Day 138 was delicious. Love & Light

Day 139 of 365- I Made It   February 5, 2018

    Snakes on the snow... It's fair to say that I had a slightly different adventure planned for today but after my morning with mom and driving home in the snow I decided to do something a little fun that required zero driving.
    In a perfect world this experience was spectacular.
On day 139 I wanted to turn sugar into a snake. You might have played with that charcoal looking snake on the 4th of July. When I was a child, it was a pretty exciting "firework" right before we lit the sparklers. I never knew the chemical reason why those little black snakes grew from the tiny pellet, but I loved them. I would stack them together to try to get the biggest one I could.
    So that's what made my adventure for the day so very exciting. I was finally getting the chance to grow a giant charcoal snake. It's so easy to make that I had to hit myself for not doing this at a younger age. I mixed 1 part baking soda to 4 parts powdered sugar. I filled a pan with sand and soaked that with some vodka. I needed an alcohol accelerant but that didn't work out well, so I used lighter fluid instead.
    Once the sand was saturated, I made a little hole in it and poured my sugar/soda combo in. I lit that sucker on fire and after a minute I got my snake. It took a bit of time to grow. It's not as dramatic as I thought it would be but when it was done, I had fulfilled that childhood dream. Day 139 was a reality that might have been better as a dream. Love & Light

Day 140 of 365- I Did It   February 6, 2018

My face, I have done a few adventures that involved some glimpses at vanity. I'm a very simple person and pretty low maintenance. I don't put a bunch of goo on my skin so it's pretty clean. Stress is my big enemy right now and advocating for mom's care is at times overwhelming. It has started to show on my skin so on day 140 I gave my face a break. I did my first ever paper facial.

Here's the deal. Homemade masks can be done with simple fresh ingredients, but I found a really cool all in one that was perfect because I didn't have to make the paper cutout and soak it. It can be done using a paper towel but that can wait until next time.

I opened the pouch and unfolded the mask with cautious hands. The material is pretty flimsy but it's also very lightweight on my skin. It didn't fit my face, so I had to fold a few areas over to compensate. I could feel the fluid immediately. It's soaked with tomato juice and other secret ingredients that I'm hoping are gobbling up all the gross crap in my pores. 10 minutes later and I pull it away to fresh tingly skin. I quick rinse and pat and I can feel the skin of my cheeks tightening.

I admit that it felt amazing and I wish it was healthy to do more often. Let's face it, day 140 was perfectly refreshing. Love & Light

Day 141 of 365- I Ate It   February 7, 2018

Surprise… Since 2005 I have been getting Kinder Surprise eggs for my kids. If you aren't familiar with the candy/toy combo watch this Kinder YouTube advertisement.

I'm so sorry for the creep factor. I'm not sure how this ad made anyone want to buy candy, but my kids went nuts on their first trip to Australia and I'll bet I bought 20 eggs. Today on day 141 for the first time ever I ate an American kinder "JOY" egg. These little suckers were banned in America about 10 years ago because parents didn't supervise their children when they ate this candy.

There's a toy inside of it and I guess American kids aren't as smart as Australian kids because the government protected us from this dangerous candy/toy experience. Thank goodness our guns are safe.

The two products are completely different, and I could try to describe it, but you should just watch the video I made. Day 141 Love & Light

Day 142 of 365- I Made It   February 8, 2018

I love adventures that take two days to create. Today, part one is making something I've never even wanted to make before, gum paste. Most people might not know what this is. I'll admit that when I started to organize these 365 days of fun, I had no idea it even existed as a thing. On day 142 I set out to make gum paste. Why?

Have you ever eaten a cake covered in fondant? I haven't but I've watched their creation on baking shows. I have always wanted to know how to do it and what it tastes like. The difference between fondant and gum paste is pretty clear once it dries.

Gum paste turns rock hard and is great for making candy flowers to top off cupcakes or other creations. The recipe is pretty simple, powdered sugar, cornstarch, gelatin and cream of tartar. Mixing all of these ingredients in the right order are what creates the magic. It has to be kneaded like dough and since I have a lot of practice from my day 125 noodle making muscles were ready.

Being made from sugar this gets extremely sticky and messy, and the original recipe called for Crisco as a lubricant for my hands. Since I would never have that in my pantry, I used coconut oil instead.

It worked like a dream and after about 20 minutes of smushing this around I had two beautiful patties of gum paste. Stay tuned to find out the purpose. When all is said and done you might just join me in making this. Day 142 was sticky and sweet. Love & Light

Day 143 of 365- I Made It   February 9, 2018

Minty fresh... If you've been waiting to find out what that gum paste was for, the wait is over. On day 143 I created my very own curiously strong mints. This was my plan all along. I went to a vendor fair and in the dark corner hidden between an overpriced handbag booth and a Pampered Chef table was an adorable woman selling homemade soaps, balms, salves and mints. She was also selling food grade essential oils which was her min gig.

I didn't want to buy anything, but it did get me thinking about how and why I didn't do this for myself.

I've already made the soaps and to be honest that's not much fun but today was actually enjoyable. I had two favorite flavors in mind, licorice and peppermint. I used Anise extract and a young living oil of peppermint that I won at a Breast Cancer fundraiser. It was a weird full-circle moment there.

The gum paste rested overnight, and I mixed the Anise extract in to it. I wanted to give these a little black licorice tint, so I used my food grade activated charcoal from. Day 121. It worked perfectly and I spent about 10 minutes blending the color evenly.

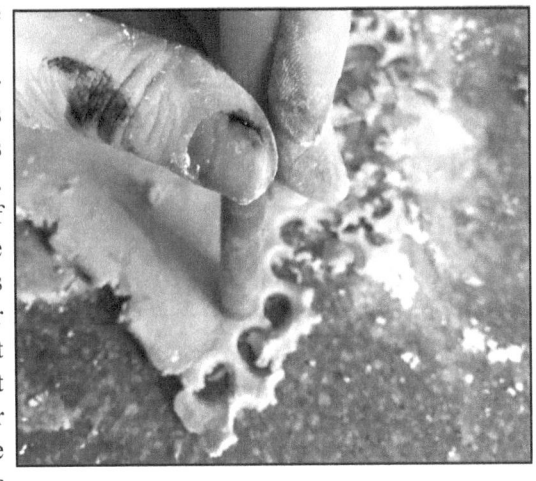

The most time-consuming part of this experience was punching out the mints. I used two straws of different sizes to make this happen. One was for cutting and the other was for extracting that cut. It was a great design and with Wonder Woman playing in the background I hand cut a few hundred licorice and peppermint mini mints.

Once they were all cut, I put them in powdered sugar to help absorb the moisture and laid them out to dry. This is an overnight process but as I type, they look amazing, and I can't wait to give them a taste. Day 143 was a total hit. Love & Light

Day 144 of 365- I Did It   February 10, 2018

    I fly… So, there are things I said I would absolutely NOT do during this adventure and skydiving was mentioned very specifically. On day 144 I attempted an indoor flight in a wind tunnel. This was my skydiving.

    The buildup was a tiny bit intense as parking in the city is a full contact sport. Maybe it's a setup to make me dizzy and test my ability to do the tunnel. Either way we made it into the actual building. That felt like an accomplishment. The staff at this facility did an amazing job of checking us in. After a quick orientation video, they gave us the cute flight suits to wear. My family came with me, and we each had completely different flights.

    The gear is basic. I wore earplugs for the noise and goggles so I could actually open my eyes inside that wind tunnel. The helmet is an obvious necessity and the flight suit is as much a tool for guiding me and it was comfort for the experience. I went into this with a healthy bit of fear and a huge amount of excitement.

    Scotty, my instructor was amazing and by using hand signals he was able to guide me in the proper position so I could feel like a flying being. Actual fly time is short, and I would have liked to do a few more minutes but this was a real true out of my box adventure. Day 144 was nothing I've ever experienced before, and I would probably do it again. Love & Light

Day 145 of 365- I Ate It   February 11, 2018

Cake pop... I've avoided this ridiculous mini monster for so long but on day 145 I couldn't resist this free first-time experience. The idea of a cake pop has to be the biggest dessert scam ever. This is what I see. As an example, let's use it as a celebratory treat. A cake pop is not big enough to count as a slice of cake and nowhere close to the size of a cupcake.

So, what's the point? "To express my great fondness of you I'm going to take a single bite of cake and put it on a stick. This forces you to eat it in one bite because two makes half fall on the floor."

Who came up with this idea?? I white knuckle drove my car this morning in a snowstorm to be with mom. I dropped my oldest kid off at Starbucks to wait for work. We took a few minutes to get coffee, and the store was offering free samples of the valentine cake pop.

This was a doughy gooey mess on a stick. True confession... it was chocolate and that was the real decision maker. I ate it and it was more like undercooked brownie. For my first experience eating one of these I would not ever need one again. Day 145 was chocolate and that was the best part.
Love & Light

Day 146 of 365- I Saw It   February 12, 2018

Medicine and Science... I'm a writer and an author. I've penned a half dozen books and I've published two. It's safe to say that I'm always writing something, and my computer is never very far away. My mother has always been my biggest cheerleader. I am spending a lot of time with her these days and in the early morning moments, as she wakes, she's had some stories to tell.

During one of those sunrise conversations, I asked her if she wanted me to write any of them down. She gave me a little half grin and said she had four stories to tell. I asked her what they were. Without missing a beat, she said let's start with this...

Knock Knock? Who's there? Brain Cancer...

It's not a joke. This is really where the story begins. On day 146 I did something I never ever wanted to do. I watched radiation therapy. This is a big part of the story. The process looked like some kind of science fiction but there's nothing fictitious about what I was seeing.

There's so much going on in the huge room. The technology would be outrageously cool if it wasn't about to destroy the parts of the body it's aimed at. There's a rotating platform that looks like a bed. Before every dose this equipment takes a CT scan of the target zone, and it's displayed on one of a half dozen monitors in the lead lined room behind it.

What does it feel like? I was told its most like the imaging done when you look for a broken bone. I never intend to experience the power of this equipment firsthand. As a witness it's all about being on the support team.

Truth be told, I hate leaving mom alone. The treatment doesn't take very long and the waiting and watching continues. The focus is all on wellness and healing. Day 146 was a struggle. I've always known my mother is a strong woman. Today, with my own eyes, I witnessed it. Love & Light

Day 147 of 365- I Ate It   February 13, 2018

Rite of passage… In 218 days, I'll be a 50-year-old woman. I've spent the last 146 days doing so many new things, but I must pause to appreciate my son turning 21. Most 21-year olds celebrate with their peers and get trashed and vow to never drink that way again.

I didn't turn 21 that way and neither did my son. He celebrated tonight with me. We honored my father who turned 80 on the same day. How do you celebrate turning 21 and 80 on the same day? Booze! I quit drinking last July. Tonight, I had my first "Rusty Nail." It's a combination of Drambuie and Scotch and it knocked me for a loop. It tastes like an old smoked pipe. My father was a pipe smoker, and I might have tasted a pipe once or twice in my life. This is a hard drink to enjoy.

I feel like we did the moment well. No naughty drunkenness, just a respectful slow sip of a wonderful man's favorite drink. Day 147 was one to remember. Love & Light

Day 148 of 365- I Did It   February 14, 2018

Thaw and freeze... I have no idea how I would have made it through the last months without YouTube. I created my own channel during this adventure so that I could share videos of the really wild and crazy things I've been doing. Truth be told, I had wilder things in mind but spending half of my day at hospitals has changed everything about my original intention.

I've encountered an immeasurable amount of science in ways that I also never intended but most of it has been about transformations. I really wanted to experiment with freezing water and watching that moment when what is liquid becomes a solid.

On day 148 I played with freezing water. The process should have been simple. Get water. Make water really cold. Watch it freeze.

Science and the forces of nature change water to ice every day in some place on this planet. I had a difficult time doing it in my kitchen. It really is all about timing. The water has to be just on the edge of freezing before I shock it into solid form. I tested 6 different bottles and had minimal success with all but 1.

Most of it was just realllly cold. One was already slushing to solid. The interesting part is that all of them went into the freezer at the same time. Science is so weird. The final bottle started to turn just as I attempted to pour it and it was amazing to watch. I call day 148 mostly successful. Love & Light

Day 149 of 365- I Did It   February 15, 2018

Feast or famine... It's Thursday February 15th, in Wisconsin. A few days ago, I almost got stuck in the foot of snow at the end of my driveway. When I look at my list of adventures, I try to plan them so I can take advantage of things like 12 inches of fluffy white snow. I should have known that if I waited, I might miss my opportunity.

On day 149 I attempted my first snowshoeing adventure. To execute this perfect plan, I loaded up my car with everything I would need to have a wild experience in the deep beautiful white snow. When I was able to get outside today it was 42 degrees. I jumped the puddles in the parking lot.

This plan was looking like a total failure, but I decided to give it a try. I'm not sure when or if this chance will come before spring. My snowshoes are interesting. They're designed to hold an average adult's weight. I feel like I'm average in size, so I secured these floppy platforms to my winter boots and stepped onto the slushy white-ish snow. Did I mention the slush? Snowshoes are meant for snow and what I ended up doing was slopping around on some muddy gloppy snow-cone smush.

It wasn't ideal but it was fun. My feet felt light for the first part of the walk. I was able to stay on top of the areas that were still deep with that white fluff. Anywhere the sunshine hit the earth today it was dirty muddy brown glop. This isn't fun or lightweight and definitely NOT what snowshoeing is about.

I continued on. I wanted to find some animal tracks and follow them into the woods but there was so much mud. I made the most of my snow adventure. If it returns, I might travel out to a local state park and take advantage of some hiking trails in the winter. That's what I was really hoping for. Day 149 was a sloppy good time. Love & Light

Day 150 of 365- I Made It   February 16, 2018

Foiling… It's day 150 and I finally got a chance to revisit my stained-glass project. I'm so excited to make progress and can't wait for the big reveal. Today I learned how to foil glass. It was time consuming and required a level of patience I wasn't sure I would have after a long exhausting morning.

I had to prepare all the freshly ground pieces. Once all of them were washed and dried I wrapped every edge with copper foil. It's a lot like taping all the trim just before you prepare to paint. If you short cut you'll end up with a bigger mess or worse yet, epic failure.

I managed to complete all 15 pieces of this experience and I'm ready to move on to the next stage. Stay tuned for the final reveal. I'm not sure what day it might happen, but it definitely will. Day 150 looked promising. Love & Light

Day 151 of 365- I Saw It   February 17, 2018

Winter fun... Who wears sneakers to a Wisconsin winter event? This girl! Who wears a fleece jacket to a snowy outdoor festival? This girl!

It's day 151 and I went to my first winter fest. Thank goodness I had a coat in my trunk. To make this adventure authentic it was actually cold and snowy because February in Wisconsin could honestly give any temperature and any storm front.

When I arrived, I was anticipating an enormous crowd. I had front row parking. This should have been an indicator of what type of event I was attending. It was definitely a family event. It was so family that there were about 4 kids to every adult and then there were more kids everywhere. I felt like a creeper.

The event had games and activities, which I thought, were intended for adults. Nope, it was all scaled to the 36" crowd. CREEPER! There were a few beautiful ice sculptures and some food vendors. I actually felt bad for the poor people sitting out in the snow trying to sell caramel corn and candy treats.

I did get a chance to carve 365 in a giant block of ice. As adventures go this one was a bust and I can say that it was a first and a last. Day 151 was cold, snowy and had a bit of pretty ice. Love & Light

Day 152 of 365- I Did It   February 18, 2018

Float ... There were a few things that I absolutely knew I would do during this 365-day challenge. It took me 152 days, but I finally got to float. If you don't know what I'm talking about let me sum it up. I visited Float Life, a 60-minute experience of weightlessness in a bath of salted water.

What made this experience worth every dollar was a complete escape from time and space. If you have the ability to let go of the world around you, it is bliss. For this adventure you strip away everything. You enter this adorable pod with earplugs, a hand towel and a spray bottle of clean water; no clothing and no reason for it. I pulled the handle that closed the top of the pod creating silence and darkness.

I don't have a fear of small spaces but once the lights went out all that you could feel was the warm water and the absence of gravity on your body. I drifted around inside the pod and my 60 minutes felt like hours. The sound of my heart beating was all I could hear. It created a drumbeat that added to the meditative experience.

It was the perfect creation of nothing. If you can't stand silence or small spaces, you might want to avoid the pod. If you've ever wondered about trying it, you absolutely should. Day 152 was the escape I needed. Love & Light

Day 153 of 365- I Made It   February 19, 2018

    Butter up... Today it rained. The buildings I spend most of my days in are so dry I welcomed any moisture even if it was outside. A few times a week I become the bringer of moisturizer when I take care of mom with lotion provided by her nurses. Today I wanted to make a gentle massage lotion for tender skin. I also wanted it to be simple, using real ingredients.

    On day 153 I made all-natural whipped body butter. I happen to cook with coconut oil, which made this an easy experience. I scooped that with some Shea butter, hemp oil and my essential oils for fragrance. I read a few articles on how to mix my ingredients, and I chose to work them at room temperature that makes the creamy last longer. My shelf life is a few weeks, which is fine since I expect this to be gone by then.

    I used my hand mixer to blend everything into a creamy frosting consistency. I decided to make three different blends, Frankincense, peppermint and a special combination of my favorite aromas. It went well and I bottled them in small jelly jars. I'll use them tomorrow when I visit my mom. I can't wait to see what she thinks. Day 153 was smooth as can be. Love & Light

Day 154 of 365- I Ate It   February 20, 2018

    Food of the gods... There are things that I've chosen not to eat because they look horrible and there are things that just never made it to my dinner table because they're impossible to find. On day 154 the juicy delicious persimmon made its way into my kitchen.

    I bought this piece of fruit in a beautiful orange hue. This particular variety is the Fuyu Persimmon. There are other varieties, but this one was all I could find in my local grocery store. In the future I might look for other varieties to compare. I cut this piece of fruit in half pulling it away from the stem leaves. The skin is pretty tough, so I cut that away to get to the very juicy fruit inside. Here's the amazing... this was so sweet and then it was a little nutty.

    The flavor was so familiar, but I couldn't place it. This is my new favorite fruit. It was reasonably priced and if I can find it again, I might just add it to my kombucha that's brewing in the pantry. Day 154 tasted so very sweet. Love & Light

Day 155 of 365- I Made It   February 21, 2018

Springing spring... Today's experience went well but it wasn't how I planned to do it. It was definitely a first, but I wanted someone special to be involved. When I invited mom to help me, she said it was too messy. She was absolutely correct, but I didn't really care about making a mess. She did and I decided to let her rest and do this all on my own.

On day 155 I let the master gardener take a nap and I made my very first seed bombs. Mom is an amazing plant whisperer and lives for gardening. She's spent many hours planning events to teach anyone about her passion for plants, flowers, herbs and things that grow in the dirt. That's why I accomplished this adventure in her honor. The process was super messy, mostly because I had to squeeze all the liquid out of the paper I made into juicy pulp.

This was very similar to my paper making adventure on day 7. I poured an entire package of wildflower seeds in after liquefying my recycled paper. Instead of sieving the pulp I hand squeezed all the liquid from the slop and pressed it into a silicon candy mold.

There's a patience factor to this day and I ignored it yet again. I popped my little flower biscuits out on to the drying rack long before I should have. They look amazing and the flower shape of the mold makes for a perfect finishing touch.

I love these messy experiences. I am hopeful that when mom feels like making a mess, she will help me pop these little seed bombs in the ground. Day 155 was another perfect first experience. Love & Light

Day 156 of 365- I Did It   February 22, 2018

Rubber Roof... I'm not a roofing expert but today I learned a bit about it. Day 156 was an absolutely blind experience that my guy registered me for. It was a women's event with a focus on heat welding. I had no idea what it was and for that reason I was totally in.

This was a two-hour event. The first hour was an endless lecture on rubber roofing materials. The speaker went on and on about the different types of rubber, PVC and other compounds used to cover a roof deck. I was the only non-industry attendee, and I felt it. I sat in the front of the lecture space and that was a mistake because the instructor must have noticed the blank stare on my face every time he introduced a new product. ONE HOUR! I was so excited when we moved out into the demonstration area.

Here's the truth about today's experience there was ZERO welding. This is glorified hot gluing. The general idea it to overlap the edges of the roofing material, use a weirdly shaped heat gun to soften the rubber and melt it together. NOT WELDING! There was no sparking and no fire. I had hoped for both and dressed in my blacksmithing clothes right down to the steel toe shoes.

You don't need steel toe shoes to glue rubber roofing together. The experience was still very satisfying, and I did learn a lot about adhering materials to a new or damaged roof. FYI, the bullet you shoot in the air lands of rooftops and can actually puncture the material. Who knew that people still shot their guns up in the air? Day 156 was educational and fun. Love & Light

Day 157 of 365- I Made It   February 23, 2018

Leather... Day 157 involved some leather, a few studs and a bit of muscle. Did you ever start a project after searching and searching for the right tool so you settled for what you could find? That's how my experience went today.

I needed to make my very first leather choker but couldn't find the hole punch. This entire project required making many holes in some very thick black leather. It's a good thing that we are obsessed with knives and weaponry in this house because I found an extremely sharp and pointy one that I used to create all of the holes I needed.

The rest of the project went well. I had planned to attach more studs but what I purchased just didn't have the strength to penetrate my leather. The experience has a purpose. I plan to wear it to a costume fundraising event. I'll add a photo once the rest of the costume is put together. Day 157 wasn't kinky, but it had a lot of leather. Love & Light

Day 158 of 365- I Ate It   February 24, 2018

Nuts... There are food items that I avoid on principal mostly because of the questionable chemistry involved in making them. (Thanks Uncle Ed) On day 158 I consumed a real troublesome food spread, Nutella. If you look at the ingredients, the first one listed is Nutella. Isn't that like defining a word by using the word? First no-no rule in English class! SMACK MY HEAD!! That was the actual split to describe the ingredients. I take it all back.

So, the mystery of what Nutella actually is, mostly sugar. I decided on this "snack break" because I knew I would never ever eat this unless it was for this experience. I opened the container, and it looks like smooth excrement. It smells like hazelnut, which is a favorite whole nut that I enjoy inside my Toffifay. This spread isn't very appetizing to me at all!

My portion was modest, and I used the little cookie breadstick to take a bit. I'm still solidly convinced that this chemistry is not worth the damage it will do to me nutritionally. I gave it a second taste just to be fair, and it was just as horrible as my first bite. As taste testing goes, I'm passing on this "spread." I'm not even sure how I would make a real snack out of this if I had a "proper jar" of it as the packaging suggests. Day 158 was a NO-go on the taste buds. Love & Light

Day 159 of 365- I Did It   February 25, 2018

Snelled… About 150 days ago I made a set of windchimes. When I set up that experience, I used fishing lead lines from a package of hooks and the looped ends worked perfectly for that project. Because I'm smart, I kept the leftover hooks.

On the 159th day I learned how to snell a fishhook. You're wondering why? I will need this skill when I use my flies from day 79 to learn how to fly fish.

I cannot wait for the day to come. I have wanted to learn since I was a kid. There's something very soothing about watching and I imagine it to be just as amazing to actually do it myself. Back to day 159… If you're wondering about hooks in fingers, yes, I did bleed for this experience. The hooks had tiny barbs that kept snagging on my finger. After my third hook I decided to file them off. I tried thread and sinew for my first attempts with the idea that it would be easier to see on camera. They didn't tie well so I shot a video using fishing line and it worked great.

As experiences go day 159 drew first blood. Love & Light

Day 160 of 365- I Made It   February 26, 2018

Shakere... Months ago I asked my mother to help me find a gourd. I know it sounds strange, but I had a very specific plan for it. When she asked me why, I was mysterious about answering and told her it was a 365 experience, and I couldn't give any clues.

She supported this adventure and found the perfect gourd for me. She even invited me to a gourd event so I could learn more, but I was already obligated to do my glassblowing adventure. On day 160 I made a shakere. I'll bet you are wondering what this is and I'm about to explain. A shakere is a percussion instrument usually "shaken" during a musical performance. This challenge seemed like it would be incredibly difficult, but it turned out to be easier than the weaving experience on day 59.

I rinsed the gourd off. I measured sixteen lengths of string two meters long. I tied one piece around the gourd to act as my anchor. The rest of the strings were looped around the first one. The rest of the experience was all about knots and creating a pattern with beads. I chose wood to give it a natural look.

I was pretty happy with the final result until I studied a few images on the Internet. I noticed the golden color and really wanted mine to look like that. This would require starting from scratch and using a lot of elbow grease. I spent about 90 minutes scrubbing this gourd with plastic pan cleaners, bristle brushes and steel wool but that sucker looks so awesome. I beaded that gourd one more time and I think you'll agree the color really looks amazing. Day 160 sounds amazing. Love & Light

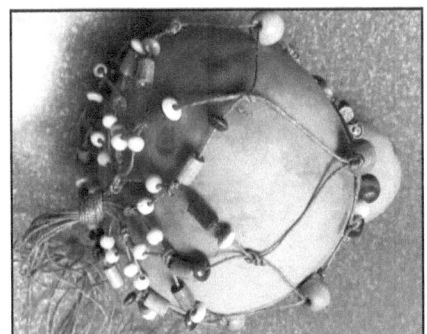

Day 161 of 365- I Ate It February 27, 2018

Soup... On Tuesday nights I play trivia with friends at a cute place called Siebert's Pub. The menu is basic bar food but it's pretty amazing. For the last few months I've had outstanding nachos, Reuben sandwiches but I've avoided their French onion soup.

Until tonight... On my 161st day I experienced my very first bowl of French Onion soup. I don't know why I've never had it until today but my best guess would be a dislike of soup that's only made of onions.

This cup of soup from Siebert's pub is presented beautifully with a golden toasted layer of melted cheese on top. I almost didn't want to crack it open. My trivia mates have eaten it many times and I've watched them roll the thick layer of cheese over to reveal soup-soaked chunks of crusty bread. It has always looked delicious. If I said the soup was served hot, I would be under-representing the word. This liquid would cool down flowing lava. It comes with a warning from the waitress. I've watched the heat roll off the top and I don't take the warning lightly.

This soup is a delight and I'm so happy that I gave in and ate it. Day 161 was a treat for the taste buds. Love & Light

Day 162 of 365- I Did It   February 28, 2018

Tap, tap, tap... The sun was just breaking on the horizon. I had a hot cup of coffee and a hotter cup of water. I was drinking the coffee and using that boiling water to heat up some plastic tubes. My mornings are pretty weird and sometimes I can't believe I'm actually still doing this challenge.

On day 162, just before the sun woke up, I was tapping maple trees. Since its part of my 365-day adventure it's obvious that I haven't done this before. I have always wanted to and never made the time or put together the supplies.

It all came together with a beautiful sunrise. The plan was simple. Drill, tap and collect. It sounds less complicated than making a cappuccino. It should have been but from the moment I couldn't find the right drill bit to the plastic tubing falling off the spire and my precious sap running on the ground, this could have been a frustrating disaster.

I made a few rookie mistakes. I drilled at the wrong angle and pounded the spires in a little deep. I don't want to hurt my trees I just want them to bleed.

The temperature was amazing and everything I read suggests that I should get some great sap. My plan is to collect about 5 gallons, and I'll let you know how that works out. If you don't know, this is the first step to making real syrup. Stay tuned... Day 162 is looking pretty good. Love & Light

Day 163 of 365- I Saw It   March 1, 2018

Puppy… It's not my first puppy but it was my very first tiny husky puppy. When we attended the pet expo on day 137, I wanted to see one of these little guys. I hoped to see a mini version of my dog Jake who was amazing, and I miss him.

On day 163 I got my puppy therapy. My sights were set on this cuddly fluff ball as soon as I saw him. I really think I would have walked out of the store with him if his price tag wasn't so ridiculous. No sales pitch in the world is ever going to make that happen. Let's talk about the mini husky. He was precious and played tug-o-war with me and he had a stuffed chicken. There's nothing more to say. Day 163 was a blue-eyed dream. Love & Light

Day 164 of 365- I Made It   March 2, 2018

Sprouts… It's another early morning here in Wisconsin. I did a bit of reading about cancer and ways to fight with food. On the 164th day I sprouted broccoli to fight cancer. When I started this personal challenge, I never anticipated the family crisis that would come. I never wanted mom's cancer fight to be a part of my reality, but it is.

I can't just sit by and do nothing, so my part is to do as much as possible to set her up to fight with all she has. Are broccoli sprouts THE answer? I don't know. What I do know is that as long as she says fight, we fight.

I purchased some sprouting seeds and a large glass and stainless-steel jar. The mesh top is ideal for helping with the growing process. The seeds will soak for 12 hours and then I will drain the water off and store them in a warm dark place. I'm using the kombucha fermenting shelf as the perfect location.

Not the patience thing kicks in. My plan is to keep a continuous grow going for as long as we need them. Mom drinks special cancer fighting drinks that my dad makes, and the sprouts will be added. Day 164 was all about getting strong. Love & Light.

Day 165 of 365- I Did It   March 3, 2018

Paychecks... I'm an artist. Making messes and creating is something I thrive on. In the last few months, I have done so many things and built a serious pile of experiences, but none compare to this. Something I also love to do is create with words. I've been a published author for a few years, and I've written for online venues. I've submitted hundreds of Op Ed pieces and although a few have been published I've never submitted an invoice to receive an actual paycheck.

UNTIL TODAY! On the 165th day of this personal challenge I submitted an invoice to become an officially paid freelance writer. It's not a dream come true. It's hard work coming to fruition. There's no lecture but here's my truth. If you want it, make it so. Love & Light

Day 166 of 365- I Made It   March 4, 2018

Sugar Shack... That's what my house has become. For the last few days I have been collecting maple tree sap. It wasn't difficult. The trees did most of the work. I was a tiny bit stressed when all of my containers were full. I had no idea it would flow so fast and abundantly. I filled so many buckets that all three of my refrigerators were full. It takes about 40 gallons of sap to make one gallon of syrup. My trees have given me about 30 gallons.

Day 166 was all about processing that sap into syrup. I've been planning this for a while, and it seemed like the day was going to require a bit of construction. After hours of online research and more hours of how-to videos and schematic diagrams I decided to go off the trail and walk the road less traveled. I poured my sap into a huge Nesco cooker.

The boiling started in the middle of the night, and I've been nurturing it every few hours. This sap is cooking off and I could smell that maple scent in my house as it started to evaporate. I boiled a few gallons on the stove and fed that in as the Nesco liquid continued to disappear.

It's going to be a very long day. The great thing about using the Nesco, aside from not building a fire pit, is that I can do other things while that pan of sap is boiling down. So far, it's looking pretty good. I have reduced the original 30 gallons of clear sap to about 3 gallons of dark liquid that smells like a pancake house on a warm summer day. In a few hours I should have this cooked to syrup perfection. Day 166 was humid and sweet. Love & Light

Day 167 of 365- I Did It   March 5, 2018

Keeping it sweet... If you've ever been to Amish country, you'll know that the home-made goods are pretty amazing and maybe some of the recipes have been passed down for generations. When we visited our favorite ranch in the state of Wisconsin, we've sampled so many amazing Amish made goodies. A few years ago we bought a gallon of maple syrup, and I was hesitant to spend the $40 bucks.

Having the experiences of the last few days collecting, boiling and preserving this delicious treat I have determined that gallon price to be a bargain. On the 167th day I thickened my liquid gold and packaged it for future use.

The final cook-down process happened in my crockpot. I left it on low heat for the day and when I came home it had thickened into something wonderful. Those hours of research suggested I filter the thin sap one time and the thicker sap once more. I followed that plan, so happy that all the filtration happened when it was free flowing. Once it hit syrup consistency there was no way it was going through that filter again.

If you've ever grown a garden that required canning, processing syrup is stickier and a little bit more treacherous. If you're wondering why, it's because I felt like Pooh Bear after discovering a honey filled hive. All I wanted to do was lick my paws. After all is said and done, I cooked about 30 gallons of sap down to 8 pints of syrup. I'm satisfied and might just do this again. I was a tiny bit stressed about getting this done for my adventures. Once the pressure is off, I might enjoy it more. Pancakes anyone? Love & Light

Day 168 of 365- I Did It   March 6, 2018

    Getting wet… Sometimes machines just wear out. We can't expect anything mechanical to last forever, ourselves included. We do have to take care and perform maintenance if we expect to get the best from anything. On the 168th day of personal firsts I got wet repairing a water softener and it wasn't my own.

    Most of the Kennedy kids are mechanical by nature; I include myself in this statement. These skills definitely come from my father, and he has never failed to be a teacher when we lacked the necessary abilities. He knows so much about so many things. The task today was to make water flow. I've never taken a water softener apart and I was surprised to discover there are so many parts involved.

    When water wasn't flowing, troubleshooting started from the end of the line and worked backwards. The space where its setup is pretty tight, and the problem was difficult to see. A few screw turns, selfie camera angles and some wrenching and the culprit was discovered. The entire house water supply runs through this machine. In order to flush out the softener the salty brine has to pass through a filter that's reduced by a plastic nipple the diameter of a paper clip.

    A PAPER CLIP! Once the problem piece was discovered, and poked with that paper clip, water started to flow, and that briny mixture was doing its job again.

    I'll admit my hands were mostly helping but I learned a lot about the mechanics of this water system. I got wet and a little bit sludgy, but the end result was a fix... for now. I see a replacement in my future. Day 168 was educational. Love & Light

Day 169 of 365- I Made It   March 7, 2018

Trapped... Spring was here just long enough to wake up the sleeping boxelder bugs. They are everywhere and they're freaking me out. On day 169 I attempted to rid my house of these pests by building traps.

This is a complete experimental experience coming from desperate moments of feeling those tiny creepy crawly legs on my arm while sleeping. You know what I think about after they wake me? I think about them crawling in my ear or nose and it's too much. THIS IS REAL!!

I know that they are harmless and I'm not going to die from them, but they chose the wrong house to invade. I've sucked them up in the vacuum and that seems just as cruel so instead I've collected some household items: an aluminum pan, dawn dish soap, water and a desk lamp. I know this sounds a little silly but here's the plan.

1. Squirt dish soap into aluminum pan
2. Fill with warm water
3. Place aluminum pan under lamp
4. Wait for them to go toward the light

Is this cruel? I don't care. They are crawling on me in my sleep. That's too much even for this tree hugging woman who caries spiders outside. I set up this trap at two in the afternoon. I'm waiting until 6 to check it.

I had another plan for the day, but these creepy crawlers have pushed me over the edge. I just want to sleep. Day 169 is all about relief. Love & Light and maybe a tiny bit of universal forgiveness

Day 170 of 365- I Did It   March 8, 2018

Rubber gloves... In the last 79 days I have probably watched a thousand disposable gloves go into a trash can. They've had blood and urine, medications and feces, lotion and bath soap all over them. That's why people in the medical industry wear them. They want to be protected.

On the 170th day of this personal challenge I'm finally broken. Without giving too much detail, we visited the hospital again. It wasn't planned and it involved hours of waiting and... patience. I'm so over being patient.

As we waited for test results I was trying to figure out if my plan for the day was even possible to complete. I watched minutes turn into hours and as 5pm rolled around I knew that it wasn't going to happen. That's when I got the idea to make something with those damn disposable gloves. Thank you YOUTUBE!!

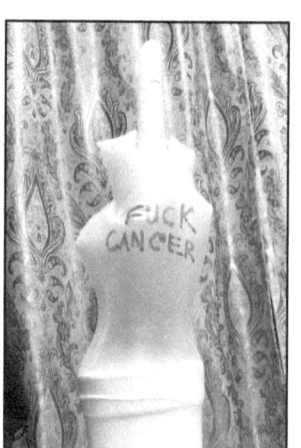

Any of you who have been following the previous 169 days will know that today will not be a cute little thing. Once I decided on using that glove the gears turned and my sassy kicked in.

The supplies for this experience were basic: rubber glove, cup, straw, tape and a marker. There was also a cat looking for attention. Get ready kids because this is about to rock your world. Day 170 blows! Love & Light

Day 171 of 365- I Made It March 9, 2018

Kiss my Lips... There are places on this planet that will suck all the life out of you and medical care facilities take the grand prize for suckage! I've spent almost 80 days in some kind of medical building and it's taking a toll on my flesh. I haven't bent myself in any kind of yoga pose so my muscles are tight. I wash my hands a hundred times a day, so they are like sandpaper.

Hydrating my body has become this ridiculous seesaw of water, lotion and lip balm. On the 171st day I decided to give my lips the luxury they deserve. I'm a Bert's Bees babe. I love the stuff especially their peppermint lip balm. That's what I decided to make.

My balm has four ingredients:
- 2 Tbsp Organic beeswax,
- 2 Tbsp organic coconut oil,
- 2 tsp sweet almond oil
- 12 drops peppermint oil.

That's it. I didn't add anything else. I melted the ingredients in a double boiler using a glass bowl and wooden chopsticks to stir. Once the oils and wax melted into a liquid, I dropped the essential oils in. After a quick stir I poured the blend into containers. I also put some of the liquid in a repurposed lip balm tube to see if I could make an actual stick. So far that worked too.

One quick note: this will soften in the heat so keep it out of the sun. It took about 5 minutes for all the containers to set and I'm very happy with how it clings to my lips. The nice thing is that I can also smooth it on the back of my hands and it's not greasy. I had a very satisfying 171st day. Love & Light

Day 172 of 365- I Ate It   March 10, 2018

Wild game night! I haven't been a vegetarian for a very long time. It's a good thing because tonight was the first time I've ever eaten many of the disgusting things listed.

On the wild game menu:

1. Kangaroo- had it in Australia and once you've seen it as roadkill it loses its appeal. It wasn't a first, so I didn't need to eat that again.
2. Buffalo loin- a real first and it was chewy. I think it could have been prepared better, and I'll have to try it again.
3. Quail eggs - total first and it tasted like... wait for it... an egg.
4. Bear sausage- absolutely not great for a first. One word, gross! Did I say gross? Just leave the bear in the woods and let it eat salmon and be free to die of old age.
5. Antelope sausage - greasy, chewy rubber band gristle. This sausage was a way for the guy to clean out his horrible antelope surplus.
6. Frog Alfredo - WHY? I'll confess that I was sure this would be gross. It was so much like chicken that I was okay with this dish.
7. Goose stroganoff - NOPE! NOPE! NOPE! NOPE! NOPE! NOPE! NOPE! NOPE! NOPE! NOPE! I remember watching a movie where the guy ate something, and he tried to wipe his tongue with a napkin to get it off. That was me and the goose. I just can't give you words to describe how much I want to never eat that again. AVOID GOOSE!
8. Rabbit Alfredo - It was just like the frog and a lot like chicken, and I enjoyed it. I'm not going rabbit hunting but if you cook it like this no one would ever know.
9. Beaver sausage - So many things to say and all of them are so very very wrong. Not my first and so salty. Do with that what you will. There was an amazing chocolate walnut brownie that made every horrible memory of that duck fade away. As firsts go Day 172 was a cornucopia. I had amazing company on this adventure and that made it one of my favorites. Love and Light

Day 173 of 365- I Did It   March 11, 2018

Go Go Go... Since I was a child, I have dreamed of packing an RV and driving for days with no course and no destination. I'm sure I'm not the only person to have this dream because on day 173 we elbowed our way through the recreational vehicle show at Burlington RV.

There is a slight hitch in this grand plan. I don't actually want to drive an RV. I want to sit in the passenger seat and navigate our path to nowhere. I want to make sandwiches while my best friend and life partner drives us down the road. I want to pee whenever I need to and maybe just pull over to the side of the road and take in whatever the countryside has to offer.

That plan will happen one day. During this event I got my first taste of RVing and exactly how insane these vehicles and their camper friends are. It's ridiculous to walk through a mobile living environment with TV's, massaging loungers, refrigerators and microwaves. These are not the pop-up campers from the 70's. As experiences go day 173 was fun and eye opening. I think I better start saving my pennies. Love & Light

Day 174 of 365- I Ate It   March 12, 2018

Fruit... I've eaten so many new things in the last 174 days. Some have been super delicious, and some have not. I try to trust my instincts when it comes to food. Most of the time I just know it's not going to be a flavor for me as soon as it hits my tongue.

Day 174 was a taste bud deception. The Kumquat, it's an interesting tiny treat, or so I thought. How can a mini orange-looking thing be bad? Why have I lived 49 years and 174 days without eating one?

All these questions were answered when I opened that small package at 7 am this morning. Here's the deal, sometimes I have to fit my adventures in because taking care of mom is priority. I actually like the food adventures that work as breakfast, but this one would have been better during margarita hour.

How do you eat a kumquat? It's like a cherry tomato. You just pop it in your mouth. That's exactly what I did, and it was so much like that first taste of lemon juice that I almost spit it out. This is the deceptive part. Because this was a personal challenge I kept chewing and the tartness of the fruit's flesh started to mix with the sweet of the fruit's skin and it was delightful!

Yep, sweet skin, tart flesh. Go Figure! Eating this fruit gave me the belly tickle of a hilly swoopy car ride. It's sort of. . . thrilling. There were about 30 pieces in the package, and I'd eaten about a dozen before I realized. My mind was trying to determine how this tasty piece of fruit could be used. I thought about a smoothie but that seemed like a waste. I also considered popsicles and that led me to a frozen kumquat margarita. I think it's a winner. I don't drink alcohol very much, so I'll keep this idea in my back pocket for a while. Day 174 was a pleasant treat. Love & Light

Day 175 of 365- I Made It   March 13, 2018

Watch it wiggle… Remember how I was telling you that I'm an artist? I promise I am even though I haven't created with paint or pastels in ages. I really wanted to do something that would get my quiet room art table messy again. The problem is that most of the day is taken with more significant priorities and sometimes it is a struggle to get this adventure right.

I'm also an author and in the middle of everything I'm working on two new writing projects. I really don't know how any of this is working and why I'm not sleeping right exactly now! On the 175th day of this challenge I wanted to make a huge mess. So, I made a gelli plate. You might not know what this is but you're about to get a lesson. Today I made Jell-O that I'm never going to eat and that will never get rotten. Why? Because I'm an artist.

The art part of the experience will come on another day since making the plate takes time. The materials are pretty simple: gelatin, glycerin and water. There's a tiny bit of science involved and that's just because you have to combine it all in the right order. It's like making Jell-O except you replace the flavoring with not edible glycerin. It took FOREVER for the gelatin to dissolve. I mixed in the hot water and poured the cooling liquid in a baking pan. I used the "make it cold" setting on my fridge to chill it fast. It still took about 2 hours to make the plate.

When I turned the pan over it stuck to the sides and tore in pieces. I now have a bowl of gloppy gelli plate material. The nice thing about this experience is that I can nuke the glop in the microwave, choose a different container and try again. Yes, I've already done this and round two is chilling in the fridge. Cross your fingers, day 175 might not be quite right. Love & Light

Day 176 of 365- I Ate It   March 14, 2018

Knock Knock Ding Dong. To set the stage for today's experience I have to share a magical childhood freedom moment. I didn't learn to drive until my second year of college.

My roommate taught me in her Volkswagen Bug using the hilly roads in Petrifying Springs Park. The lack of an automobile in high school didn't really matter because I rode my 10 speed everywhere. I bought a how-to book and tricked that red rocket out! What's the point? I didn't need a car to establish that feeling of freedom. One of my best memories of childhood was hopping on that bike and riding to the little country store to get my favorite treat.

On day 176 a childhood dream came true. The spirit of all things terrible to eat created the Ding Dong ice cream sandwich. Stop laughing. This is a real dream come true. If you've ever had a Ding Dong cake you know that eating it frozen is ideal. That crunchy chocolate coating over the crumbly cake covered cream filling, I can actually taste it from sense memory and it's worth every real-life calorie.

How did I find them? Fate? Destiny? I'd like to think so. Truth be told I was doing a good deed, and it paid off with a 5 pack of ice cream sandwiches. I brought these suckers home and poured the box into the freezer, they are ice cream but that's what you do in my house with regular Ding Dong cakes. Remember crunchy chocolate it ideal!

The disappointing moment was watching the treats fall out of the box. Those little treasures weren't wrapped in the aluminum foil of my youth. Come on, you know you opened that foil and worked for minutes trying to smooth it out into the original square shape. I do that with my Dove chocolates. Thank goodness someone still appreciates a foil wrap.

I felt joy when I finally opened the plastic pouch. All I'm going to say is if you share this dream with me, you should find a box and try to eat just one.

They are perfect and the ice cream is flavored to taste like that cream filling, and the volume is what I've always wanted in my cake treat. I'm hungry now and this is the most time I've spent writing about Ding Dongs. . . EVER! On Day 176 I discovered dreams can come true. Love & Light

Day 177 of 365- I Made It   March 15, 2018

Another purpose... I've been doing something new every day for 177 days. When I turned 49 a few of my friends, who are wonderful and really get who I am, gave me this beautiful sign that's been propped up on my porch.

Every time I go in my front door, I feel all those words, but I also see it propped on a plastic table waiting to be honored with a proper stand to hold it. On the 177th day I created my first repurposed pallet project. I love using power tools and it's been a few months since I've pulled out my construction arsenal.

This was soul food, and I didn't realize how much I needed it. I will admit that my end result needs tweaking, and I'll wait for my blacksmithing partner to help me put on the finishing touches. The base of the stand is an old 5 gallon plastic bucket. I used grey in hopes that it would blend in with the pallet wood. I made 15" cuts to the slats after ripping them off with a pry bar.

Like I said, so satisfying! I used some old belts from our monster belt sander and stapled them to the backside of every slat, one band across the top and another for the bottom.

The rest of the project was balancing the weight of the sign with the narrow bucket base. Eventually I plan to fill the bucket with cement mix about halfway, put in some drainage holes and plant some seasonal flowers in it.

You'll have to stay tuned for that update in mid-May. Until that time, I have loaded the bucket with some massive rocks. I built something purposeful on day 177. Love & Light

Day 178 of 365- I Made It   March 16, 2018

Gnocchi… There's something delicious about making food from scratch. I'm trying very hard to create passion for the process. Can you learn to be passionate? On the 178th day I discovered I am too impatient to be passionate about making Gnocchi. This experience was time consuming. I had an amazing cinematographer who took some great shots and it's always fun to have a partner on one of these adventures.

To start these little balls rolling I boiled a few pounds of potatoes and riced them using my grandfather's ricer. I've had the thing for years and never used it, making this a double dunk of firsts. That ricer was built to last, and I made quick work of those golden spuds. It did take a little bit of muscle to squeeze by hand, but it was extremely satisfying.

The recipe called for 2 large egg yolks. Mine were small so I used 3 along with some finely sifted flour. With gentle hands I mixed it all together being careful not to overdo and make tough little dough bombs. Using small globs of my gnocchi dough I rolled it out in a snake, chopped it in half and made small misshapen cuts. I forked the rest. They made darling little potato dumplings.

Here's the disappointing part. I put the first batch in the boiling water and overcooked them. That made potato glop. The second, much smaller batch turned out well and I cooked them with some shrimp and roasted brussel sprouts. Day 178 was a great exercise in patience. Love & Light

Day 179 of 365- I Did It   March 17, 2018

    I'm not quite ready. Not so long ago a good friend of mine told me that when the apocalypse arrives, she's going to come to my house. Why? That's pretty simple, I have the perfect setup or so she thought. On day 179 I attended a survival expo.
This is how the day worked out. The venue was pretty big and filled from wall to wall with everything I'll need for the end of days.
    I found just about any book I might need to create the fully prepped living space. I didn't spend a ton of time here because I use Google and all the answers are just a quick search in the palm of my hand. I know, when the apocalypse comes the net will be gone. I should be all prepped by then. I met a cool inventor and enthusiastic survivalist who showed me how to use the tiny stove that he designed. I will admit that I bought one of these because he impressed me with this pocket-sized treasure. I plan to use my foldable camp stove on a future experience so stay tuned for that.
    I have a strategy for browsing through these expo adventures. I work from east to west and accordion fold the room. I navigate this way so I don't miss any of the exciting displays or demonstrations that might be tucked off in the corners.
    This survival expo had 1000's of products I didn't know I would need when the end-of-times comes. It made me wonder if I really want to play the "Just Survive Somehow" game. The table that didn't really surprise me, the endless line of paper targets being offered for shooting practice. Every shape and size were on display at a reasonable and disposable price.
    I don't shoot often but anything works as a target, just check out day 90. I expected more weapons for sale at this event but what I saw most were gadgets. If I love anything, it's those little pocket size save the world necessities.
    I played with tiny can openers and every kind of multi tool and "emergency" kit that you can imagine. If I had the cash, I would be wearing a backpack equipped to clean water, dig a trench and close a massive wound.
    That's PREPPED! When the end comes, food and water are the essentials and there were quite a few pails filled with packets of dehydrated meals. The meals in pails need clean H2O so don't forget the purifier since all clean water will cease to exist in an apocalyptic situation. Are you getting anxious yet? That's what the expo is trying to do. It's trying to freak you the hell out!! We made it halfway through before running into a table filled with medical supplies. Have you ever started an IV or sutured a wound?

The average prepper is learning to do this and I'm trying to figure out why? I guess the world will have a lot of sharp pointy things to get cut on post-apocalypse. I Googled these two procedures and I'm pretty sure I'm not going to save your life if either one is necessary. Remember in an apocalypse to hydrate and avoid cut-y sharp edges.

On day 173 we went to an RV expo and that event didn't have the tricked-out end-of-days cruiser that my survival expo had. This retired military monster had everything you'd need to drive your way to safety; minus the food and water, but it has a satellite dish. It made me wonder if the grid is "off the grid" when the end of civilization comes. Googling this might have been a mistake. Don't Google the end of days and satellites. That's some scary shit!

There were more tables filled with knick-knacks and knives. Most of these were meant to appeal to the people who watch the walking dead and shows like that.

Don't get me wrong, I watch them but I'm not going to buy a damascus bowie knife or a shovel that also works as a hammer, hatchet, saw, pry-bar, carabineer, grappling hook, zip-line, cleaver and machete. As experiences go, this was so much fun. I would do a survival expo again just because the vendors are enthusiastic and I'm not quite ready for the end of days. Day 179 was eye opening. Love & Light

Day 180 of 365- I Did It   March 18, 2018

It's a bird... It's a plane... It's a Parrot? I've had expectations for this experience, and I think I set myself up to fail. It's 6:15 am and my little experiment for day 180 is charging in the kitchen. My heart is racing with excitement and I'm so impatient.

That's when reality hits. My adventure for the day was to fly my very first drone. I've done a little research and shopped around for months. On a whim I stumbled upon this tiny Parrot Mambo. It's got a 10-minute flight time and will shoot 720p video. The price was pretty great, so I decided to make it the adventure for today. It came charged but I still hooked it and the controller to power and topped each device off. I wanted to use my phone as an alternate controller, so I downloaded the app for that. You cannot fly a drone out of the box. There is pairing and syncing and ALWAYS a software update. Thirty minutes later I was almost ready for my first flight.

"Device not found" Really? I shut everything down, just like rebooting a wireless router and BINGO we were in business. This little drone is pretty versatile. It has a bunch of add-ons at a reasonable price. If I can get it to work properly, I might get the "NERF" dart attachment.

Back to my first flight, it wasn't anything to celebrate and all I could get it to do was hover. Just as an FYI it does this no matter what. I was getting a tiny bit impatient, as none of the controller options would connect with the device. Another reboot of the drone and it finally connected to the wireless controller that it came with.

Mission control, we have lift off!   Houston, we have a problem... After all of that hovering the battery went into critical levels and my drone dropped like a rock. I think the "drone gods" are laughing at me because I tried to squeeze this adventure in at 6:30 in the morning. I wanted that sunrise shot. Kelly Branyik from @travelbranyik was with me and took some pretty cool first flight pictures. She also reminded me that every sunrise would eventually bring a sunset. What a little ball of sunshine she is. My drone never flew again.

If you're shopping for one, you'll need to make sure it has auto-stabilization because without it you might hit a barn or something like that. As experiences go, I had hoped this would open the door to drone use on future adventures. This went back in the box and back to the store. Day 180 was amazing for almost a full minute. Love & Light

Day 181 of 365- I Made It   March 19, 2018

You are what you see. A few weeks ago, I wanted to attend an event that would help me assemble a Vision Board. The idea behind this experience is to create a space to hold images and words to help motivate you to achieve your goals.

Today, on my 181st adventure I gave the vision board a little twist. I helped my mother create a board for her room. I've been talking to her for the last few weeks, collecting her dreams and ideas.

This was no small task and a few of my family members helped. I started with a large dry-erase foam board. The idea is that as mom heals she can change the words on her vision board. Right now, she's a fighter and that's what I wrote for her. My mother is a master gardener, so her board's vision is to be back digging in the dirt planting her flowers and growing her herbs. As experiences go this one was more about loving my mother and wanting more than anything for her to achieve the visions that are hanging on her wall. Day 181 was a gift. Love & Light

Day 182 of 365- I Did It   March 20, 2018

I'm halfway there. On the 182nd day I made an impression... in metal. There are no accidents in the way that all my adventures come together. I had a list of things that I wanted to do and try but the spirit of this personal challenge takes control, and I find something that I've always wanted to do landing right in my lap.

Today I made a metal charm intended to be a pendant. Since I'm not much for jewelry I decided to sew it to my backpack. The idea came from my sister, and I love it. This was a little bit of a challenge because my tools were tiny. The kit came with  everything I would need including metal alphabet stamps. I have always wanted a set and so has my kid. I think he is going to be a tiny bit jealous.

I set up my equipment on the table and read through the instructions. It's not complicated but the pressure to keep the letters aligned was intense. I screwed it up on the first strike, so I just went with it. The actual letter stamps are 1/4 inch so the margin for error is about 1/4 of an inch. I made quite a few errors, which in the art world "give character."

This charm has a lot of character in the two inches of material. I like how it turned out even with the imperfections. It's also a reminder of the work I'm doing with Just Live, Inc. The halfway point has come, and I marked it in metal. Love & Light

Day 183 of 365- I Ate It   March 21, 2018

Amazing Grass… This morning's experience gave me a new perspective on the old saying, "the grass is greener." I went into this adventure "full on" eager to be energized. It was mostly just gross.

On day 183 I consumed my very first wheatgrass drink. This is how it went. In powder form the little packet of greens looks harmless. I poured it into a mason jar so I could add water and shake it. It smelled a little like grass clippings on the mower deck after rain forced you to stop cutting. Not an inviting flavor profile. My sister thought it was delicious; I'm questioning her sense of taste.

The packet suggested adding it to 8 ounces of water. I opted for 6 and I'm so glad that I did because this stuff still hurts my tongue. Remember how I wanted to wipe that duck off on day 172, I wiped my wheatgrass tongue on a napkin. After shooting the last of this concoction down my throat, I drank a LOT of water so maybe the pro of my wheatgrass experience was getting my daily-recommended dose of H20. As experiences go day 183 was definitely not the kind of grass I will continue to enjoy. Love & Light

Day 184 of 365- I Saw It   March 22, 2018

A peep show… It's almost Easter. When I was a kid there were a few things that were holiday essentials. The Life Saver candy storybook at Christmas and marshmallow peeps for Easter.

On day 184 I went to my very first Peep art show.
This was AMAZING! The Racine Art Museum is a small place, and the exhibit was even smaller, but it was so fun. The art pieces were all over the place when it came to themes. Harry Peepter, Jurassic Peep, a Peep flip book, Olympic peeps with a curling team and so much more.

I loved the T-rex made from purple peeps and the Wisconsin state map made from little hacked up bits of bunny peeps. It's a bit disturbing when you really look at it close up. The best art piece was the Tide Peeps. I nearly peed my pants with laughter. As experiences go day 184 was exactly what art should be, something new and a treat for the spirit. Love & Light

Day 185 of 365- I Made It   March 23, 2018

The things you do for love. I love peanut butter, but I really don't like peanuts. I had no idea that 1 ounce of peanut butter has 8grams of protein. I'm monitoring protein, not for myself but for my mom. I do a lot of things for her these days and on Day 185 I made peanut butter.

This wasn't a complex thing, but I really wanted to see how difficult it was and if I purchased organic nuts, could I make organic peanut butter on my own. This was successful and not only did it turn out delicious it was as creamy as butter.

If the world was a perfect place and my mother had the strength, this would have been the crunchiest peanut butter ever made in any home. I couldn't make that for my first batch, but I plan to in the future. My mother deserves every crunchy nutty morsel. If you're interested in making your own, I just filled up the food processor with nuts and let it go. I'd say it took about 3 minutes. The best part of this experience is that my peanut butter is made from one ingredient... peanuts. Day 185 was smooth and nutty. Love & Light

Day 186 of 365- I Made It   March 24, 2018

Gelli paint... About ten days ago I made a fantastic Gelli Plate. I didn't share what the plan was for it but today you get to find out. My 186th adventure was getting my hands dirty and printing with my Gelli plate. The process was extremely fun and if you've got a budding artist, I suggest you try this on your next day together. I stored my plate in a giant Ziploc and since it's gelatin it stuck to that plastic bag. It was a little like having a ball of booger stuck on your finger that you just can't shake off. Once I defeated that container, I laid my plate on a hard surface.

Since spring arrived a few days ago I chose some paints to represent this time of year. I spread the colors across the surface of the Gelli plate with a brayer (hard rubber roller). I cut a few cardboard stencils to score the paint. On day 7 I started making my own paper from shredded recycled junk mail. I have a pretty impressive stack of it and that's what I used to make my prints. They turned out so amazing and I hope you'll give this messy experience a try.

Lesson learned about my Gelli Plate, don't fold it. I cracked it in half. The best part about making it with gelatin is I broke it apart, heated it for a minute in the microwave and poured it back in the pan to harden it again. Day 186 was all about making the best art fun!!Love & Light

Day 187 of 365- I Made It   March 25, 2018

Healing power of food. I do a lot of things to my body that aren't necessarily great or even good. It's mostly because those things are exciting, and they taste or feel good. In the last 187 days I have chewed, sipped, licked, sucked and bitten some really intense things.

I've pushed myself to be outside of my bubble of comfort and that's making this challenge extremely personal and... well... challenging. What I realized was that I had not explored the healing properties of the food that I eat. Why today? I had an experience with the negative effects of food. My goal is to fight food with food.

On day 187 I made bone broth onion soup. Why bone broth? One magic word, PROTEIN! Why onion? The busting up of unwanted mucus. Our bodies are fantastic machines that can endure a fair amount of abuse and we are designed to self-repair. The key to this reparation is to put clean food in. I can't use cheap fuel and expect the machine that I am to run well.

The process of this soup was as simple as can be. Bone broth is now available and it's organic. I'm trying to keep the base ingredients free from GMO's and chemical growing techniques. I was excited to find onions, garlic and vegetable broth that met the criteria.

I chopped a purple onion. I used this type because I love the flavor after it has been caramelized with garlic. My house smelled amazing as the bone broth simmered in with the other ingredients. I'm bringing the entire batch of soup to a slow boil in my crock pot, and I'll let is warm on low overnight. What I'm hoping to do is bust up the phlegm from a dairy imbalance. My fingers are crossed. Day 187 is an experiment in self-care. Love & Light

Day 188 of 365- I Made It   March 26, 2018

Something's sour... What's your favorite bread? Have you made it yourself or do you buy it at the store? Have you read the ingredients?

Believe it or not I have never made sourdough bread and on day 188 I started to do just that. If you've been reading all my posts so far, you'll know that I enjoy multiple day experiences, but I am extremely impatient. This bread requires something called a starter, which requires time and patience.

Back to my pantry, where I'm growing kombucha, broccoli sprouts and now festering sourdough bread starter. The thing is my kitchen closet and the temperature inside are amazing at creating these fermented goodies.

The recipe: water, flour and time. As I type, the goo is growing and in a few days, I will spoon it into the dough ingredients and bake a lovely loaf of sourdough bread. Day 188 was pasty, and I hope it goes sour. Love & Light

Day 189 of 365- I Did It   March 27, 2018

Hakuna Matata... I'm a little under the weather today and posting from the tiny bubble that I've closed myself in to get over this cold. My amazing niece brought some cheer and her ukulele and taught me to play a little song. I wasn't sure I would make my challenge goal today as I'm tired, achy and my head is pounding.

The song she taught me is a classic and also a cheerful one. Hakuna Matata It's five chords and if you've never played a ukulele, it's fun and a little tricky. There is no recording or me singing but I made it all the way through. What a great little instrument to play. I did it. Day 189 was a sweet song. Love & Light

Day 190 of 365- I Did It   March 28, 2018

Angels and butterflies... I've got these amazing beings in my life that give me great joy. Today I got to spend time with one of them who taught me how to build angels and butterflies with a computer.

On the 190th day I learned how to 3D print. In an undisclosed location we scanned into the computer lab. This super high-tech environment had rainbow spools of material in a cabinet filled with exciting supplies.

The technology involved looks intimidating and I wouldn't want to have to service it, but my hands were twitching with excitement. Technology and I are best friends, and I have wanted to do this for a very long time.

I found an angel template on www.thingaverse.com that I thought would be perfect. The project file was loaded into the software program. A few mouse clicks and adjustments were made and 15 minutes later we had a little angel.

You will never understand how satisfying it is to 3D print until you actually do it. We printed a rainbow of angels and also added some butterflies. Such sweet little delicate things were printed from plastic that's the diameter of weed trimmer line. This is freaking cool!! Day 190 was an amazing boost of techno energy. Love & Light

Day 191 of 365- I Made It March 29, 2018

Mobile and Lucas Oil… I learned to use a 3D printer on day 190 and decided to make something from those tiny creations. On my 191st day I built my very first 3D printed mobile. The best part of this adventure was using the materials I printed along with a spool of wire I had in a box of craft supplies.

If you've ever made a mobile, you understand that balance is essential to making it work. I'm not balanced lately but after hours of bending and clipping wire this angel and butterfly mobile is. I attached a crystal pendant and a tiny Celtic knot to add a few universal energies. I'm planning to hang this somewhere special.

When all was said and done this experience was fun. I don't suggest you build one unless you have the patience required to make it hang perfectly. I can't even tell you how much wire is wrapped around my recycling bin.

If this wasn't enough, I had my very first glimpse of the Indianapolis Colts football stadium. What's so cool about that? It's right outside my hotel window. Why am I in Indianapolis and not just passing through? Stay tuned! Day 191 was an exercise in persistence with a new view. Love & Light

Day 192 of 365- I Saw It   March 30, 2018

  Almost and not… Day 192 was my very first adventure in Indianapolis, Indiana. I started my morning at the Pop Culture Association conference. This full circle moment brought me to a lecture about the characters in Buffy the Vampire Slayer. The Buffyverse is a huge part of who I am, and I was excited. The discussion went a bit off course, and I'll admit it was a little disappointing. Not every adventure is a good one.

  After my trip down memory lane I had an amazing moment of pride listening to two extraordinary women discuss representation of LGBTQI+ youth in television and movies. It was pure joy to sit and listen to ideas and solutions. How refreshing.

  I almost got into comic con, and I didn't get thrown out; two more funny firsts. The Indiana Comic Convention just happened to be across the street from my hotel. I went through the downtown mall to enter the venue. It wasn't difficult to find; I just followed the cosplayers and bumped into all kinds of crazy characters. I tried to get kicked out by security, but the guys were so nice and didn't want to throw me to the curb. When I asked them to look menacing, they just smiled and posed for a picture.

  Why didn't I buy tickets? The venue was only open for another 30 minutes and they were still charging $30 to enter. It felt like a waste of money, so I just walked through the open areas and enjoyed the costumes. Since it was the first time in Indy, I decided to explore downtown and it's a great city to walk through. The architecture is impressive, and the sights are plentiful.

  I stumbled upon Dick's Last Resort. This restaurant chain is one short raunchy sexist penis joke. The initial thought was to pop in for a quick dessert menu item but the more I looked around the bar and waiting area the more I realized this place is an example of why objectifying human beings has become normal. I didn't stay for dessert. As adventures go, Day 192 was loaded. My feet are sore, but my heart is very full. Love & Light

Day 193 of 365- I Saw It   March 31, 2018

A festival of vegetables… Since last September I've had the most interesting days and experiences. Some have been planned and some I have just stumbled upon. On day 193 I intentionally stumbled upon Indiana's Vegfest. First let me say that I followed the Facebook post, which originally had about 450 interested likes. In my head I thought this was going to be a grassroots experience with a couple of hundred people and a few tables with food samples.

I was so wrong. When we arrived the parking attendant sent us down the road to a secondary lot. There were cars everywhere and it became very clear that this wasn't going to be a small affair. Once we actually made it inside it was impossible to navigate the tightly packed crowd.

I've attended quite a few fests and events in the last couple hundred days, but this one was by far the most intense and least enjoyable. Maybe it was all the hungry vegans and the smell of the amazing food, but it was nearly impossible to enjoy this event at all. I was able to sample a small sip of coconut tea and the tiniest bite of vegan espresso chocolate. These bitty treats were hardly worth the visit. It's not that I was impatient; it was more that the intensity of the crowd made me eager to exit the tight venue.

When I asked the volunteers how long they'd held this event they said this was the second year. I was very surprised and also impressed to see how large the Veg community is in Indianapolis, Indiana. I left the event with a souvenir T-shirt and an empty stomach. On the drive home we stopped at a delicious Veg restaurant in Chicago, The Chicago Diner, VEG free since '83. This visit made up for the miserable lack of dining that out festival offered.

I had a vegan chocolate shake that brought a smile to my tummy. The Vegan BLT and Mac & Cheese made me wish I had a second stomach. If you haven't eaten there, you should give it a try. Day 193 was filled with tasty firsts. Love & Light

Day 194 of 365- I Made It   April 1, 2018

Experiments... Today is a complete exercise in food science. A few days ago, I started growing sourdough bread starter. It required a little more care than I had time for, but I managed to make the funky grow.

On day 193 I attempted to make my very first loaf of sourdough bread. I added my starter mix to the bread flour and olive oil. The recipe isn't very involved. Here's where it all went to hell. The recipe called for rest, not for the baker... for the dough. I left the dough to rise for 3 hours until it doubled in size. I was pretty pleased with what I saw but it felt very sticky.

Following this recipe required enormous patience. Baking this bread is never going to be in my top 10 list of things to do. Back to the instructions, which required me to cut the dough ball in half, and another hour of resting to let that dough rise again. At this point I'm tired of waiting and I've still got an hour of baking in the oven.

In a perfect world I made the most amazing loaf of sourdough bread. What I actually ended up with wasn't quite perfect. The bread tastes a little sour and it's a bit dense. As first time experiences go this wasn't awesome, but the starter is still growing, and I'll make another attempt in the future. Day 193 fell a little flat. Love & Light

Day 195 of 365- I Ate It   April 2, 2018

What's this green all about? It's been twelve days since my last green drink overload. I can still taste the dirty wheatgrass flavor on my tongue. If I'm being honest, I'll tell you that I have a new aversion to consuming green anything.

On the 195th day I had my very first drink of Matcha. This was on my list of things to try during the 365 adventures. I knew it was coming. Since my days have a tendency of running together, I often find myself at the entry door of a local Starbucks ordering drinks. Today it was my very first taste of Matcha.

At Starbucks they mix their green tea powder in milk. I chose coconut milk. It's such a shift from the horribleness of wheatgrass that I wish I'd tried this first. I think I found my new summer drink. Day 195 was quite delicious. Love & Light

Day 196 of 365- I Did It   April 3, 2018

Games people play. Today's adventure was a card trip across the dining room table. On the 196th day I learned how to play the most entertaining and challenging card game, Bandido.

Here's how it plays. In the box of cards, you have a double-sided bandit in a cage. Each side has tunnel openings. What's the point? The point is to close off every tunnel opening using the stack of tunnel cards. It seems like an easy game to play but we lost both times. It's a cooperative game but the challenge is that you don't know what the other players have in their hands. One minute you've got it down to a single tunnel and then you're trying to close off six.

This game is super compact for travel but requires a full-size table or floor to play on. I recommend it for any family game night. Day 196 wasn't stacked in my favor, but I'd play it again. Love & Light

Day 197 of 365- I Saw It   April 4, 2018

It's a small screen world. I'm in Vegas baby. It's not my first time but as you can imagine this Midwestern girl is going to bump into many new experiences.

On day 197 I became part of Television City. The experience is this. I lined up to be part of a group. The adorable ticket agent walked me into a room, mine happened to have 12 stations. I signed in on the super hi-tech iPads and followed screen prompts that indicated I would be watching and reviewing the TV series S.W.A.T.

My viewing summary: The episode seemed out of context and selected at random. The characters lacked development, and it was difficult to connect with any of the action. While watching I had a little box with a dial that I turned from 1-100 based on how much I was enjoying the episode. I never turned beyond the 35 mark.

The experience was interesting. As a funny side note there were a few participants who were pissed to be watching this particular show and they pouted and huffed through the entire hour. As experiences go this was enjoyable. I'd hoped for a new show. I've never watched S.W.AT. before and this didn't make me a fan. Day 197 made me feel like part of the television machine. Love & Light.

Day 198 of 365- I Did It   April 5, 2018

Fast Friends... Have you ever been to an event alone? I have and it's excruciating for an introvert like me. On day 198 I experienced speed friending. Here's the setup. Hundreds of strangers file into a room. They stand face to face in two enormous snaking lines. The event coordinator shouts out conversation starting questions and you've got a few minutes to bond and become instant friends.

That's how my adventure played out, but there was a tiny spin. I was one of the people volunteering to keep all these strangers in line. Who knew moving to the left could be so complicated? It wasn't easy but I also managed to meet a few people in the process. Day 198 was all about new friends. Love & Light.

Day 199 of 365- I Saw It   April 6, 2018

I'm trying to narrow today down to a single first experience. I'm attending my first Clexacon and standing beside thousands of human beings who are asking to be seen. It's one of the most humbling and invigorating experiences of my life.

On day 199 I made my LGBTQI+ connection. What does that mean? I met the editor of TAGG. This bi-monthly magazine based in D.C. is expanding across the country and looking for more representation on the rainbow spectrum. I'm beyond excited to have an opportunity to be a part of it. I can't believe this is me and I'm finally coming out of my own shadow. For those of you who have followed my journey, today was a life changer. You never know when you'll have an opportunity to see yourself in a new way. On day 199 I found myself and I didn't even know I was lost. Love & Light

Day 200 of 365- I Ate It   April 7, 2018

Super fan and Pho... I'm still in Vegas compiling a list of firsts that you'll never get to hear about. It's impossible to share everything that happened to me and for me today.

I'm passionate about my mission to find help for depression awareness and suicide prevention. Mental health care is pushed aside and underfunded. Today I met an amazing actress, Mandahla Rose.

Her bravery, while sharing the story of a tearful failed suicide attempt, touched me. I was standing in a room filled with 700 people who experienced the same moment of honesty. I am humbled by her courage. This extraordinary actress took the time to speak with me today. If she didn't know, I made it my mission to tell her that what she said and how she said it was important.

There were so many other firsts. I finished it with my very first Pho. It was joy on my lips after a very long day. My 200th day was life altering and soul honoring. Love & Light

Day 201 of 365- I Did It   April 8, 2018

Pen to Paper... It's day 201 and I attended my very first workshop led by show runner Emily Andras. If you don't know who she is you need to watch Wynonna Earp. It's an amazing series on the Syfy Network. I'm a HUGE fan of just about every aspect, from the womanpower characters to the positive representation of the LGBTQI+ community. I could go on and on, but you be the judge. Season 1 is on Netflix. Watch it.

My afternoon was all about writing, pitching and writing some more. It's what you'd expect from a workshop, but this was special for me.

The energy was incredible, and the information was invaluable. I respect the honest attitude toward teaching the room of writers that collaboration requires humility and compromise. As experiences go day 201 was a dream come to life. Love & Light

Day 202 of 365- I Did It   April 9, 2018

It's day 202 and I beat the Vegas odds. I'm a terrible gambler and I think it's because I play the stupid slot machines. I don't know why I do this anymore because I've never walked away a winner. Today was the day to break the streak when I played my very first Vegas table game, Roulette!! My plan? Bet on even and bet on black. I've got no reason for betting on either, I just felt like it was going to be a win.

I wanted to buy in with $10 but the table required $20. I got my stack of orange chips and put $4 on odd. Bam! Just like that I was a winner. I moved my pile to black. Bam! I hit it again.

This is where I would generally blow it all by betting more. Truth be told I needed to go to the airport, so I cashed out with an $8 advantage. I'm no high roller but I did walk away with $28. Day 202 for the win. Love & Light

Day 203 of 365- I Did It   April 10, 2018

Never let them see you sweat. In the last 5 days I've traveled to Vegas. I attended an amazing convention, Clexacon. During the event I knew I would be on the go and decided to use this to experience another first. On day 203 I experienced the crystal deodorant stone. This little sucker is the size of a bar of soap and fit well in my travel kit. Did it work?

It did. I ran my ass off all weekend and never felt or smelled stinky. You might not want to know the details but if you want to stop using chemical deodorant this is the BOMB!! Day 203 didn't stink. Love & Light

Day 204 of 365- I Did It   April 11, 2018

It's not easy to contain my excitement. I've got an incredible hobby that never feels like work. Since my favorite partner has gone off to have his own adventures, I've been trying to find someone to work with me.

On the 204th day I gave my very first blacksmithing lesson. I didn't want to scare anyone, but I also wanted them to understand that everything around the forge gets hot.

I'm not talking about boiling water hot; I mean bubbling flesh hot. The forge gets over 1500 degrees Fahrenheit. When you burn flesh at this temperature that heat causes serious damage. We don't mess around. This shit gets hot. After explaining what not to touch we put on all of our safety gear and lit the fire. I burn a gas forge so most of the mess comes from the work we are doing.

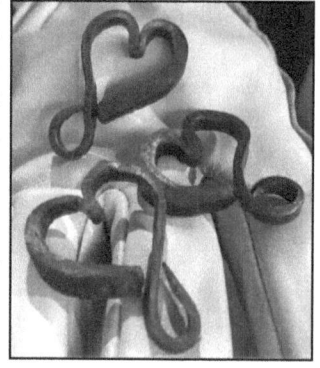

When you heat metal and hammer it, the impurities come off in flakes and chips called scale. As the bits are popping off with every hammer strike, they can cause burns too. Like I told my student, everything around the forge is hot enough to burn you.

The project that I demonstrated was a heart made from a horseshoe nail. There are quite a few steps involved. They listened, watched and performed exactly as instructed.

The best thing about playing with hot metal is that if you make a mistake, you heat it back up and hammer it again. This project is very forgiving for a beginner.

We spent two hours at the forge and when we finished my student had three pretty little hearts. I had the best time sharing something I'm so passionate about. Day 204 was hot... hot... hot! Love & Light

Day 205 of 365- I Did It   April 12, 2018

     Don't stand so close to me. It's day 205 and it has been a very long one. Since I was a child, I have been athletic. I've had moments of "woman power" strength and "I'm down for the count" weakness. One thing I have never been brave enough to try is a handstand. Here's how I feel about this. Hitting my head and hurting my neck are huge fears. When I was in grade school, I could do so many gymnastic exercises, but never once did I try to stand on my hands because of the fear of the fall. Today I am letting that 40-year-old fear die.

     With a little bit of execution help I made it up the front of the door and on to my hands. One foot on the wall and I was almost up on my own. I'm calling this a win. The fear isn't gone completely but I held my own if only for a brief second. Day 205 was amazing, hands down! Love & Light

Day 206 of 365- I Ate It   April 13, 2018

     It's not junk email but oh did it taste like junk. SPAM. I'm not sure how Friday the 13th, my 206th day, became salty chopped up meat day but here's my first experience with it. I'm not going to tell you what the ingredients are in this "meat" but they are, as a general rule, shit I just don't eat. I will always say no to hot dogs, sausage or "parts is parts" chopped up bits of animal stuffed in a casing.

     Why SPAM? Yum? Under any other circumstances I would not surrender to my fear of this canned nasty, but this is an adventure, and I've got 159 left. My first dilemma was how to cook it. It's got a slimy snot consistency in the can, so I prepared it in a frying pan. It smelled a bit like ham and I'm guessing it's the ridiculous amount of salt in it. The longer it fried the more it smelled like ham. I thought it might be good.

     Nope! This is the saltiest meat substance I have ever eaten, and the experience confirms that SPAM is not for me. If you've ever eaten this and loved it, I'm glad you survived. I can actually purchase some unprocessed meat for the same price as this small can so I'm not really sure why anyone would eat this. Day 206 was like licking a salt lamp. Yum! Love & salty light.

Day 207 of 365- I Saw It   April 14, 2018

Hog day should always follow spam day. It's day 207 and I went to my very first Harley Davidson event. It's raining. This should be an indicator of how the experience played out.

When I was in grade school my brother rode motocross and raced. I wanted to do the same thing. I have a picture somewhere of me on that bike, dreaming of riding like him, but I never did. I rode the little RM-80. I have to admit I didn't enjoy the speed, so I gave up that fantasy/dream. Why Harley Davidson in the rain? Why not! The event wasn't very exciting. They had a table set up with a raffle, a "parts is parts" sausage sale and discounts of Harley gear.

I did get to look at the beautiful bikes and the salesman was nice. As events go this was an opportunity to buy a bike and I wasn't really shopping for one. Day 207 was all bikes and no dirt. Love & Light

Day 208 of 365- I Saw It   April 15, 2018

Sex, drugs and . . . Day 208 was a definite leap into new territory. On my Hog excursion yesterday, I drove by an adult's only video, sex toy and smoke shop. Have you ever been? I definitely have not which made it a perfect "out of my comfort zone" experience.

Without over sharing, I don't need most of the toys hanging on the walls inside. There was a huge section that some might find entertaining for a bachelorette party. Interesting enough I have way more questions after being inside this store than I did before it.

I enjoyed walking through the smoke shop. They sell a huge selection of pipes for "tobacco" smoking. If you need water pipes, they have them. So many are made of blown glass, and they are beautiful. Setting up for a hookah party? You should visit this store.

I was schooled in so much. I had no idea. I tried to take a few pictures but everything inside is TOP SECRET. I was scolded like a naughty kid. It just added to the awkwardness of the experience. Day 208 was a bounce around my comfort zone... Love & Light

Day 209 of 365- I Made It   April 16, 2018

    Roll, roll, roll your bowl. When I was in high school, I took a pottery class. I learned how to place a huge chunk of clay in the center of the wheel and form it into a pot, or mug or vase. I gave all my creations to my mother. I was thinking about this when I was playing with my plastic dough today.

    After 209 days I am determined to make it to the end and today I had my first baking clay experience. In my head I was going to create these adorable little dishes that I could use for all the hobbies that I have. Before starting this experience, I had a few but now I have a few hundred. I'm not kidding, I have learned how to do so many crafty things, but I have no free time to explore them further.

    When I turn 50, I plan to craft in all of my free time. This baking clay is as hard as a brick, and it took about an hour to soften it enough to roll it out. The colors I bought were boring, so I tried to use them to mix my own. They came out a little muddy so next time I'll spring for the premixed ones. I curled the snakes of clay in a ball and used a rolling pin to make a colorful patty of dough. Shaping the actual bowl was not my strongest moment. I made three attempts and I'm sure this blog is the only time you'll get to look at them.

    After the bowls baked for 15 minutes and hardened up, they still looked horrible. I think they are something only a mother would love. I'll ask her tomorrow. You'll get an update. Day 209 was proof that I am not a bowl maker. Love & Light

Day 210 of 365- I Did It   April 17, 2018

Oh vanity. On day 27 I had single hairs threaded off my face. It was horrible. What I didn't realize at the time was that those little deep-rooted follicles would grow back in an aggressive bristle brush way.

On day 210 I tried to fix this error in judgment with facial waxing. I know you're trying to understand how I could live 49 years without ever trying this. Wisdom!

I own tweezers. I've plucked away one or two unattractive lip hairs in my life. I think my face is pissed at me for the threading situation because I've got new hair that wasn't there before. Don't get me wrong. I didn't manifest a unibrow, but I swear I didn't have hair between my eyes. I decided to go to an actual spa. I don't know what the hell that means aside for $$.

I'm pretty sure that being thrifty when it comes to cutting hair or other vanity driven experiences could lead to disaster. I shouldn't care about having a hairy face, but I do. The complete experience didn't take very long. Warm wax was spread across my brow in a small tolerable amount. Little strips of cloth were pressed on and seconds later ***Rip*** and the hair was gone.

It felt like punishment for giving a shit about how my body is changing. I think I'll try to age with grace and pluck those bristly hairs on my own. Day 210 was hairy, not scary but a lesson in what's important. Love & Light

Day 211 of 365- I Made It   April 18, 2018

I've discovered myself in a bulb of garlic. Let me preface this by saying that day 211 started at 5:00 am and my senses might have been heightened. For the last few weeks, I have been making bone broth onion soup. I usually start in the afternoon sweating my onions and browning my garlic so it can slow cook overnight. Everything is grown organically and is considered medicine in the cancer fight that continues in our family.

What does this have to do with a 5:00 am wake up? Today I wanted to try something new for me and for my soup. At the butt-crack of dawn, on my 211th day, I roasted garlic. Don't think this wasn't an adventure for me. This was a process and if nothing else I realized after 18 years of living in this home I have no idea how to use the timed cooking feature on either of my ovens.

I tried . . . I really did. This is where I had to pry both eyes open and stay awake. My parents are incredible gardeners. Mom has always had plants growing everywhere, some that appeal to the eyes and some to satisfy the belly. When I was a young girl, I remember both of my parents working outside in the huge vegetable garden that they planted. I had no idea what a gift the memory would be. My dad grows some things of his own, his pride and joy, garlic. It makes sense that his loving hands would tend to the medicinal bulbs that I roasted today.

I will admit that I had to do research for this experience. I didn't want to screw it up. I wrapped three bulbs in aluminum foil and dropped a nice clump of coconut oil in the middle. I turned the oven to 400F and set a 45-minute timer. Everything I read gave an estimated time, but one said to let your nose tell you when it was ready. At 5:00am this made me laugh.

I went upstairs to get dressed and in about 30 minutes that "nose knows" suggestion became very clear. The scent of that roasting garlic had risen to the second floor and even though my door was closed I understood. My house smelled like an Italian home. I've cooked garlic in a pan 100's of times, but it's never smelled so delicious.

I waited the additional 15 minutes and when I opened the foil it was beautiful. After only one experience, I have a roasted garlic problem. I might just do it every morning so I can feel like I'm in my mother's kitchen. I can't wait to taste how it changes the flavor of the soup. I didn't forget to slice the onions and sweat those together with that garlic. After all, this was about making onion soup. It was definitely an incredible way to wake up. Day 211 was a sensory experience. Love & Light

Day 212 of 365- I Made It   April 19, 2018

Herbs and edibles... This was the most challenging experience to date. When I decided to go to today's event it was to create something for my mother for Mother's Day. I had no idea the roller coaster that was in store for me. The Ladies night event was held at the Burlington Garden Center and for my 212th experience I was assembling a vitality bowl.

As an experience I have all the necessary skills to put this together. As I walked through the building, I couldn't help but remember the last time my mother and I were there together. My eyes clouded over and I had to stop.

If it wasn't part of my 365-day challenge I wouldn't have stayed. This is one of my mother's favorite places. These are her people and for the last few years she has invited me into her green thumb world. The garden center isn't very big, so mom and I covered most of it during our last tea and talk about plants. When I went back to the plant area where the vitality bowls were being created, I couldn't hold the tears back.

The amazing woman guiding the mini workshop approached me and asked questions that I struggled to answer. I explained why I was there, and she cared for me with a kindness that almost hurt my heart. I had not prepared myself for all these emotions. I felt lost in this world of plants that mom always led me through. I'm sad to say that I don't remember the name of the woman who helped me, but we talked about mom and herbs and edibles that might be helpful while she is fighting cancer and all the side effects of radiation.

It felt good to put my hands in dirt. I chose herbs that smell amazing when I rub my hands against them. The volume of knowledge inside my mother's head humbles me and I can't wait to share this with her. Day 212 was a mixed blessing. Love & Light

Day 213 of 365- I Did It   April 20, 2018

I'm on fire… It's 4/20 and I'm sober as can be. I should have planned a more appropriate experience to honor the date but instead I did my first nighttime glow run. This event was Superhero themed, so I wore my Wonder Woman shirt and cape.

My event was at Six Flags theme park, and it felt like opening weekend. The lines were typical and there was nothing to do until the sun set. Once we actually started to walk the chill in the air kept us moving at a pretty good pace. I think it was meant to be a 5k, but I didn't check my Fitbit before we started walking. Day 213 was a fun run that I walked. Love & Light

Day 214 of 365- I Saw It April 21, 2018

You never know when your first time might also be the last. I had my first glass of Pinot Grigio for mom, but that's not today's real first. On the 214th day I experienced the one and only thing I never wanted during these 365 days and thousands after. If you've been following my journey, you know that mom has been fighting. In the early morning of day 214 my mom found peace and her fight ended.

She was a force. On the last day of her life, she fought with every breath to stay here. She taught me how to be kind. She taught me how to find joy in the little things. We had so many adventures together and in the last months I got to know her without boundaries and pride. If you never got a chance to meet MaryAnn Kennedy, you missed an amazing human spirit. She made me want to be better and work harder.

If you knew her, you met a real living, walking, breathing angel. Her greatest gift was the ability to make you feel perfect as you are. She loved the idea of this 365-day adventure. She was one of the first people to write feedback and when she was awake in the hospital she would listen to me read my latest post. I already miss her words of encouragement.

On Tuesday April 17th mom said, "I love you" as I hugged her. That was the last time she spoke to me. The sound of her words fills my heart. Being loved by her was a gift.

Today I held her for the last time, kissed her, felt the warmth of her skin against my hand and let her physical presence go. Day 214 Love & Light

Day 215 of 365- I Did It April 22, 2018

How do you summarize a life? How do you capture extraordinary humanity in a single photograph? On the 215th day of new experiences I planned a funeral for my mother. She was the planner in the family. She was such an organizer that she had labels on her label case. Her hand-written tags are attached to most of the boxes in her office. She wanted to know how and where to find the things that were important.

Our family drafted a short explanation of who mom was in her 79 years. There is so much, and she had passions that stretched all over. There is no way for you to understand who she was in 500 words but somehow, we managed. We looked through 1000's of pictures, each sorted by family and event in a quest to find the perfect image of my idol.

She was something special and the true Wonder Woman in my life. By the end of the evening my father, my sisters and I assembled what feels like a snapshot of my mother in word and image. It was a long day. She was amazing, this is the hardest experience of my life, and I keep waiting for mom to come in and rescue us from our floundering. Love & Light

Day 216 of 365- I Ate It April 23, 2018

Not your cardboard granola bar. For the last month I've been protein obsessed, not for myself but for my mother. We were doing everything possible to control the calories and content of the food she was eating. My uncle found an amazing plant-based breakfast bar loaded with 22grams of protein.

On the 216th day of my personal challenge I ate one of them. Why did I wait so long to try one? These bars are freshly made without preservatives and ridiculously expensive. I wanted to save every single one for mom. I never wanted to eat one. It took up to 14 days to manufacture them and another 7 to deliver by Fedex. It was a process and to make sure there wasn't a gap we decided to get a good supply. We ordered 6 cases of 12. My mother passed away before the order arrived.

I thought she liked them. Today I ate the raspberry hazelnut bar, and I understand why my mother loved to eat them. They are delicious and as I sat with my sister, drinking a latte I thought about mom. She should have been with us at the table. Day 216 was a break. Love & Light

Day 217 of 365- I Did It   April 24, 2018

Tied up in knots... This day has been pretty long. I managed to get through most of it without any idea what I was going to do. I have to admit that the next few days are going to be pretty difficult for so many reasons.

On day 217 my cousin Colleen came to the rescue to teach me to crochet. This is something that I have wanted to learn for most of my life. She taught me the double crochet stitch. I spent a lot of time making a chain of yarn with the hook that I could have done faster by hand. My cousin was so patient, and I felt successful at the end of my lesson. The rhythm of crocheting is much like weaving chainmail, and I found it very relaxing once I learned how to be less horrible at it. This experience is going to take a little more than one day. Day 217 was educational. Love & Light

Day 218 of 365- I Ate It   April 25, 2018

Fancy Moon Clover... That's my unicorn name. I discovered it today while accomplishing my 218th experience, unicorn cereal. NO, I've never eaten the delicious unicorn. My original intention behind the purchase of this treat was to help my mother play some sensory games. I learned them from her speech therapist. We started with bowls of sugar, oatmeal and cheerios. Our goal, stimulate the senses and start a conversation. We did everything but hear my mother speak. She was not talking.

After that morning experience I saw a post online about the Unicorn cereal. My mother played with a unicorn ball popper so that creature became a part of our healing arsenal. Once I saw the cover of the cereal box, I knew mom and I were going to have a great time with these. The problem, I couldn't find them in any store. I had to special order them from Amazon. I didn't know it at the time but these little loops of pink, purple and blue wouldn't arrive until after my mother passed.

As my experience today, I played with mom's food. I poured a big bowl of cereal added some organic almond milk and ate that delicious breakfast. They're actually pretty delicious and after a conversation about them with my cousin, she bought me 5 more boxes. I think my mother wanted all of us to take a taste. We're going to mix them in melted marshmallows and make Unicorn cereal bars. If you can find a box, you also have to check out the side panel to discover your unicorn name.
Fancy Moon Clover. I'll take it. Day 218 fulfilled a promise made. Love & Light

Day 219 of 365- I Did It   April 26, 2018

To the point... On day 84 I made a beautiful knife. Life happened and that experience was left a tiny bit incomplete. On my 219th day I finished putting an edge on that blade. The experience required a teacher. My dad and I have spent many days together in good times and in very bad. He's someone pretty special and he knows so much about so many things.

Today he taught me how to use a whetstone so that my knife would cut. The process was pretty simple once he explained it. I did get a tiny bit confused about the direction that I should use when pulling the steel across that stone. It worked. It's sharp. Success. Day 219 cuts like a knife. Love & Light

Day 220 of 365- I Did ItApril 27, 2018

    Sphero… I bought this experience almost a month ago with the idea of tearing up the room that my mother was living in. Things changed but I had to achieve this experience. Day 220 was all about the sphero. This is a little robot, mine happens to be a replica of the Star Wars BB-8, which makes it 1000 times more adorable.

    This mini bot should have been amazing. It was not. My little rolling friend kept losing his head. I guess by design it needs to float around the spinning ball. It was fun and frustrating at the same time.

    If you were in the market for one of these, I'd pass. It's cute but the fun fades as you chase the head of your bot around the floor. Day 220 kept rolling and rolling. Love & Light

Day 221 of 365- I Did It   April 28, 2018

One last time... Day 221 was my chance to visit the places I remember as a child. That's not a first. Today was about the one time I would take my mother on her last tour of the country life she lived. The women in this family are extraordinary. I give my mother credit for that. We picked mom up this morning from the funeral home. She was cremated and we walked out with her in a beautiful red rose decorated vessel. The four of us took our positions in the vehicle and as my sister carried my mom to the back seat I pointed out that mom never rode in the back because it made her sick. We all got a chuckle and fastened the lap belt in front of the urn.

Theme of the day? W.W.N.D.   What Would Nana Do?

As a child the drive from Antioch had two routes, the quick and the scenic. My mother loved the slow speed winding country roads. Today we DO the scenic route. It's April 28th, 50 degrees and Garage sale weather. Believe it or not, Nana would DO a garage sale.

We stopped, we shopped, and Nana had her last hurrah in the rummaging world. Our next stop was the one restaurant in Camp Lake that everyone knew. If you had a party, wedding, funeral or just needed a six pack you went to Marchuck's. The place was dated; wood paneled and an all-around hole in the wall joint. It was where everyone knew you and made you feel like family. It also burned to the ground a few years ago. Nothing gold can stay. The view from their hill was beautiful. Our next stop was my Grandparent's home. It took us a few laps around the neighborhood, but we finally found it. Our moment was a bit sketchy. We snapped the picture and got the heck out of there.

Mom's next adventure was a quick drive by one of our family homes. I was a baby when we lived there. We didn't stop. That old sucker needs to be pushed over and made new again. I didn't take pictures because the memory of yesterday is so much better. Next stop, ice cream! Last year the most adorable ice cream parlor opened in Wilmot. Mom loved the place. Hansen's has a variety of flavors, but we all got a scoop of Black Cherry just for mom. She loved Door County cherry, but that flavor is seasonal. Last fall mom and I talked about doing the all flavor sample dish as a 365-day experience. I don't think I'll be able to do that one. I'm going to miss my ice creams with mom.

Since we were in the sleepy town of Wilmot, we decided to take mom to her alma mater. I must imagine that so many things have changed since she attended because I don't recognize the old building from my high school days. U Rahh Rahh Wilmot High!

We stopped at my parent's current home so mom could be among her flowers. Just before she passed, I brought her photographs of everything in bloom. Yellow tulips were her favorite, but they haven't blossomed. I'm sure mom has already found a place in her eternal garden.

Mom's next adventure was a walk to my childhood home. I haven't been back there in a dozen years, and everything seemed small. As a child, our modest home felt like a mansion. As it stands today, it feels like a dollhouse. The property is big, and the tour was bittersweet. Mom had a secure place in the baby stroller and my heart wanted to keep the real image of that home. We left without taking a picture.

Tonight, my mom is with my brother. That was our last stop, and I think it's only fitting that they have some time together. He was her only son. We all say goodbye in different ways and not all who wander are lost. I will miss those winding scenic drives even though most of the time I ended up getting car sick. Life is funny that way. Day 221 Love & Light

Day 222 of 365- I Made It   April 29, 2018

Some assembly required. My triple deuce day was an escape from everything around me. To be honest, this experience wasn't even on my radar. I was looking for some family photographs and stumbled upon a kit to make a kaleidoscope.

At first glance this seems pretty simple. I imagine that my mother got this kit as a gift and planned to assemble it on her own. After reading through the instructions, I understand why it's in the box. This kit's instructions were written and illustrated by two different people who had no intention of collaborating on getting to the end result. At no point do the instructions match the pictures and there isn't much logic to the order of things. All that aside the parts went together with patience. That's how I know this was a gift from beyond. Only my mother would set me up with a task that would require me to slow down. She didn't really ask me to do this today but when I found this unassembled kaleidoscope it couldn't go one more day in pieces.

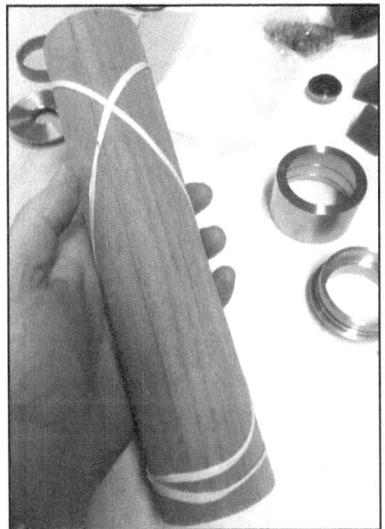

The most exciting part was assembling the mirrors. The reflective triangle felt like a thing of magic. Once it was glued together, I could get a real feel for how beautiful this was going to be. I can close my eyes and see the joy mom would have had on today's adventure and as I worked, I could feel her right there with me. This kaleidoscope would have made her very happy.

Day 222 gave me a new perspective.
Love & Light

Day 223 of 365- I Did It   April 30, 2018

    I delivered a eulogy today. I can't even come up with a single thing that's good about eulogizing my mother. She was placed in a columbarium that already had her name etched in stone. This was one of the longest days of my life and it happened in the blink of an eye.

    I'm still waiting for mom to come outside and call us in for dinner. I'm not going to say that I didn't take my mother for granted. I'm 49 and honest enough to admit my imperfections. I consider myself one of the luckiest people because her blood is in my veins. I also sat with her for many days and had the privilege of seeing how strong she was. I had no idea. Tonight, we ate every grandchild's favorite breakfast . . . banana splits. Nana would approve. Day 223 Love & Light

Day 224 of 365- I Ate It   May 1, 2018

    May day! It's the first day of May and also a great day to sample some delicious treats. On the 224th day of my adventures I decided to sample one of nature's most amazing sources of protein.

    ANTS! Here's how it played out. I've been sitting outside most of the afternoon. It was a gorgeous day, and I watched these tiny little bugs creep across the ground. Why eat one? Why not! I grabbed a tiny creeper crawling across the floor. It wriggled around in my hand. I really wanted to try it but wasn't quite sure I could.

    How do you make an ant taste delicious?   Chocolate. Really delicious?   Dark Chocolate! That little sucker went down easily. My cheering support team told me not to chew but I did anyway. No harm no foul. As experiences go, ants will not become part of my new diet. Day 224 was crunchy. Love & Light

    Nutrition of Ants.

Ants offer a high nutritional value. Scientist have proven that eating insects, such as ants offers great health benefits and should be encouraged. Ants are super rich in protein and minerals and they have way less cholesterol than pork or beef.

Nutrition of Ants | Ant Proteinantprotein.com/nutrition-of-ants/

Day 225 of 365- I Read It   May 2, 2018

It's a little bit funny... For the last few days we have been sorting through all the things that my mother used in the pursuit of a happy life. In all her little bits and goodies I found a mini edition of "50 ways to a Better you, for dummies."

I've never needed a "dummies" book until I became my mother's "techie." She struggled with anything electronic even though she managed to use a computer at work for 20 years. She called me on the phone when I was living in Colorado to help her get rid of the blinking light on her VCR. My mother was so amazing and brilliant, but she bought a lot of "dummies" books. As firsts go, finding this book was a surprise and it wasn't. My mother may or may not have read this book. If she did, she took it to heart. If she didn't read it, somehow, she was already living all of these things.

On the first page two ideas are listed: You need to work toward finding happiness in your life and discover common elements in happy people. It seems pretty simple. My mom seemed to do it without effort, but she never did learn how to program her VCR.

My 225th day was my first solitary "dummy" experience and I feel like it might be the best experience I've never had with my mom. I feel like she led me to it today. If you believe in the possibility of guidance from the afterlife, I know this book is in my hand today for a purpose. Love & Light

Day 226 of 365- I Ate It   May 3, 2018

Why did I do that? It's day 226 and I tried, I really tried. I had a delightful evening with three beautiful people. This isn't new but the conversation was. I've discovered a few things about myself in the last 135 days and the most important is to be an authentic human being.

Have you ever tried to explain who you are and actually felt heard? That happened tonight and it felt amazing. While this conversation was happening, I also had to reach over and sample two very new Italian dishes.

Chicken Cacciatore and Spaghetti ala Carbonara. Here's the deal. . . Chicken is really chicken. When it comes to smothering it in (sugary) sauce the only thing that can really ruin it is too much salt and too much sugar. This dish was balanced, and the flavor was wonderful. The spaghetti ala Carbonara was a different story. There was so much salted meat in this dish that you could call the deer home to feast. I'd never order this again.

My food experiences have been hit or miss in the last 226 days. I have discovered that I can do a lot of different flavors and textures, but I can't do aggressive salt. Why have I never tried either of these firsts? I'm a simple person with simple needs and both meals were a little busy for my taste buds. Day 226 was sweet and salty. Love & Light

Day 227 of 365- I Did It   May 4, 2018

Lost... It's the 227th day of personal challenges and I had my very first metal detecting adventure. Why? I was looking for a lost memory and I didn't find it. I'm not sure it will ever be found because the person who lost this item is suddenly lost to us. The treasure happens to be white gold and the only way to find it is to make it ding. I've never operated a metal detector and as this piece of equipment didn't come with instructions, I had to feel my way around the How-to part of it.

I put on my gloves, dialed in the sensitivity on high and floated that little sucker over a box of rotten food. Yep, that's where we think the lost item ended up, in a compost bin.

I found a lot of junk in that pile but the only thing that went ding was a rusty nail. I spent another 30 minutes searching the garden boxes around the yard. I found a few rusty screws, probably from the construction of the boxes, and a broken plant hanger. Junk! I think it might be helpful if I had a better device. I don't know if I will ever be able to recover what's lost. Day 227 was a fruitless adventure. Love & Light

Day 228 of 365- I Ate It   May 5, 2018

Moment seized... I have a variety of tea bags in a kitchen cabinet. I don't have them because I have a tea problem. I have them because my mother did. It wasn't a problem so much as it was a dislike for many of the herbal blends that I would buy. We drank a lot of tea. She LOVED drinking tea, growing herbs to make tea but most of all she found great pleasure in sharing tea with others.

On day 228 I made my very first pot of Numi blooming tea. This was beautiful and I can't believe that my mother and I never shared them. What a missed opportunity and if I didn't have so many other tea times with her it might make me sad.

I'm disappointed that this first happened without her but I also believe she would have loved all the women in the room who drank this delicious drink.

If you haven't had this tea experience you should treat yourself to one. Seize the opportunity. Make time for yourself. Day 228 steeped to contentment. Love & Light

Day 229 of 365- I Ate It   May 6, 2018

Drinking an angel… For most of my life my father has had stories to tell. He's been on this planet for 80 years and has a thousand times as many tales to share. He's had many careers and experienced some things that seem impossible, but he was a photographer, and he took pictures. In his lifetime dad tended bar and in that environment, he learned a thing or two about mixing a drink.

On day 229 dad made me a cocktail. This might sound unbelievable, but I've never had a mixed drink with my dad. We've had our share of beer and that's something I enjoy, but I'm not a huge consumer of liquor.

What did he make for me? The drink is called an Angel's tip. It has 3 ingredients: crème de cocoa, whipping cream and a maraschino cherry. I'm not going to go into a lot of detail but this drink has a few names. You can Google it if you have questions. The theme of this house has been angels long before my mother's passing. She wouldn't have cheered for my alcohol consumption, but she would have giggled about the drink. She was adorable that way. My Pop made the drink.

I think he wanted me to experience how he floated the cream on the top of the crème de cocoa. It's a simple drink because once the pour is complete you top it with a maraschino cherry and drink it. It's pretty to look at and warmed my belly as I drank in one long sip. My father is amazing. I could listen to his stories every day and the sound of his laugh is pure joy. Day 229 Love & Light

Day 230 of 365- I Did It   May 7, 2018

Hammer time... Oh I had the best time. Day 230 I let my hammer smash an old tube TV. I have always wanted to hit one of these suckers and after the week I've been having this was almost therapy.

I dragged the television out in the yard and removed the plastic housing. This particular unit had a VCR built in, so I ripped that sucker out too. Once the glass tube was removed, I laid down a tarp and placed the glass on top of it. I didn't want to make a huge mess and risk driving over the shards while mowing. I chose a lovely 4-pound hammer and with my best ax pitch I launched it right at the bubble of glass.

I missed. Just as I was about to launch the hammer for a second time my cell phone rang. Good thing I wasn't mid-throw because the call turned the video camera off. Call answered. I set myself up for a second throw and that TV tube popped and it was AWESOME! The video is so great. Day 230 was wicked. Love & Light

Day 231 of 365- I Did It   May 8, 2018

Thy will be done... It's been 17 days since my mother passed. I've sorted through thousands of pages of paper loaded with 10 times as many ideas to fill the days of her life. From the piles on the table, my mom thought she had 50 more years to live. In all of the leaning towers of paperwork we unearthed mom's plan to create a will.

Do you have a will? Have you determined who gets to sort through all of your shit when you die? Have you written that lucky sucker's name down so that the surviving relatives don't start World War II over a wicker basket and a pair of gloves?

On my 231st day of this personal growth endeavor I helped my father establish a plan by writing a will. The workbook we used was written in 1993. My parents had this as a "to-do" item for 25 years. In my head this will is written. The court system prefers the will in writing. We're about to remedy the situation. My thought on today's experience is this, death is inevitable, make it easier on all the people who you'll leave behind and tell them what you want... in writing. Day 231 Love & Light

Day 232 of 365- I Did It   May 9, 2018

Picture that... There's always a picture to be taken. On day 232 I used a smartphone rig. The unit has three parts: a boom microphone, and LED light and the rig frame to hold it all together. The only thing missing from the picture is the camera; I'm holding that. I plan to add a Bluetooth remote to make it easier to activate the camera. I could have purchased each piece individually.

I took a walk around the yard to capture the sights & sounds of life in the subdivision. The camera feels stable, and the microphone captures audio with amazing clarity. I have plans for this little gem. Day 232 looks and sounds marvelous. Love & Light

Day 233 of 365- I Did It   May 10, 2018

Paddle... I'm not a water sport person. I don't enjoy wearing a swimsuit especially when it means I'm getting into the water. Nope! Not my thing. On day 233, the 10th of May I had my first kayak adventure. When I was a kid, I spent most of my summer in a pool or the lake. It was before air

conditioning and if you were hot and wanted to cool off, you got wet.

When I was gathering ideas for my 365-day experiences I had a kayaking goal. That plan capsized when my wonderful niece told me that she owns a kayak and that she would take me for my first trip.

I believe I had the best tour guide. I'm a bit of a cheater when it comes to paddling and I had a terrible time alternating with a consistent rhythm. My extraordinary niece Becca was patient, and I hope she had as much fun as I did. We toured areas of the lake that I've never seen from the water, and it definitely felt like a first for me. Day 233 was good to the last drop. Love & Light

Day 234 of 365- I Made It   May 11, 2018

Whip it... It's just a bit of joy. My mother inspired day 234. She had this amazing little glass-whipping container in her kitchen and today I used it for the first time.

If you've ever made whipped cream, you know that it requires a firm whisking but also attention to the process. One mistake and you've got sweet vanilla butter. No mistakes were made. The Speed E Whipper works like a dream. I might experiment with different types of milk and maybe add some chocolate. Day 234 was saweeet! Love & Light

Day 235 of 365- I Saw It   May 12, 2018

It's academic... I've raised two amazing human beings. They have dreams and are fearless about chasing them. No apologies and minimal regrets have led each of them to finish college. On day 235 I watched my first-born child graduate Magna Cum Laude with three Bachelor of Arts degrees, one in philosophy, one in history, one in anthropology and a certificate in ethics.

This kid weighted 6 pounds at birth, a little scrawny and jaundiced but once the learning began there was no running away from the quest for knowledge. I'm certain I stopped comprehending this kid's thought processes just after 7th grade.

We fed that mind just like Johnny number 5 from the Short Circuit movies, "Need Input!" I sat in the auditorium today reminding myself to be in this moment, present to how my life changed because of this human being. It is possible to be overflowing with pride. I experienced it on the 235th day. Love & Light

Day 236 of 365- I Did It   May 13, 2018

How do you hold a moonbeam in your hand? If you watch The Sound of Music, you'll hear this question asked in regards to the main character. It is the ultimate Mother's Day movie. Maria becomes a mentor and the woman who will choose to be a mother to those seven children.

I've never watched the Sound of Music from this perspective. Motherhood is different for us all. I've had some pretty amazing firsts in the 49th year of my life. I've pushed beyond my fears and learned about weakness. I've seen, tasted, touched, smelled and heard what seemed impossible. My 236th day was, is and will always be redefining. I am officially without my north star.

I can no longer seek the wisdom of a woman who knew me from the moment I was made. It feels impossible until I stop, close my eyes, and I see her sitting at her table. I smell the cup of tea in front of her. I hear the sound of her laughter. I've had 49 years to infuse my soul with the strength of a real Wonder Woman. She was my mother. I visited her today. It was my first time alone at the cemetery. I sat without her physical presence and thought about our last Mother's Day together. It was so much the opposite that I found a sense of joy in every moment that we had before she died.

She loved yellow tulips. A few years ago, I gifted her with three hand blown golden blossoms in a flowerpot on her porch. We planted tulips in my garden almost 10 years ago. This morning, I cut one and I left it at the cemetery just as a sprinkle of rain began to fall. Day 236 Love & Light

Day 237 of 365- I Did It   May 14, 2018

    Getting schooled… I've got a pile of old comic books in my house. I don't know much about them, so I decided to take a trip to the local comic book store and get an education. I watch The Big Bang Theory. The characters are always standing around in a comic bookstore and drooling over whatever it is they are reading.

    The problem with comic books as I see it; it takes 20 issues and loads of time to tell the story. I can't do the patience thing, just tell me the story and DO IT NOW!! I'm a chapter book gal all the way. I definitely need someone to tell me if it's time to let these old, yellowed pages go. The store clerk was generous with his knowledge and went through the pile that I had.

    I have books from the 70's, 80's and 90's along with my amazing Buffy the Vampire Slayer season 8 & 9. I'm not a collector but I wanted that show to stay on the air forever. As we sorted through the pile it was interesting to learn that every ding, dent, fold smudge and tear made a difference in the value. It's not like I want to sell them, but I do want to know if they should be tucked away.

    According to the clerk he wouldn't give this stack of old comics to a child, but I'm not going to take any extended vacations from the proceeds either. Day 237 was entertaining, Love & Light

Day 238 of 365- I Made It   May 15, 2018

    Not in my garden… If I confess that I've neglected my home and yard it means that I see the leaning tower of clutter and the bed of weeds growing around my porch and now I have to deal with them. I've been distracted. This is where I share how much I hate using toxic solutions around my home. Does chemical weed killer cause cancer? I'm not a scientist but if it makes plants shrivel up and die, it can't be good for my body.

    Day 238 was all about non-toxic weed decimation.

The simple ingredients include: 1 gallon of white vinegar, 1 cup of salt and 1 tablespoon of dish soap. I measured the salt in a 2 cup container and added the vinegar. I stirred this until all the granules dissolved. I mixed in one tablespoon of soap and poured the solution back into the bottle of vinegar and gave it a good shake to mix it all together.

    The real test started after I sprayed the front bed with the mix. It isn't immediate which sets off the patience alarm that this 365-day challenge created. I want those little green weeds to go away. I really don't want to pull them out. I absolutely hate pulling weeds, which is why I poured 3 tons of rock around my home. This is going to be a process. So far, the sun is shining. Day 238 should be killer. Love & Light

Day 239 of 365- I Saw It   May 16, 2018

We go on… Not so long ago I wrote and published an article about being a mother titled, "Watching you go." I penned this piece after watching my child leave for a semester overseas. She was gone for four months but it felt like something more. In the last few weeks, I've had to say goodbye to my mother, to friendships and to family.

When I woke up this morning, I had a plan to go to the grand opening of Ikea in Milwaukee. I watched the news and the broadcast put me off on the whole idea. They reported about the traffic, and it wasn't even 6am. I rolled over in my bed and contemplated an alternate plan for day 239.

I abandoned Ikea. I think my partner in crime, aka husband and driver, was relieved. I absolutely hate crowds, and he heard a report that it could be just like a black Friday event. I'm out! That shit isn't fun anymore. I rolled back over in bed and closed my eyes. I woke up and started to tackle my bookwork, as I made my way to a second cup of coffee, I heard the buzzing of my phone. 8:14 a.m. and life changes again. On day 239 my daughter was officially offered a space in the master's program at the University of Edinburgh in Scotland. The last few weeks have been heavy with emotions, most of which were sorrow.

Today we celebrated. When Victoria was in Scotland in 2016, she purchased a bottle of scotch with the intention of opening it when she received her grad school acceptance letter. Tonight, we cracked that bottle open and shared it with many of the people who have been support for my kid through this stage of life. I see greatness in the future. I also see some overseas travel. Day 239 was Joy.

Day 240 of 365- I Did It   May 17, 2018

So, write… As experiences go today's hits my heart in a joyful way. I've been writing most of my life. As far back as I can remember I have dreamed of telling stories that create hope and inspiration. On the 240th day of this unbelievable journey I became a contract writer for SBS Australia.

What does this mean? It means that I need to work on having something to say. Right now, I can't think of anything. This can't last for long, right? It wasn't a long and drawn out experience as it was all about signing that contract. Watch out world, I might have a few international things to say. Day 240 Love & Light

Day 241 of 365- I Ate It   May 18, 2018

    Teatime… Today felt like a crazy one. I had a visit from local law enforcement. The story in summary, some guy fled a traffic stop and ran across my property. This is alleged and I never saw anything, but the cops did have a walk around the property.

    Believe it or not this wasn't actually a first for me. THAT story can be found on Facebook in 2014. Since a visit from local law enforcement couldn't be my experience for the day, I decided to try something that my mother and I had talked about doing.

    Day 241 was all about harvesting and drinking dandelion root tea. I will be honest when I say that I was relying on my mom for guidance. Since she didn't have any dandelion tea bags on her shelf. I'm pretty sure her interest was mostly about having this 365-day adventure together. First things first, getting the roots. The harvesting part of the day was pretty simple since I seem to be farming those golden weeds with no effort at all.

    It was a bit tricky to get large portions of the root, but I got enough to make it worth the effort. Just for your information I don't use any chemicals on my yard so these roots a free from herbicides and pesticides. <u>Mini info infusion:</u> Dandelion root improves digestion and aids in weight loss. It eases congestion of the liver, helps to purify the bladder and kidneys. It reduces the risk of urinary tract infections and contains calcium, magnesium, iron, zinc, potassium, vitamins B and C. It helps to purify the blood, regulate blood sugar and improves blood circulation and helps with aching joints.

    There are a few other things but as summer celebrations get into full swing you might want to brew some root to help detox that liver. Just a suggestion, I pulled out about 30 rooted plants and after cutting off the greens I had a 1/4-cup of cut root. I read quite a few articles to determine that I could do this a few ways. I decided to roast the cut root at 250 degrees for about 30 minutes. I added a tablespoon to boiling water and waited about 10 minutes for it to steep.

    If you're curious, this tea absolutely tastes like dirt. I scrubbed those roots pretty clean, but it still tastes like the smell of the container I keep my night crawlers in for fishing. This would fall into the medicinal tea realm. Maybe I'll add a touch of raw honey next time. I'm going to give this a try for a few weeks to see if it improves my aching bones. Day 241 was dirty and not quite so tasty. Love & Light

Day 242 of 365- I Saw It   May 19, 2018

Built and eaten... Day 242 was quite the adventure. I attended a K.L.U.G. event and had my first dining experience at a local tourist stop. I really thought that attending an area LEGO event would be an adventure. It turned out to be less than exciting. The displays were amazing if you're a brick fanatic like I am. Most of the building was focused on trains and as much as Lego is wonderful, trains don't really excite me.

The highlight of the morning was the medieval village built using close to a half million bricks. The architect was enthusiastic, and the display was impressive. This could have been my thing for the day, but I wasn't satisfied. It fell a little flat. To round off the afternoon we made our way to a place called Apple Holler. I have driven by this place thousands of times, but I've never eaten there.

Why? Because of the thousands of cars parked along the highway. It is definitely a tourist trap come mid-June. Since its mid-May, and there was parking available in the actual lot, avoiding this adorable food barn ended today. I had a wonderful sandwich and although I wanted to eat some apple pie, I was too full to give it a go. Day 242 was a double dip. Love & Light

Day 243 of 365- I Read It   May 20, 2018

Recipe for fun… In March of 2017 I sent a book to my mother. I visited a few amazing human beings who shared this book with me and the moment I read through it I knew that mom would love it and hate it all at the same time.

Honestly, I was being naughty when I sent it. My mother appreciated every part of the book and marked a few pages with post-it notes and business cards. I can't tell you how excited I was to see it sprawled on her butcher block just a few weeks after sending it to her.

We bonded over the vulgarity and laughed at the recipes. This book is one of the few that I wanted to keep after she passed. For my 243rd first time experience I decided to try one of the recipes inside this cookbook. I didn't have to go solo; my freshly graduated college kid was my right hand. What did I decide to make? Tea Smoothies. I know that it doesn't seem like a recipe, but this was close to my heart and mom would have been right with me on this new twist to Earl Grey tea. I have never made a tea smoothie, and I should mention that this is a vegetarian cookbook, so all of the ingredients are animal free.

The entire experience took a few hours and the recipe as it is written is so hilarious you should go to the library and grab a copy. I blended the smoothie in my Ninja and served it in a wonder Woman glass. It felt absolutely perfect. I'm so grateful that my mother had a sense of humor and that we shared it. Day 243 cooked. Love & Light

Day 244 of 365- I Did It   May 21, 2018

Science
Technology
Engineering
Art
Math

Day 244 was all about kids and science. I had an amazing time volunteering at a local S.T.E.A.M. event. I've been very fortunate to have the support of my cousin who has been feeding me so many adventures. Today was an absolute treat. It started earlier than I like my experiences, and it was also pouring rain. I arrived at the school with enough time to eat my breakfast and puddle jump into the office.

It's been a very long time since I've been a school volunteer, but my cousin was there to greet me and set me up with my official visitor badge. In the back of my mind, I thought there might be some cool robots that I've never had a chance to play with. It turns out I actually got some time with K'nex.

Don't laugh because until today I have never played with these before. If you're wondering how that's possible, it has a lot to do with the TONS of LEGO I have stored in my house.

Since I have ZERO K'nex experience I needed to do a fast Google search to get the basics and construct something to display when the kids came in for their fun. I built a pyramid and a spinning top. They were great icebreakers, and the rest of the day was a blast. Kids really are amazing and if you put toys in front of them, they really do know how to play. It was educational for me and every school should take the time to expose students to science and technology. Day 244 Love & Light.

Day 245 of 365- I Did It   May 22, 2018

It's a go! I have exactly 120 days left of this 365-day personal challenge. It hasn't gone exactly as I thought it would and I'm admitting right now that I wanted more action in my 49th year.

Today I made a commitment to take a few more risks and use the healthy body that I have. I'm not going to jump out of anything moving or off of anything stable. I do plan to try that hot air balloon ride that I said I never would and maybe run a zip line or take that Royal Gorge helicopter ride. In order to give you my best "new" perspective, on the 245th day I am learning how to use a GOPRO.

I haven't played with one of these aside from watching someone else use it. I invested in the model that gives me a few more features and will shoot in high resolution. That's the extent of my knowledge. I am a serious NO pro at the Go Pro.

I brought my purchase home and had a giggle of a time just opening the package. Don't laugh, there is a tiny blue line on the bottom of the box that doubles as a clever pull tab. I can think of a few people who would get a great laugh out of my inability to open this freakin' box.

Once I cracked the package seal, I discovered that it took a half dozen engineers to build the packaging for a camera that is 2" x 3." Like many new electronics the instructions have no words, just little pictures. No judgment but I like a good user's guide. Google it is!

This camera comes with absolutely no accessories. For the price it should have an SD card and maybe something to mount this camera to. It did come with a USB cord but no adapter to plug it in to the wall. I guess the company assumes I already have something that adapts a USB cable for charging. The camera is packaged with one mount and two sticky mount bases. That's it kids. You can search this camera on the net and see what I paid. It should have a few accessories and a user's guide.

Moving on! Out of the box the camera needs charging, so I stop everything and wait for that. As a side note I packed my charging block, so I used a battery backup to charge the camera, and it was at 85% in about 30 minutes.

While all the charging was taking place, I could pair the camera with my phone and setup remote sharing between the two. That should be great for editing and uploading to the net.

As I was fiddling around with all the settings and buttons, I accidentally shot my first video. This was not my plan. My first go-pro movie was going to be something cool, instead it is a video of my head. I have never felt so out of touch with technology. That's as much time as I have to play right now. As the afternoon wears on I will read, watch and play some more. This adorable little camera is tucked in my suitcase ready for some action. Guess you'll have to stay tuned for tomorrow's adventure. Love & Light

Day 246 of 365- I Saw ItMay 23, 2018

Sleepless and Seattle… The time change is wonderful. It's 6am. I'm in Seattle and the window of the apartment is open. I can hear the sounds of Pike Place market. What's a chick to do so early in the morning in a city she's never visited?

Starbucks! If you're a coffee drinker, and you enjoy Starbucks this is the town to HIT-IT! I've been told that the line out the door of the original store can get hours long. It's a little like waiting for a roller coaster at Six Flags.

I ordered my regular cup after marking my order the cashier launched the cup across the room to barista. It was engaging and exactly what this tourist was anticipating. The best part of a 6am Starbucks visit in Pikes Place, Seattle? No line. I was able to take quite a few pictures and act like a complete tourist, and the barista was a real gem. Next stop... THE MARKET.

From the apartment I can see the back side of the official public market sign. Up and down the street in every direction the vendors are set up to sell their wares. The fresh cut flowers are everywhere and even with the seafood I can appreciate the Peony blossoms. This is an absolute delight for the senses. Because I'm in Seattle I had to take a hike to the Starbucks Reserve Roastery. This is a serious site to see. You don't have to be a fan of the company to appreciate the aroma busting through the open door. I'm so buzzed on caffeine I can't think straight, and it feels so good. Day 246 was the adventure I was hoping for. Love & Light.

Day 247 of 365- I Saw It   May 24, 2018

Glass and needles... Seattle is a typical big city. Endless opportunities for food, stop and go traffic and old and new architecture of every form.

On day 247 I got a chance to explore two classic Seattle locations: Chihuly garden & glass and the Space Needle. The garden and glass location was pretty spectacular. Dale Chihuly is a masterful artist and the gallery at the base of the Space Needle has an overwhelming display of blown glass art.

After our walk through the garden of glass we took a turbo charged elevator to the top of the Space needle.
Our tour had backstage access to the construction area. They are in the process of installing glass floors and benches for an absolute "pee your pants" experience.

I've never been to the top of any tower like this and having access to the outer deck was a knee shaking experience. As first times go I set my fear aside and just did it. Day 247 was out of this world. Love & Light

Day 248 of 365- I Did It   May 25, 2018

Fillet of fish... I have never held a whole uncut salmon. I have eaten many fillets but never learned how to cut one. On my 248th day of experiences I had my moment as an apron wearing fish wife.

If you Google that term you will read that there are a few meanings. Many are appropriate to me and that inspires a few giggles.

This morning was exciting and a tiny bit intimidating as I walked beside heaps of beautiful seafood. The salmon are piled high, and my teacher is already hard at work cutting the fish for smoking. This guy isn't messing around and after a few quick demonstrations that knife is in my hand and I'm chopping the fins and head off this giant fish.

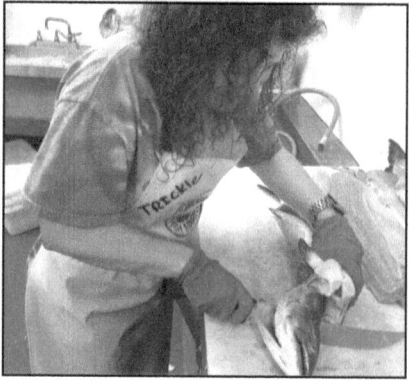

It's amazing and for all my PETA pals I'm not apologizing for how delicious their smoked fish tastes. Eyeballs and all I cut away all the unnecessary bits to reveal a beautiful piece of fish. Day 248 Love & Light

Day 249 of 365- I Ate It   May 26, 2018

    I am not an Island, and neither is the destination of today's adventure even though it is called Bainbridge Island. After 249 days I finally had an island/non-island adventure by ferryboat.

    This day was jam packed with firsts. I walked uphill both ways. In Seattle it is completely possible to walk from one end of the city and back again and hit hills in every direction. I've been experiencing this for the last four days and I find it exhausting.

    Why did I go to Bainbridge Island? Vodka, Whiskey & Gin, Oh yeah! I arrived on the island and made my way to the distillery on foot. I had no idea what the walk would be like and that's a good thing. I just couldn't have planned a more amazing trek. The Bainbridge Organic Distillery is located right beside a brewery, winery and a bakery. I did a 50/50 and hit two of the four.

    My first stop, the Organic distillery. I had my first taste of Gin, and it was something pretty special. The tour was short, but our guide was eager to share her enthusiasm for the company. She likes her gin too. I sampled all four of their products, but I have to say that the "Oaked" Doug Fir Gin was a flavor I've never experienced before. I don't know if people sip gin, but I do.

    The rest of the afternoon is a bit fuzzy from gin, vodka and whiskey sampling but I know that it involved a bakery, and the most delicious blueberry fritter I've ever eaten in my 49 years.

    If you're ever in Seattle and want to take a ferry to Bainbridge Island and walk two miles uphill to a wonderful distillery. Go to Bainbridge organic distillery. Just go and see Erin and take her tour and have the sample of the OAKED gin. You won't regret it. Nope, not one bit. Day 249 Love & LIGHT

Day 250 of 365- I Made It   May 27, 2018

Waffling… It's a travel day and an early one. The morning was cool and with suitcases in hand I made my way to experience number 250, waffle cone making.

It's 730am. The iron is at baking temperature, and the batter has been mixed. I've already tasted the flavor of the morning, vegan lavender ice cream. This was a first flavor for me and as tasty as it is I would rather have a giant scoop of the mint chip or the black licorice.

The sample of treats are gone and I'm ready to roll this adventure into a waffle cone for someone to eat later today. At the Shy Giant they roll these cones by hand. The crisscross of the griddle is smoking hot, and the batter only takes a few minutes to cook into a floppy moldable flapjack.

I've got about 20 seconds to handle the unrolled cone before it starts to get hard. It's hot, and I mean glove hot, but I wrapped it bare handed. It took a lot of wrong to get this right, and even after all the attempts mines were only passable. My teacher, Hillary, who can roll a perfect specimen in seconds, is beyond patient with my failures and fixed every single goof-up that I made, and I made quite a few.

My reward for learning the technique was a tiny sample of ice cream and cone. Truth be told I've had so many scoops of this delicious ice cream in the last few days that I was absolutely on board with my samples. Day 250 was hot and pretty cool. Love & Light

Day 251 of 365- I Did It   May 28, 2018

Migraines... If this was a perfect world so many things would have been different on day 251. Every year the small town of Burlington holds an event called Chocolatefest. I have lived in this area most of my life and I've NEVER been to this insane celebration of chocolate.

Today I joined the annual festival parade, which also lands on Memorial Day. Here's where the headache begins. Heat and sunshine are a perfect combination for dehydration and a trigger for migraines. Don't you worry, I walked that parade and I handed out the most delicious chewy candy, pencils, bracelets and promo materials for Just Live, Inc.

The rest of the morning was meant to include more chocolate and a walk through the festival grounds. Instead, I got a fun migraine and a little bit of heat exhaustion.

PARTY! I've never taken a cold shower in my life but after an attempt to cool off with ice I had to turn it all around and hop in that steady stream of cold. I'm not sure it was the perfect thing to do but it helped. Day 251 was hot, cold and hurt like hell. Love & Light

Day 252 of 365- I Made It   May 29, 2018

Don't worry. As a kid there was a plaque on the wall at my house that read:

> *Go placidly amid the noise and haste and remember what peace there may be in silence.*
> *As far as possible without surrender be on good terms with all persons.*
> *Speak your truth quietly and clearly; and listen to others,*
> *even the dull and the ignorant; they too have their story.*
> *Avoid loud and aggressive persons, they are vexations to the spirit.*
> *If you compare yourself with others, you may become vain and bitter;*
> *for always there will be greater and lesser persons than yourself.*
> *Enjoy your achievements as well as your plans.*
> *Keep interested in your own career, however humble;*
> *it is a real possession in the changing fortunes of time.*
> *Exercise caution in your business affairs; for the world is full of trickery.*
> *But let this not blind you to what virtue there is; many persons strive for high ideals;*
> *and everywhere life is full of heroism.*
> *Be yourself.*
> *Especially, do not feign affection.*
> *Neither be cynical about love; for in the face of all aridity and disenchantment it is as perennial as the grass.*
> *Take kindly the counsel of the years, gracefully surrendering the things of youth.*
> *Nurture strength of spirit to shield you in sudden misfortune.*
> *But do not distress yourself with dark imaginings.*
> *Many fears are born of fatigue and loneliness.*
> *Beyond a wholesome discipline, be gentle with yourself.*
> *You are a child of the universe, no less than the trees and the stars; you have a right to be here.*
> *And whether or not it is clear to you, no doubt the universe is unfolding as it should.*
> *Therefore be at peace with God, whatever you conceive Him to be, and whatever your labors and aspirations, in the noisy confusion of life keep peace with your soul.*
> *With all its sham, drudgery, and broken dreams, it is still a beautiful world.*
> *Be cheerful.*
> *Strive to be happy.*
>   ~ Max Ehrmann, Desiderata ~

Why am I sharing this today? For my 252nd experience I learned how to make No worry dolls. I was inspired by Desiderata and after having a very emotional morning I wanted to redirect all my energies.

I've had a tiny container of these dolls since I was a young girl. Are they magic? Maybe. I believe in the possibility of all things and try to respect them even when I find it confusing. My magic non-worry creations are not as complicated as I thought they would be and as I assembled the materials, I felt the calming effect that usually follows my creativity.

Making the little string and wire beings started out well. I guess I can overthink a project because my first attempt turned out to be a tiny bit misshapen. I have enough materials to make another and I'm happy with how it turned out. Day 252 was a reminder to not worry. Love & Light

Day 253 of 365- I Did It   May 30, 2018

Raindrops on skin... It's been an interesting day. So often I make plans, and something seems to get in the way. Today I got in my own way, and it felt pretty wonderful. On day 253 I stripped away everything and had my very first naked rain dance.

This wasn't a whimsical decision. It has been on my list from the very beginning. I didn't know when it would happen but for some reason today felt exactly right. It was a moment of real freedom. I wouldn't say that I have body issues, but I tend to be modest, so this is a definite out of my box experience.

The storm today was pretty beautiful and after running my errands the clothes came off just as the rain came down. It was the most luscious warm rain and as my toes curled around the fresh cut grass I felt wholly connected to the earth. If you've never done this, you should.

Make note that I live on 18 acres and am surrounded by trees. You might want to be somewhere secluded... or not. FYI mosquitoes really like naked rain dancers. Day 253 was a soul cleansing experience. Love & Light

Day 254 of 365- I Did It   May 31, 2018

If the shoe fits… Today I had an adventure at one of my favorite shoe stores. I was on a mission that had absolutely nothing to do with shoes and there it was…A MAGIC SLATE

I flashed back to my childhood, to the plastic and cardboard that kept me entertained for hours. As I did a Google search for this post I couldn't believe there were so many different styles, and I screen grabbed the Donnie & Marie slate because I wished I had one.

If I remember correctly mine was very generic. Why am I having magic slate flashbacks? On the 254th day of adventurous experiences I magic slated my feet! I was actually on a quest for empty cardboard boxes and stopped at my favorite shoe store to pick up a few. As I was waiting for help one of the amazing salespeople had this new but old device on the floor.

It stopped me in my tracks because all I could see was the magic slate from my childhood.

Ahh… the universe works in great ways. I needed a bit of joy, and it landed right in my lap. For the next few minutes, I had the most fun measuring my feet. I had sandals on, so I put on a pair of nylon socks, and the peel-apart film base took a pressure image from heel to toe. It was amazing. Perhaps it was the return to childhood that made it so wonderful. I really didn't care. The device actually has a purpose; aside from entertaining me it also measures how wide your foot is, shoe size and your arch height. Who knew? Day 254 measured out to be fun. Love & Light

Day 255 of 365- I Did It   June 1, 2018

Rip it up and turn...Today, on my 255th day I got down and dirty on the Skidsteer. My expectations were mixed. I've always wanted to drive one but to be completely honest these suckers scare the crap out of me.

First step... climb inside this monster. I'm not a big human being. I'm all of 5 foot 3 inches on a good day and this machine was designed for a person with much longer legs. I attempted to adjust the seat so that my feet would actually reach the pedals and I came up short again.

I'm pretty sure this machine should not be driven on tippy toes. I surrendered to the fact that this was going to require my entire body to maneuver. I'm still scared, and I haven't even turned the key. Starting the engine is a process because this beast is diesel and has glow plugs and once it turns over the sucker rattles like rocks in a glass. Every part of me is vibrating and none of it feels good.

Next step, foot pedals, which lift and tilt the bucket that is necessary for me to even move. Remember my feet aren't actually touching the pedals so there may have been some clinking and banging during this learning process. Bucket up and now because I'm beyond scared out of my mind, I have to learn to drive this in REVERSE!

I'm so glad that I waited 255 days to experience the Skidsteer. I'm not sure I would have had the courage a few months ago. Also, SNOW. When all is said and done, I actually drove this sucker, scooped some dirt and scraped the potholes in my driveway. I was pretty happy when I was done and even happier to park this beast and finish my experience. Day 255 Love & Light

Day 256 of 365- I Made It   June 2, 2018

A study of nature... its day 256 and I learned a new blacksmithing skill. It is impossible to express how happy I am when I have a hammer in my hand and hot steel on my anvil. I don't think I really understood the joy until today. When I attend a workshop there are always a few dozen students trying to work at a half dozen stations. The firepots are crowded, and the anvil is always hot. It can be frustrating.

Day 256 was completely different, and it was a gift I didn't know I needed. Today's students were divided in two groups, beginner and not. I was in the not group of which there were a total of 3. For the first time ever, I had my own workstation and didn't have to wait and watch my projects burn like fourth of July sparklers.

I have been playing at the forge since my son was 14 and built one in the yard. That clever kid assembled a pile of scrap into a working coal setup and taught himself how to be a blacksmith. How did I get addicted? My kid invited me into that world, and I've been a curious blacksmith since. I'm on my own these days so when a workshop comes up, I attend because it is the one environment where I'm happy to be the student.

The projects today were introductory hooks and latches and... leaves. Oh, those leaves, I have avoided them because they seem impossible. I can say that because I have never made one until today. To call this a spiritual blacksmithing moment would hit the nail on the head.

I made a tiny pile of scrap metal while I worked today. That's not new for me but the instructors spent a lot of time breaking down the process into steps that I could follow and duplicate. Little by little my square became round, and my flat took on the shape of a chubby little aspen leaf. I got a tiny bit frustrated, and my teacher took me for a short walk through the patch of trees and brush. He picked a leaf, and we studied the physical structure. We talked about texture and

symmetry. It was almost spiritual and spoke to the artist in my soul. I spent 3 hours making a leaf that should take 15 minutes, and it was amazing.

Once I finished, I started another and by the end of the day I had three leaves, two of which felt like pieces of art. From failure comes success. It was almost perfect. Day 256 Love & Light

Day 257 of 365- I Ate It   June 3, 2018

      Once you go charcoal… With no destination in mind, I got in the car with my dear friend Christina, and we landed in the perfect place. On my 257th day I had my first Main Street Coffee adventure. I say first because this was the most adorable location, and they also serve great coffee and I intend to go back many times. If I said that we stumbled upon this business, it would be true. From the outside it doesn't seem like much but inside it's spacious and still feels cozy.

      Without a real plan I would usually spend about a half hour in any coffee house. At Main Street I was there for four hours. The music is low, and the staff moves through the store with attentive purpose. This is a great place to relax and have great conversation. The menu is diverse and filled with clean real food and the drinks cover a wide variety of flavors. The real treat, the long list of lemonade.

      I drank my very first glass of charcoal lemonade. It was black and tasted just like… lemonade. Is it going to do all the things that the sign on the wall suggested?

Probably not, do I care? Absolutely not. It's about the new experience. If my colon gets a cleanse, good job! Like I said at the beginning I didn't have a plan for the day, and it was the perfect plan. Day 257 was sweet, tart and a little bit dark. Love & Light.

Day 258 of 365- I Did It   June 4, 2018

Rage… sometimes emotions rule. Not so long ago I let mine go and today's experience was all about repairing physical damage to personal things. I've got an awful lot of them. On day 258 I bought into an infomercial product in an attempt to repair a broken wheelbarrow. You thought this was going to be some intense family thing?

Today it isn't. Well, it is a tiny bit but mostly it is fixing something that made me so angry that I broke it even more. The world is flooded with plastic and although it makes things lighter and sometimes less breakable, it was not the case with my very new-wheeled transport. I kicked it and knocked the bottom right out. For about $15 I bought this roll of wonder rubbery flextape. Yes, I did and turned it into an adventure for sure. If I had pulled out my cheater reading glasses, I would have read that this roll is only 5 feet long.

I should have bought two, but the original cost of the wheelbarrow was only about $40 more. Maybe I should take an anger management class before this 365-day challenge is over. As per the package instructions I cleaned the surface and fit the broken pieces together. I measured the length of each strip and that's when I realized 5 feet was ridiculously short and I'm not sure what anyone could fix with it.

My repair didn't look the way I'd planned. The instructions recommended dry fitting, and I am so glad that I followed them. This shit is sticky as hell, and I have an amazing ability to roll tape onto itself and make a wild mess. At $3 a foot I didn't have an inch to spare. Yay for following directions.

The rest of this repair went well. Once the adhesive started to stick there was no moving it and I used my brayer to roll out as many of the bubbles and creases as possible. The package also suggests weight and time will create a stronger bond, so I piled in some forge metal and left it for the next 24 hours. Check back to see how it works. Day 258 was some sticky business. Love & Light

Day 259 of 365- I Made It   June 5, 2018

    Magic presence... I've been doing this challenge for 259 days and I've had quite an extreme ride. It feels very much like a roller coaster with amazing highs, lows and the breath-taking infinity when you're suspended in between.

    I heard a song the lyrics are, "I said remember this moment, in the back of my mind." For the last nine months I have tried to be present (remembering the moments) in every new experience and keeping this web page has been an important part of staying in the now.

    On day 91 my mother was diagnosed with Glioblastoma, an aggressive form of brain cancer. On day 92 she had a craniotomy to remove it. Love kept me present, to be there for her and not run away. On day 146 I watched as medical professionals radiated my mother's brain. I stayed present. I soothed her face when they were done burning cancer from her body. Every few days I would read my blog posts to her, bringing the outside to her nursing home room. Sometimes she gave thumbs up, or quirked a grin but always she was listening, present.

    On day 190 my mother was diagnosed with Influenza B. How does that happen? I had no idea that 24 days later she would be gone. I was present for her and I didn't need any song to encourage me to be. She was the most beautiful woman I have ever loved. My mother died on day 214 and this 365-day adventure seemed like the most selfish thing I've ever done. Continuing felt, and every day still feels impossible. I buried my mother 36 days ago.

    When I visit her and read my posts at the cemetery, I am the only one present. It takes every ounce of courage for me to continue.

    The loss is so big. On the morning of this day, number 259 I decided to make something to bring a bit of magic back into my life. I decided to cook a batch of nectar for my hummingbirds. They have not been present since last year.

    The process is amazingly simple, and I don't know why I haven't done this before. 1part sugar and 4 parts water cooked to boiling. That's it.

    Did I add red dye? NOPE! From what I have been reading artificial coloring is damaging to the little hummingbirds. That's what prompted the at-home experience. The nectar has cooled and is hanging in the yard. Do you know how impossible it is to be present for a hummingbird encounter? I've got a few hours of empty feeder videos to prove it. These beautiful little birds are my reminder to continue to be present; to give myself the time to reorder my days and to be patient and to understand that every measure of love requires bravery. Day 259 I am sticky, and I am just being. Love & Light

Day 260 of 365- I Ate It   June 6, 2018

I put that in my body. It's day 260 and I'm eating things I should say no to. Item number 1: Chicken chalupa

You've seen this nightmare on TV. I know I have, and I've been curious. Purchasing this was an accident and just as my kid was about to take a bite I said, "I've never tried one of those," and day 260 began. Here's the thing. This is an offense to the body. I know it. Someone took a lovely cut of chicken, beat that sucker flat, breaded it with something unnatural, fried it and transformed it into crunchy deliciousness.

This particular variety had a spicy kick. I only ate that first bite and as much as I enjoyed it I didn't want the bomb of calories that it measured out to be. Next up? I washed that crunchy feast down with mouthwatering SMILE water. I eat a lot of salads and vegetables so I'm pretty good on fiber. Today's thirst quenching "naturally flavored" SMILE water is also fortified with 5g of fiber.

As I'm writing this, I'm realizing how much I may have just destroyed the next 24 hours of digestion. Why does my taco need a flattened chicken shell? Why does my water need fiber? I wish I had an answer to either, but I feel like consuming these two things just created unanswerable questions. Day 260 Love & Light

Day 261 of 365- I Did It   June 7, 2018

Breaking wind. This has nothing to do with the fiber adventures of day 260. On my 261st day I used the "incredible" air lounger. Yes, this is a thing and even though I was 100% certain it would be an epic fail it wasn't.

Out of the package the design is cool. It collapses into a drawstring backpack so you really can take it anywhere. Here's the challenge, inflation. If you watch the commercial all you have to do is hold it in the air and it fills up like magic.

No magic happened. I jumped. I ran. I flapped like a bird. My  lounger would not fill. I handed this floppy mess to my son, and he bolted across the field and filled that chair to maximum capacity. A couple of twists turns and clipping the latch and the incredible lounger was born. It's comfortable. Keep sharp objects away. Day 261 Love & Light

Day 262 of 365- I Did It   June 8, 2018

    Han shot first… Star Wars is the movie series of my generation. I can still remember the line that stretched down the
sidewalk as we waited to purchase tickets for A New Hope. I wanted to be a Jedi even though the back-story hadn't been written.

    I didn't want to be any single character. I wanted to be part of the Star Wars universe. On day 262 I dragged my family in to the wild world of Han Solo and the gambling moment that earned him the Millennium Falcon. The Han Solo card game isn't like anything we've played before. I thought it might be a bit like UNO, but it isn't even close.

    With two cards in hand, I tried to accumulate the lowest number of points. Green cards have a positive value and red are negative. Zero as a card total is the goal. To make this game more challenging you roll dice every hand to determine if you get to keep the cards you've collected.

    It is unpredictable which kept me engaged and I like that on family game night. As a footnote I have to question the engineering of the box this came in. Once all the pieces are punched out of the cardboard frames it doesn't fit in the package. It seems very odd. Day 262 was a very good deal. Love & Light

Day 263 of 365- I Made It   June 9, 2018

Still thirsty... Today's adventure involved so many mosquitoes. In fact, it feels like the entire planet of that insect population has turned up on my property.

What did I do today? I drank from the bark of a birch tree. It was perfect and I learned a skill that increased my apocalypse prepping street cred. Here's how it's done. Harvest the bark. That's when the mosquitos had their feast. My camera crew looks like a skittle pock commercial with welts all over. After the harvest I had to scrape away the outer white layer to promote a more flexible piece of material. Birch bark fresh off the tree is very flexible.

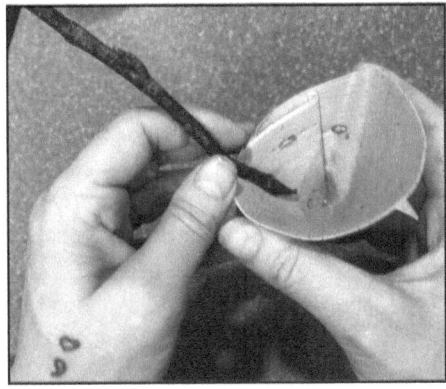

I cut my cleaned bark into a circle and double folded it to create the cup. This is why it was very important to keep it thin but also free from cracks and knots. Holes are the enemy on day 263. I used a piece of birch tree branch to create a pin to hold it all together. It also doubles as a handle. That was the simple plan. It came together so wonderfully aside from the tiny hole that created a drip. If I was scooping this from a basin of boiled water, it would work well, and I could also use it to fill a canteen.

This felt a bit like camping, with the mosquitoes and the wooden cup. I did disassemble the project when I was finished and wrap that patch of bark back on the tree. In a real-world environment, I wouldn't do that, but I like the birch tree in my yard. There is a learning curve, and I feel educated in a leaky way. Day 263 was thirst quenching. Love & Light

Day 264 of 365- I Made It   June 10, 2018

Tied up... I'm an artist more than anything else. I love to make messes that touch the heart. Writing every day, even just focusing on sharing my adventures, is art that messes with the heart and not the dining room table.

On day 264 I messed with string art. From the outside this looks pretty simple. Poke some pins and tie some string. The execution is a little more complicated and if you've been around me with rope, yarn or string you know I'm the absolute best at tangling them all.

I used embroidery floss for this project, and I did end up with a twisted clump on my third color. It was going so well. This was a kit that I purchased mostly for the step-by-step instruction guide. I used foam board as the base and regular push pins as my anchor points for this piece. I chose the 8-pointed star and got to work. Every part of this experience was relaxing until the tangle. I wrapped and rewrapped until each layer of color came together.

If you haven't tried this, you should. There are hundreds of YouTube videos and the materials you need are very inexpensive. I might try a project using my leftover pallet from day 177. Day 264 was the perfect rainy-day experience. Love & Light

Day 265 of 365- I Made It   June 11, 2018

I am 100 days away from meeting my goal. I'm excited and also a little hesitant for this to become a part of my past.

On day 99 I learned how to juggle. What I accomplished was a rotation of three balls and nothing more. I haven't tried it since and to be honest it reminds me of the hospital room mom was in as she was 7 days out from a craniotomy. I've decided to let my juggling drop for a while. On day 265 I focused on building a pair of Poi spinners. When I started planning this, I felt like I could double up and learn to use them at the same time.

Ha, what a fool! As I researched today's grand plan, I chose a rather complicated braiding pattern for the tether of my poi, that's the cord connecting the handle and the ball. I'm terrible at doing any kind of braiding and still I chose to do a 4-strand version.

Oh, did I mention that I have two cats that never show their faces unless I'm trying to do anything with string or yarn? They turned up to complicate this just a tiny bit more. I begin to make a braid with 4 feet of yarn, 14 strands per color, it's gonna get tangled. Add two cats to this insane mix of adventure and I spent most of the morning combing through an abundance of knots.

What was I thinking? I could have made the damn braid my experience for today because I'll bet I attempted them two dozen times. After about two hours I made a successful poi spinner. The thing is, I needed two. Did I mention the cats and knots and tangles? I made two tethers, and they are the same length. I'm giving myself a perseverance award because I could have tossed this aside and chosen a different experience.

The rest of my poi assembly wasn't half the challenge the tethers were. I weighted and wrapped the ball end making it as round as possible. I chose Wonder Woman fabric to finish it. The handle end is a very basic pompom. I figure I'm probably going to hit myself many times I might as well smack myself with WW.

As experiences go this was only frustrating because of the cat tangles and my inability to do a very basic braid. Wait for the actual spinning. It's coming soon. Day 265 Love & Light

Day 266 of 365- I Did It   June 12, 2018

Spinning round and round... On day 265 I made the most beautiful and symmetrical Poi spinning ropes. The process of making them was challenging but the real fun was actually learning to use them. My arms are a tiny bit sore. I have pummeled myself with the soft and round end of my poi spinners all for the good of day 266.

I think my video says it all. Love & Light

Day 267 of 365- I Ate It June 13, 2018

The delicious devil... It's been a long few weeks since mom passed away. I feel her presence everywhere. Sometimes it feels wonderful and other moments hit me with such finality it takes my breath away. You can't imagine all the places that I've shed tears.

Today I made a quick stop at the grocery store to buy some supplies for testing a blacksmith experiment. I stumbled upon a childhood memory that became my 267th experience. When I was a child, I wanted to try this can of horribly processed meat. In my head it was going to look like liverwurst which mom and I ate all the time.

This was so far from smooth spreadable meat that I was ready for a second spam experience. Mom would have laughed at today's experience because she would never let buy this for me. Perhaps she was trying to protect me from myself. It's a pull-tab can so it was easy to open. Maybe this is an apocalypse item. I popped a fork into the can and gave it a stir. This is for sure some kind of demonic food spread, and I understand why it has a pitchfork-wielding demon on the label.

It smells like ham and as I take that first bite, I am happy and sick at the same time. This is truly a can of evil goodness. I didn't want to eat the entire container, but I did. It is the saltiest "meat" I have ever eaten, and I could not stop myself even though I did pucker from the flavoring.

This would be an amazing emergency food item. PACKED so intensely with sodium if you need a boost. If you watch your salt intake this might keep you set for a few days. I tried to cook it because it seemed so much like the meat in canned corn beef hash. It wasn't. It just turned in to bubbling greasy salty goop that never got crunchy. It was hot deviled ham, and I ate all of that too. Like I said, this is demon food, and I don't think I should buy this again. Day 267 was devilishly delicious. Love & Light

Day 268 of 365- I Did It   June 14, 2018

Go, no Go… Day 268 and I've officially attempted to understand what the Pokémon go app is all about. On a wonderful sunny summer morning I downloaded and installed the app on my phone. True confession... I have no idea what the point of this game is, but I hope to figure that out during this experience.

I am throwing around countless balls and trying to bop an unpronounceable creature into submission. They will become members of my Poke arsenal. I played this game while walking through the town of Lake Geneva. There were creatures and stops and gyms all over the place. I collected balls to throw at monsters so I could get more monsters and grow them into powerful monsters.

I think this is the goal. I'm still kinda guessing. I've never played the Pokémon card game so most of this virtual experience is just following directions. I collected many creatures and made it to level 7. I did this by stopping in the middle of the sidewalk and throwing my balls around. This is a real thing, and I did enjoy myself until my cell battery went dead and it left me with no gaming and no cell phone. If you're going to play this game, have a wingman that carries a battery backup. Just my suggestion. Day 268 Love & Light

Day 269 of 365- I Did It   June 15, 2018

    Wondering what to make. I visited a mill shop today with the invitation to build whatever I wanted. Having no experience with the machinery in the workspace I was at a loss. I walked in with no plan in hopes that the amazing crew would steer me in the right direction.
    I have the best friend Kim, who knows me well and after a short conversation and a few introductions we were on the way to the design desk. Internet searches are wonderful and the artist behind the AutoCAD setup the perfect project. The software is so much like Adobe Photoshop in how ridiculously complicated it is, I would still be there outlining the graphic.
    I was content to be the student asking a ridiculous number of questions. I understood about 25% of what the professionals were talking about. I'm okay with that. I have complete respect for their skills and watched in awe. What did we make? It'll be no surprise. On day 269 we cut Wonder Woman to hang over my forge and it was the best shop experience.
Love & Light

Day 270 of 365- I Did It   June 16, 2018

Sweet and sour... Every day seems to have this strange duality. There are many moments of joy and discovery and then moments that remind me that change can feel like an impossible hurdle. Today was another roller coaster ride.

I've had 270 new experiences; actually, I've had a few more than that because some days were a two for one. Those are accidental because it can be extremely difficult to accomplish just one. Today I had an unbelievable experience at an annual Chalkfest event. It's one of the coolest experiences and every year I try to attend with one art idea in mind. The street is shut down and all the attendants spend a few hours filling it with creative chalk designs. This year I came ready to go with my first every spray cans of sidewalk chalk.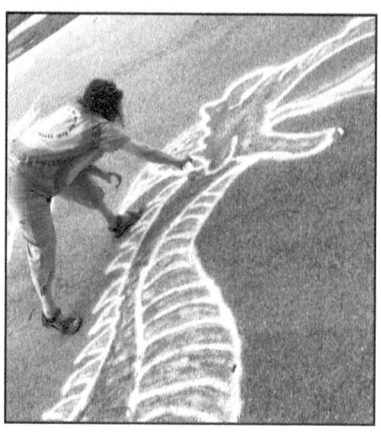
What I didn't have for the first time ever, was a plan or even an idea of what to create.

The spray can is AMAZING! My first doodle was a flower. I've made them in the past, but they usually take about 30 minutes because regular sidewalk chalk isn't very intense in color, so I use water and sponges to make a paste.

It was so fast with the spray, and I was able to layer my colors. I was ready for more. I decided to make a dragon and used the World Wide Web for inspiration. I started at the curb, and the first lines were drawn. I haven't had this much fun in ages. I would still be there if I had a bigger pallet of colors and more cans. This takes sidewalk chalk to a whole new level.

After hours of fun, I made my way to experience number two.

No suspense on this one, I drank a pickle juice slushy from Sonic. I thought this was going to be the highlight but after the chalk it just couldn't compare. I ordered a small because I was sure this would be a tummy turner. The first sip was amusing and because my mother always scolded me for drinking from the pickle jar, I had a moment of sense memory that made me happy and sad.

That happens very often, and the inner conflict hurts my heart. Mom really is so attached to the human being I am. I drank my icy pickle juice slush, and it brought the adventures of day 270 to an amazing end. Love & Light

Day 271 of 365- I Did It   June 17, 2018

The better to see you with... Plastic has saved me from some big messes. I've dropped so many bottles of miscellaneous food and beverage items that plastic has prevented the need for hours of mopping and the "cleanup in isle 7" at the grocery store.

But it isn't always wonderful. I've got a 1968 Volkswagen with glass headlights that look like I put them In yesterday and I have a ten year old Chevy with plastic headlamps so discolored it's like driving behind frosted glass.

Well, it was. On the 271st day of experiences I got a better view of the night road with Rain-X Headlight restorer. The directions suggest I wash the lenses with a damp cloth and a circular application of the white paste.

I was 100% skeptical of this product. I've watched the infomercials for a similar product at four times the cost. Headlights are crazy expensive to replace if it isn't necessary so for about $5 it was well worth a try. This stuff is impressive, and I was surprised when hours later I could see inside to the lamp bulbs and reflectors. For those of you who keep a car longer than 5 years this stuff is a great investment. I'll let you know what happens after a few days. Day 271 Love & Light

Day 272 of 365- I Did It   June 18, 2018

    I did it to myself. I should know better by now when it's a good time to introduce new technology into my life.

    Now is not the time! On day 272 I decided to use my first digital pen and tablet combo. Here's the exciting part. I have always wanted to take my photographs and try to create more than the eye can see. Being an artist is what makes me happy, but I've never tried digital art. This 365-day experience is teaching me so much about intuition and in order to create opportunities to escape my comfort zone I have ignored my intuition quite a few times this year.

    On day 8, I made cheesecake. I don't like cheesecake, which is why I'd never made it before. I spent about $10 on ingredients, had the experience and moved on. It didn't change my desire for cheesecake. On day 11 I attended the light festival. In my head this was a great date night with a beautiful display of flickering lanterns in the sky. We sat for hours. It was beautiful. It generated a massive pile of exhausted lanterns. We stumbled over them on the way back to the car. They fly less than 100 meters. It's a horrible mess and a waste to the environment. I do regret the aftermath of day 11.

    I really could go on for a few more but that's not the point. What I'm saying is that as I've grown into my womanhood, I have also been aware of what I don't and won't allow on my life path.

    I shouldn't have used technology like this. I just don't have the patience. I started the installation of the hardware at 7:30 am. It is 9:20 as I begin writing my blog post and I have not processed a single photo yet. I'm a MAC user and my computer does not come with a CD-ROM. I attempt a software download, but the website source comes up as non-trusted and I'm not opening the door to some hacker in Russia.

    I stop the download and set up my external cd drive and put in the software disk. Here's where this gets even funnier. The disk is dated 2014 and requires an update before I can open the driver files. I've stopped for coffee. I had two cups.

    Back at the computer it requires a reboot, which it would have been nice to know while I was drinking those cups of coffee. It's 8:15 and I haven't even connected the tablet yet. It feels like the old PC days when adding a driver for a piece of hardware cleared all my loved ones from the house. I may or may not get a tiny bit hostile when drivers and hardware are involved. Apple could solve this problem with a touch screen MacBook. My cats are hiding under the living room table.

At 8:25 I take a photo of the touch tablet making contact with the USB port of my MacBook. It should have been magic but... High Sierra. More updating and a solid confirmation that the App store is a magical place made for preventing tech frustrations! I love you Apple and I'm so glad you're here. Reboot. More coffee which should be gin or vodka at this point. Bathroom break. It's 8:45 and I have moved from my living room floor to my dining room table because there is so much packaging, CD's, portable devices and paperwork that my lap couldn't handle all of it.

In order to get the free software that comes with this device I have to register the product. Yep, you guessed it... more coffee. This little gem has a registration key and an SBD key.

Neither of them are easy to locate or log in with. I had to Google the SBD, which is the Software Bundle Download code. It is a ridiculous combination of numbers, letters, dashes and spaces I thought I was getting into Russian counterintelligence because the number is actually hidden on the inside flap of the box. Why don't they just put it on the CD rom envelope like they did in the 90's?

WTF! It's just the Corel website. I made it in, and the software is downloading. It actually installed without a hitch. It's 9:15. Corel's software requires an authorization code. Oh yes you guessed it. My hands are shaking because I never drink this much coffee.

I log in to the account that I just created to install the tablet and in a quiet little corner of my virtual library there is another magical product key. This sucker is just as ridiculous as the others and now I feel like Lara Croft and I'm about to raid a tomb of art treasures when all I really want to do is make a pencil sketch. It's 9:20. I'm exhausted. I stop to write this blog. I can't believe I was ever tech savvy, but I will not be defeated. Wait... For... IT!

It's 11:11 and I admit defeat. I thought it might be a software problem, but I think it is actually a tablet problem. I have set up and reset this sucker a half dozen times using multiple software programs. I can get it to do really fat lines but when I attempt my own art it looks like a primary school project gone wrong.

SO VERY WRONG. Instincts are telling me that this is a device fail because when I stop using the pen and draw with my mouse it works. So why do I need the pen or the touch tablet? Bottom line, crap is crap, and I spent most of my morning determining that this is not going to make my 365 days any better or the rest of my days to be honest. This is a "follow my instincts" moment and I'm letting the tablet and touch pen win.

As I type this final line, I will admit that I asked my tech savvy offspring to check my work (so humbling) and he gave it the middle finger too! Day 272 penned out to be a disaster. Love & Light

Day 273 of 265- I Did ItJune 19, 2018

One foot in front of the other with some assembly required. The last few days have been ridiculous with rain. I've been staring out my window watching the height of my grass grow. I can't wait for the new generation of mosquitoes spawning in all that standing water. Can you tell I'm feeling a tiny bit trapped? On day 273 I took the opportunity to build a foot- pedal only stationary bike. Here's the thing, this sucker is tricked out to sync with the smartphone app and a Fitbit.

Don't worry this isn't for me. It's actually a present but because I'm the "some assembly" gal I did take this new device for a virtual spin. After the technology disaster that was day 272, I felt like I needed to redeem myself, if only for myself.

Mission accomplished. This sucker weighs a ton and although it didn't have a lot of moving parts it did require a screwdriver. I was not surprised when the screw holes did not line up, but I made it all work. Now for the fun. I downloaded an app, which I wasn't terribly happy about. I hoped it would sync with the Fitbit directly. That would have been perfect. Have you ever ridden a Bluetooth stationary bike? Neither have I.

This might be a half or quarter bike but why split hairs. This sucker is designed to fit under the desk of an overworked professional. I think it will and once it synced up, the personal challenges inside the animated app were fun. Day 273 Love & Light

Day 274 of 365- I Did It June 20, 2018

My face... Remember when I was talking about the hordes of mosquitoes breeding on my property? They are here and along with them come the necessary slathering of bug spray. I use deet-free repellant made from sweet almond oil, lemongrass, tea tree and eucalyptus. It smells wonderful but I have to go out of my way to keep it from getting in my eyes. The problem with all this oil and sweating in the heat is that my skin isn't happy.

I tried the tomato facial on day 140, but I really wanted to use more of that 12-ounce bag of activated charcoal that I bought for day 121. On day 274 I made a super sticky facial mask using activated charcoal and gelatin. I used a tablespoon of each and 2 tablespoons of hot water to dissolve the gelatin. It stirred into a beautiful dark slurry. I spread it on my face taking extra time to keep it from my eyebrows.

My mixture was a tiny bit thin and after the first application it began to drip, and my facial looked like a melting candle. I have never put gelatin on my face. This mask took about 30 minutes to "set." Once it did it felt like rubber, and I was a little frightened to remove it.

To say that I could feel this peel away is the understatement of this 365-day adventure. I don't think I needed such an aggressive facial mask but after it was cleared away my skin felt amazing. I loved this experience, and I would do it over and over. Day 274 Love & Light

Day 275 of 365- I Made It   June 21, 2018

Fluxed... I started this particular experience in January and although it isn't framed my work is complete. On day 275 I learned to solder stained glass. If you've been following you will remember that I started on day 124 just learning to cut glass. In my head I was going to complete this experience in a single day. Little did I realize it would be hanging over my head for so long and that my end result would change purpose.

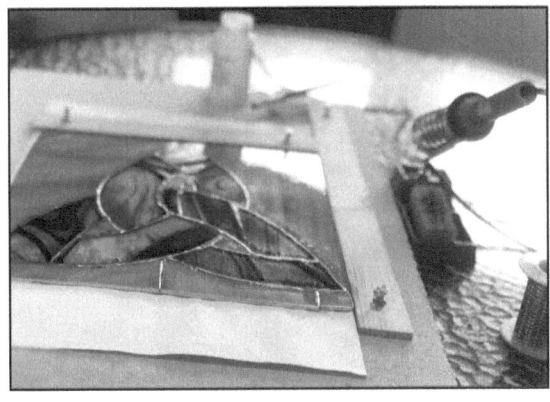

On day 128 I learned how to clean the edge of the glass by grinding it. This was my least favorite part and if I was better at cutting the glass I might not have needed to grind so much. All my cuts didn't fit together quite right but filling the gaps would be an experience for another day.

There was a lull in my progress until day 150. That was foiling and it was fun. If you're a stained-glass person and need your parts foiled, I'm your gal! My project took a very long (125 day) rest while my life fell to pieces. I was making this stained-glass project for mom. I wanted it to hang in the window of the "tree house" that my father built for them. She loved looking out the windows at the flowering gardens she planted.

This would have looked wonderful in her home highlighted by the glow of the sun. So today as I worked, I thought of her. I thought about the symbolism of the Celtic knot I was soldering together. Those huge gaps and flaws in the cut and foiled glass have come to symbolize my imperfection as a human being.

The triple goddess as a Celtic symbol honors the maiden, mother and crone, three parts of womanhood. That's what attracted me to it as I was choosing the design. Making it a gift for my mom it more appropriately represents the trinity; the father, the son and the Holy Spirit.

I imagine she and I would have had a wonderful conversation about this masterpiece over tea and shortbread. I would thank her for being all three parts of womanhood and also for loving me from a place of spirituality that honored the sacred trinity.

It is June 21, summer solstice and the longest day of the year. It seems appropriate that all the pieces would come together now in a perfectly imperfect way. I am so very proud of this experience. Day 275 Love & Light

Day 276 of 365- I Did It   June 22, 2018

It all happened by accident. I had no idea when I popped the package this morning that doodle tops were going to be my experience. It was all pretty innocent, and I was reserving them until one of those late nights when I had nothing done. What happened at 6:30 am turned into an hour of bleeding these tiny spinning markers dry.

Doodle Tops! Doodle Tops! Doodle Tops!

I cannot believe my mother never shared the joy of these toys. She loved tops. She had a box of them with a tray designated just for launching and keeping the dizzying spinners on the table. It was magic and so much a part of her that we had them at her funeral.

This package was among her things and in fine Nana fashion it was unopened waiting for some child to play. In walks her youngest child. The date on the package says 1996. The odds are great that these suckers are bone dry after 22 years. I am not embarrassed to admit that I tried these on a little piece of scrap paper because I didn't think they would work. I can't believe I was this casual after 276 days. I was so unbelievably mesmerized that I got a 24"x24" piece of paper and laid it on the floor to spin more designs. I recorded about 20, 60-second videos of a doodle top spinning.

Don't judge. I've already ordered a 6 top kit because this is my new therapy. I've got about 100 yards of 24" paper. I'm set for a while. If I don't answer my phone or reply to your emails, I might be on the floor with my Doodle Top or I might be chasing the cat that has stolen the spinning thing on the floor. Barbarian! If you have a kid in your life, now's your chance to justify buying these. No one will ever know. *winks* Day 276 is spinning out of control. Love & Light

Day 277 of 365- I Did It   June 23, 2018

Getting high… It's day 277 and I have finally accomplished a high ropes course. My experience started at Aerial Adventures in Lake Geneva. The place has a Climbing tower, free fall, bubble soccer, zip line and a high ropes course. I was only interested in the high ropes, but the admission price included everything.

Just to make sure I hit that ropes course with jelly legs I did a quick climb up the 35' tower. The team didn't give me a break. Instead of taking the stairs down they have a lovely free fall. The guide transferred me from the belay line right to the free fall. A few seconds later and I was back on the ground.

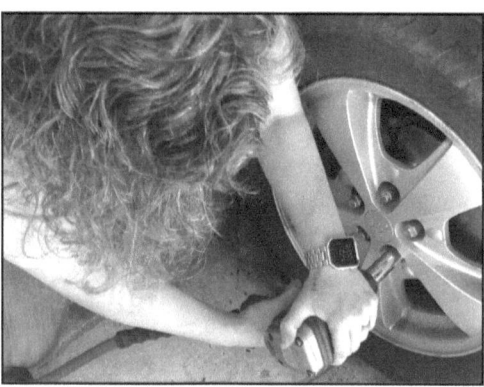

That was the start to my morning. I had a few minutes to catch my breath while the rest of the blue team took their turns. Everyone had a long hesitation just before dropping off that free fall. The climbing instructor's advice, "don't think, just do it." That was my mantra for the rest of the afternoon.

Next up was the ropes course, my reason for being there. The split-level structure had 6 obstacles. Heights have always been an issue for me but today I tackled the whole thing. The staff focus on safety made me more comfortable as I stepped across high beams and swinging rope obstacles.

Because I spend a fortune to keep my hip and neck in place, I decided not to play bubble soccer. While we were waiting for our time on the zip line there was an accident on the ropes course, so the adventure ended. I will say that I didn't witness what happened but after being on the course I really can't understand how it happened. Day 277 stretched the sides of my box. Love & Light

Day 278 of 365- I Did It   June 24, 2018

Braking... My adventure on day 278 involved an impact wrench, rotors and new brakes. I have never worked on a car's brakes. I can change oil and tires but when it comes to taking them apart, I have always been apprehensive. I don't own the tools required for this job, so my father was in charge of the morning. My son was the muscle and we got to work.

Everything was rusty but not so much that we couldn't get it apart. I had fun taking my son's car apart and making it work again. I didn't do this by myself, and I was happy to have my father's wisdom and my son's muscle. We make a great team.

The process was pretty simple. Loosen the lug nuts and remove the tire. Finding the bolt that holds the brakes and rotor in place was a bit of a challenge. The right tools make all of the difference, and the entire job took just a few hours. I have to admit that using the pneumatic tools was exciting and SO LOUD. Day 278 was greasy good fun. Love & Light

Day 279 of 365- I Made It   June 25, 2018

I am grateful... When I started this personal journey, I never thought that I would lose my mom. I didn't think that the relationships with most of the people I love would change. I only looked forward to pushing myself to try new things and to take myself on an adventure that would launch me into the next part of my life.

Grief is suffocating. Trying to put on a brave face is exhausting. The worst part is the loss of the voice of reason that my mother always was. As part of this journey, I wanted to write to mom. I wanted to put down in words all the memories that she gave me. My strength and self-confidence came from watching her achieve her own successes. I have wished for her council every single day since her death. The void is often larger than I ever thought possible.

She was in the hospital for over 120 days. I was there for almost all of them. On day 279 I wrote the gratitude letter to my mother that was intended for Mother's Day. I wanted to put it on special paper and make it as beautiful as she was. I had huge plans and after her death I wasn't going to write it at all. It seemed silly because she would never read it herself.

All the fun foods that I learned to cook were meant to celebrate my mom with a special meal. In early September of 2017, the week before this adventure began; I made a list of ideas to help me get through the year.

One of them was a gratitude letter to mom. She deserved so much more. I wish our last experience together wasn't fighting cancer. I'm not going to share the letter here. I've already read it to the ether. What feels perfect is that I had all that time with her at the end of her life. I would do it all again. I hated the hospital. I hated her nursing home. I really hated the lack of compassion in the administrators who managed her care, but I loved her and even when she struggled to say it those last days of her life, my heart knew. I know. Day 279 Love & Light

## Day 280 of 365 -I Made It	June 26, 2018

So it glows… It's day 280 and I'm making messes again. This time I wanted to try something I saw on social media. I'm not jumping off a roof, although I did jump from a rock wall on day 277. On day 280 I made glow in the dark bubbles.

They actually do glow in the jar. Before you get anxious with thoughts of how toxic this is, I took precautions. I also mixed this with bubble solution, and I never want to get soap in my eyes. This is how I did it.

I poured the contents of a 5-ounce bubble container and my two glow sticks into a glass jar and mixed them all together. That's it. Not complex. Now I'm waiting for total outside darkness to see how affective this is. I did make bubbles in the bathroom, which made my mirror, sink, floor and toilet look like a Hubble image of the universe.

After the sun set it was pretty amazing. I mixed in some fresh glow stick solution, and we were blowing glowing bubbles. You have to look closely, and maybe in the dark. The camera had a hard time catching them. Day 280 Love & Light

Day 281 of 365- I Made It   June 27, 2018

Watch it wiggle… Today is an all-day adventure in patience and I won't know success or failure for many long hours. Day 281 is all about making edible drinking cups. Why?   Why not! I used Jell-O for this experience and the family approved.

I chose the Captain America berry blue mostly because it's blue but also because they didn't have Wonder Woman. I'm not surprised. I mixed the liquid using half of the suggested water and added a teaspoon of unflavored gelatin.

If you're planning to make them for yourself you can add alcohol, just remember that you have to balance the liquids to keep the gelatin from being diluted. Mine are alcohol free. As I planned this, I decided to make small cups using 5 ounce as the base and 3 ounce as the spacer. I filled the base cup half full of Jell-O mix. I set the 3-ounce spacer inside and added water to it.

The weight of the water pushes the small cup down until the top of each cup meets. I centered the smaller cup and taped it in place. I poured blue mix until the cup was full. Now I'm hoping for success. I have never liked waiting for Jell-O to set up. I've never had great success with making firm Jell-O treats. And then there is the patience part that has been the true test since 7:00am this morning.

I won't lie. I have peeked a few ties and it's getting firm. 5:00pm and I have something that resembles a cup that jiggles like Jell-O. I sprayed the cups with cooking spray to prevent sticking as I pulled them apart. It worked but I should have added a tablespoon of gelatin because although they look like glasses they split when I fill them with liquid. I might just make some whipped cream and eat them. Day 281 was an intentional and unintentional flop. Love & Light

Day 282 of 365- I Made It   June 28, 2018

Hoppy wort... Day 282 was almost therapeutic as I spent most of the morning and afternoon making my very first home brewed beer.

Science in combination with my 365-day adventures seems to be working out. My very wonderful friend Christina who has home brewing experience led me down the path of wort making today. Why wort?

This is the boiled combination of grains and hops that will eventually ferment into delicious cream ale. I'd like to say that it was hours of very complex mixing and measuring but it wasn't. I boiled water, dropped in a mesh bag filled with grains, boiled it, added malt syrup, boiled it and poured that cooled down hot mess into a sterilized 5-gallon bucket. Easy as can be.

I did have to time it carefully and stir the foam out of it. The warning about boil over was severe so I watched that pot like a hawk. Now I wait two weeks for it to have a science-y good time and ferment. Check back to see what happens next. Day 282 Love & Light

Day 283 of 365- I Made It   June 29, 2018

Tied and tangled... Today was all about satisfying curiosity and finally figuring out how to tie, weave and braid a very specific type of bracelet. I have wanted to learn this forever. When I started to weave Byzantine chain mail, I was also intrigued by corded weaves that look like my braided metal.

YouTube was my inspiration and after a few misguided instructors and a pile of tangles I found a great video that helped me create a cardboard jig. It works like a loom but is also primitive enough to cut from cardboard. Once I fell into a rhythm I couldn't stop. I bought a rainbow of floss colors and proceeded to make a half dozen bracelets in a variety of color combinations.

I could take and make this anywhere. It's great for killing time and doesn't require batteries. Day 283 Love & Light

Day 284 of 365- I Did It   June 30, 2018

Crying over spilt milk. Success and Failure often go together. Since the beginning of this personal challenge, I have accomplished a variety of things and had a chance to take the mystery out of some of them.

Day 284 was not a mystery-removing day. It turns out that my goal of pouring a little heart on top of a cup of coffee would actually become a lesson in properly steamed milk. I had no idea. I happen to own a beautiful espresso machine. I have made foamy frothy milk for many cups of coffee. I've never tried to control that process and I learned why. It's a tiny bit complicated and it requires patience. I was so impatient with this experience and unrealistic in my expectations. I expected to have amazing hearts after just one lesson.

WRONG!

I used an entire half gallon of milk and never made a proper heart. However, I did learn to make steamed milk for the pouring process. It's supposed to be shiny. Here's the real deal, I don't do dairy. I was worried that if I tried it with alternate "milk" I might screw things up.

It was all screwed up anyway and I guess I'd rather dump cheap milk down the drain. Yes, I dumped a lot of hot lattes down the drain. I drank a lot too, which is why my hands weren't very steady on the last half dozen pours. I made 13 attempts before I ran out of supplies. I froze some of the coffee to use as ice cubes for my cold brew from day 25. On the 284th day I learned that some things take practice, and foaming hearts fall into that category. Love & Light

Day 285 of 365- I Did It   July 1, 2018

The power of water… It's 95 degrees outside. For the last few weeks we have had a ridiculous amount of rain, trapping me inside. The temperature isn't giving me much of a break. On day 285 I literally beat the heat with a power washer.

I HAD NO IDEA! This is a tool that I will add to my arsenal of absolute necessities. I love using it. I started on my front porch. It went well and I moved around to my deck. This is where all the ick has been collecting. Half of the deck is in shade and moss tends to grow. When this part of the deck gets wet the moss makes it slick. I may have taken a tumble once or twice.

Not anymore. I started in the corner and that slippery green mess just washed away. I couldn't stop. I know a few spots will require sanding, but it beats having to replace the entire deck. I finished spraying every board, but I couldn't stop. I moved on to the patio furniture that didn't make it in the barn last fall. It looks beautiful now.

I managed to power wash some kids' toys, a concrete patio, a few welcome matts and a rug. I could do this all day. Fortunately, I stopped with enough time for the rug to dry before the rain came again. Day 285 was very satisfying. Love & Light

Day 286 of 365- I Made It   July 2, 2018

Written in pencil… On day 286 I created a character for the game of D & D. I can't even believe I made it through because I had no idea what I was doing. My kid is a serious gamer, actually both of them are and I've never understood it. This experience is all about fantasy and imagination and READING!

Dungeons & Dragons is not for the faint of heart. My kids started playing before they were teenagers and I never gave them credit for researching through the volumes of books required to escape into this fantastic world. My character comes from a race known as Dragonborn. Sounds cool, right?

Over the next 90 minutes I read through a 300+ page handbook of very detailed characteristics that my Dragonborn Sorcerer would possess. Oh Yeah, this is serious business and I'm ready to do something with this magical creature that I rolled a crapload of dice to create.

It's a process and as complex as this part was I can't wait to learn how to play. But that's another adventure. Day 286 Love & Light

Day 287 of 365- I Made It   July 3, 2018

    Who needs a quart? Ultimately, I did. On day 287 I painted a chalkboard. I made many mini chalkboards. They worked so well that I continued making chalkboards.

    Why did I make 20 mini chalkboards? I got a chest of drawers from my family and although it is intended to keep all my crafting supplies in order, there are so many drawers that I can't remember what's inside any of them. I wanted to label each drawer in a way that made it easier to change it. I searched a few big box hardware stores but couldn't find what I wanted.

    Enter the chalkboard paint. I intended to get a pint of this stuff and cut little wood panels to glue on each drawer. Chalk paint only comes in quarts. I was certain I would never use all of it, so I looked for a spray version. I was excited when I found it. I should have purchased the quart because the paint is wonderful. I can turn almost anything into a chalkboard. Throw in some liquid chalk markers and my drawer signs look amazing.

    I continue to find experiences that are so wonderful that I would like additional time before moving on. When this year comes to an end, I won't have a problem finding something to do. Day 287 Love & Light

Day 288 of 365- I Did It   July 4, 2018

    I might have blown up my family. It seemed very fitting on the fourth of July and my 288th day to play "Keep talking and no one explodes." This is one of the most fantastic cooperative games for PlayStation and it incorporates that VR headset that made me motion sick on day 98. The weight of the Virtual reality goggles is disorienting and when the game goes live you open your eyes to a room with a few VR manuals. This is pretty wild and if I wasn't sitting down, I would have probably fallen over.

    I am not a gamer. I grew up with the single button Atari joystick that moved through one playing field. This is not the game of my childhood, and I was schooled in the ways of bomb diffusion in the VR world. It's actually a combination of puzzles and clues that you solve. A timer is set and the player wearing the headset has to explain to the rest of the team exactly what is on the screen.

    There is no time to make mistakes and if you cut the wrong wire too many times that game ends in an explosion. It's all VR so no Angelicis were damaged during the playing of this game. It was perfect fun. Day 288 was the bomb. Love & Light

Day 289 of 365- I Made It   July 5, 2018

    Today was an opportunity to honor another plan that my mom and I made together.

    It's not a secret that she and I spent time having our own mini adventures. She loved life and she fed the curiosities in her heart and mind. Very often she invited me to tag along. She was also in charge of establishing some smile inducing traditions. One that held true for most of my adult life was to celebrate our birthdays together. We were both September women, strong Virgos with many attributes in common.

    Mom understood me and for many birthday celebrations she would include some type of LEGO set. I was in my early 30's with two young children, and she still wrapped up a little set for the bottom of the gift bag.

    It was my job to find her some new exotic tea that didn't have a half dozen ingredients that gave her the sniffles. Hibiscus in her cup was a no-no. For so many years we went back and forth surprising one another with new and old gift ideas. Day 289 was all about embracing a tiny treat that mom never forgot was my favorite, honey sesame sticks.

    Last September, just before turning 49, I took a trip to Italy. I found two special things for mom to celebrate her 79th year. When we met for our birthdays, we exchanged surprises. My gifts to her included those Italian goodies. Her gift to me continues to be an inspiration.

    In a small Wonder Woman gift bag, my mother had a ceramic plaque. Tucked just beneath it was a package of sesame seed candy. The plaque was intended to inspire me on this 365-day journey. It reads, "She believed she could, so she did." Mom must have been psychic because I look at that wall hanging every day and remember my strength comes from her. The second part of that gift was the sesame seed candy. She told me how simple it was to make, and we decided it would be one of my experiences.

    So, I made this candy using sesame seeds and a jar of pure honey that I bought for my mother while she was ill. She never got to taste the honey. She passed away two days after I bought it. The recipe is so simple that I can't believe we never made them together. I toasted the seeds until they were golden brown. I brought the honey to a boil and added the seeds while it simmered. No patience required.

    As the mixture started to cool I poured it on a parchment-lined pan and rolled it out like dough. I waited 20 minutes to cut it to pieces that resembled the original treats. They taste amazing. The richness of the toasted seeds limits me to one or two pieces. Day 289, I believed I could, so I did. Love & Light

Day 290 of 365- I Did It   July 6, 2018

Warning today is about guns!

I have mixed feelings about today. The summer between my sophomore and junior years of high school I performed CPR on a gunshot victim. I was 15 years old. I held that man in my arms as he convulsed, choked on his tongue and turned a color of blue that haunted me for years.

I don't have to imagine what gun violence looks like. I was too young to know much about life or the circumstances around why this man was shot but the incident shaped my relationship with guns.

I graduated with a Police Science degree and part of the program was firearms training. I was very good at shooting, but I could never forget the lifelessness of the man I eventually saved. The memory of his blood on my pants, stabilizing his neck as I tried to breathe life into him replays every time I hold a gun in my hand.

I didn't shoot him. I wasn't in that field when it happened.
It hasn't stopped the memories. It's impossible to be in law enforcement and be hesitant to fire a gun. On day 290 I took a concealed carry firearms course. I want to put this chapter of fear in my past. I was fortunate to find an instructor who would come out to my home to teach me.

He is someone pretty special and aside from being a certified firearms instructor he is also a Rabbi. He pulled up on his motorcycle with a rolling firearms equipment bag strapped to the side. His instruction was dynamic and although I felt comfortable with the material, I still can't shake the past.

I completed the course and filed for my card. I'm comfortable with that. Will I carry? I guess the concealed part of that will just have to stay a mystery for now. Day 290 Love & Light

Day 291 of 365- I Saw It   July 7, 2018

It's a grand slam. It's America's favorite pastime. No, not social media... baseball. Today I attended my first Kingfish baseball game. This isn't the big league. It's minor and the scale of the crowd maxes the stadium at 3200. That's not a typo; just over three thousand two hundred is the max number of spectators at a Kingfish game.

I did have seats that included food and drink, which always helps. I'm just not a fan of watching baseball. I had something they called funnel cake fries. They were fry shaped but also cooked in the same oil as the cheese curds making the flavors combo not quite delicious.

The Kingfish won tonight's game, which also adds to the excitement. They also set off a great fireworks display. Don't tell my husband but I'd sit in those seats again. Day 291 was a solid hit. Love & Light

Day 292 of 365- I Did It   July 8, 2018

Balls... Few people would be surprised to know that I own a crystal ball. I've had it for years and it's been part of my meditation space. It's beautiful and until my 292nd experience I've never used it as a tool for photography.

Let me start out by sharing that I have a few superficial burns on my hand and the top of my lawn table is melted. Holding a crystal ball in the sun is ridiculously stupid but I did it about 100 times in an attempt to capture the perfect crystal sphere picture.

I have a few amazing photos, but my hand is also resting on ice. The table is going to need a little touchup paint. I started in the back yard and played around with the trees and greenery, but the subject was too broad. Since most of the flowers in my yard are weeds, I decided to use a vase of colored daisies I received from a friend.

There was a learning curve, and I felt like this might turn into a flop of an experience but then the sun hit just right, and I couldn't stop. I filtered the light, changed some angles and suddenly my table was melted. That sphere of glass might be calming but it will also create some intense heat. As experiences go, I'm not sure how to carry a crystal ball around but it would make an amazing accessory in my camera bag. Day 292 and absolute win. Love & light

Day 293 of 365- I Did It   July 9, 2018

Batter up! In the last week I've had quite a few experiences with baseball. It's supposed to be America's pastime. I think social media has taken over that particular category. Since I'm not a huge fan of watching this game, I have taken on today's experience with hesitation. On day 293 I assisted as an umpire in a machine pitch softball game.

As a young girl I lived for this sport, but I have never played the catcher position and until today I have never umpired a game. I don't know why anyone would. It's no fun at all and everyone around can call the game better than you.

My personal experience with the coaches was okay. I'm sure they knew it was my first time. I'd like to say it went well but I really can't judge. I didn't have to do much but count pitches, outs and innings. This is a thankless job and as easy as machine pitch plays, I wouldn't want to umpire a game that has more action and criticism. Maybe every coach should be required to umpire just to see how difficult it is. Day 293 Love & Light

Day 294 of 365- I Saw It   July 10, 2018

Just one seed or thousands… You never know where adventures will lead. On day 294 I visited the Museum of mustard with my friend Becky. I wasn't sure what to expect but I was excited when I entered. The walls were lined with bottles from across the country and around the world. Mustard from everywhere!

I had no idea so many types existed. Wisconsin had the largest collection by state followed by California. After spending time with the plethora of examples downstairs in the display room I went up to the tasting room. This is the bonus because every item sold in the gift shop is part of their free sample selection. I had some amazing flavors. I would go back just to try another dozen. I could only eat so many before they all started to taste the same.

The museum is located in Madison, WI and worth the trip. It's free to enter and after a few samples you'll leave with a bag of deliciousness. I love their motto; Peace, Love & mustard. Day 294 was tasty. Love & Light

Day 295 of 365- I Did It   July 11, 2018

It all makes sense, finally. I've used the phrase "par for the course" many times but today it really was, and I finally get it. On my 295th day I had my very first golf course experience, in a cart, off the T and I never hit the sand.

My friend and mentor on the course, Kim, was an excellent and patient teacher. We started on the first hole, and she went through everything I needed to focus on while playing. I watched and she smashed that first hit beyond the halfway marker.

We took a spin in the golf cart and finished the hole with a few long putts. I've played mini golf, but this isn't a playground, and no windmills are spinning my ball out of the hole. I did that all on my own with an overenthusiastic swing of the club.

We drove to the second hole, and it was my turn to give that driver a swing. I'd love to tell you that I had a 100-yard drive, but it spiraled 15 feet sideways into the brush and trees. Not a wonderful start.

As the afternoon went on, I felt like I was improving. I didn't expect to enjoy it as much as I did. Perhaps it was my patient teacher. Mercy came in the form of skipping half of the course and we went right to the clubhouse.

As experiences go, I would do this again. I enjoyed the long drives over short ones, mostly for the margin for error that landed in my favor. Day 295 was a home run. Thank you, Kim. Love & Light

Day 296 of 365- I Did It   July 12, 2018

Fun and games… Since day one I have had some amazing human beings supporting this journey and coaching me through many adventures. I've had some eye-opening moments. On day 296 I followed my daughter onto a virtual battlefield while playing Shogun II: Total War.

My kid is a gamer and subscribes to conquering innumerable decades and centuries of foes. My adventure played out in 16th century Japan with Samurai swords and archers. I've never played a game like this and I'm not sure I understand the setup completely. She helped me select an army and the game sorts them by group based on their soldiering skills. I have the ability (I use this term loosely) to maneuver these battle-ready packs and advance them toward the enemy.

My first attempt was a slaughter, but I learned a bit of strategy for my next battle. As games go I might play this for fun but I'm not a strategist. This could be an amazing teaching tool if you are willing to look beyond all the little corpses strewn across the battlefield.

We bonded over battle tactics. I'm not a quick study but the kid has many years of gaming experience to guide me through my second battle and a victory. I'm not going to run out and buy every Total War game in the series, but I might sit down and watch a real gamer play this through. Day 296 hit the mark. Love & Light

## Day 297 of 365- I Did It	July 13, 2018

    Bucket to bottle… On day 282 I mixed up a batch or wort, the first step in the process of home brewing delicious beer! On day 297, Friday the 13th, I opened that 5-gallon bucket and pumped that brew into bottles.

    The setup is pretty simple but also time consuming. My amazing friend Christina was kind enough to open her kitchen for this process. She's such a trooper. Somehow, she managed to amass more than 50 empty amber glass bottles for beer. I spent the morning, with the help of my kid, washing and sanitizing those bottles.

    While the pristine containers dried, I opened that 5-gallon bucket. This was sensory overload. I wanted to climb into that plastic pail and drink my way out. It smelled amazing. I know that the beer needs to carbonate so I moved the contents of the original container to the bottling bucket and added the sweet corn sugar boiled into simple syrup. I forgot how much I love the smell of beer.

    The bottles are placed in rows on the floor and gravity feeds my new home brew into each one. Did I mention my adoration for beer? I managed to transfer 5 gallons into about 50 bottles without taking a taste. I was informed it wouldn't be good, and I didn't want to ruin the first sip.

    I have a few six packs down in my basement. They need to be in the dark until all the delicious chemistry inside evolves into bubbling beer! Joy! Day 297 Love & Light

Day 298 of 365- I Saw It   July 14, 2018

Bonjour... On day 298 I had an experience at the Bastille days festival. The first adventure of the morning was finding a place to park in downtown Milwaukee. It's always the least exciting part of any festival.

After the car was parked under the shade of a tree I walked to the event. Festivals in the park always have two things: food and souvenir vendors. I hit the food first and I had two new treats. My first, a crepe. It was more like ice cream with a doughy shell. It was disappointing. My second treat, a beignet and this first was delicious.

We walked around the festival for a while longer. The schedule board showed music, but I didn't hear much. Children were performing on the tiny stage but as festivals go this one was a little dull. I stopped to take a picture of the replica of the Eiffel tower, which felt like the only attraction. I finished off the afternoon by walking through the vendor tents.

Without a theme, this was just like any other market in the park. Day 298 was a total one & done. Love & Light

Day 299 of 365- I Ate It   July 15, 2018

8,111 feet I live at 751 feet. I'm in Colorado and I've got a Rocky Mountain high, on life. For my 299th experience I took a long hit of bottled oxygen.

I'm not 100% sure this makes a difference while I'm resting beside a roaring river in Mount Princeton. This is the first Colorado visit of my 365-day adventure. I had planned for more, but I have to stay in the NOW. My day started at 3:30am. I flew to Denver, Co by way of Nashville, TN. Don't ask questions, I'm not sure how this is economical, but I went about 550 miles south to go 1,000 west. It's a head scratcher.

Why is this important? I'm well over a mile above my Wisconsin altitude. I figured this would be my chance to hit the oxygen bottle hard. I saw a photo on the wall of the train at the Denver airport advertising "Boost Oxygen." I didn't think much about it until we were driving into the mountains. It was a silly joke but after a wonderfully informative conversation with "Siri" I found the product at a local grocery store.

As I hold this can in my hand, I realize that I paid $15 for air. I bought a can of air. It's all around me. This might just be the silliest experience so far. I took a hit, and it was like spraying myself in the face with the air compressor hose in my barn. It's oxygen. Oxygen is a colorless, odorless, tasteless gas essential to living organisms. Day 299, Love & Light

Day 300 of 365- I Did It July 16, 2018

It's day 300 and it feels like the impossible has become possible. If I'm honest there have been moments when I felt like I'd never make it this far. Day one was the base of an enormous mountain and today I can finally see the summit.

To celebrate my 300th adventure I dipped myself in the Hot Springs of Mt. Princeton, Colorado; definitely a first but not a last. What I experienced about naturally occurring hot water is that it's freakishly HOT. I've been in a few Jacuzzi tubs and most of the time the chemicals used to keep it clean prevents me from staying in for very long.

Not here. In the mountains of Colorado, it's the sunshine and freakishly hot water. I enjoyed both... in moderation because I've got 65 adventures remaining and sunburn is not on the menu. There isn't much to explain when it comes to hot springs. You get in and if you're smart you get out before the staff needs to carry you out. I enjoyed the exhilarating difference between the ice-cold flowing mountain river and the little pools of earth-heated water, perfectly symbiotic. Day 300 was hot and wet. Love & Light

Day 301 of 365- I Made It   July 17, 2018

    Not what the Jetsons had in mind. I am staying at a beautiful mountain resort. My room happens to be one of the most recent additions to this property, so it has some modern conveniences. On day 301 I had the first and only EVER experience with the Nespresso coffee machine.

    My impression of pod coffee makers; they generate horrible waste. I also think of the machine at my former job and how nasty it got after a few months of indifference in a community kitchen.

    The Nespresso machine is compact and for a hotel I wonder, why? This can't be a money saver. Maybe so few people own this machine that it prevents them from shoving the extras in their suitcases. What makes good coffee? GOOD WATER! The water here is so chlorinated that the brewed pods taste like last week's dregs.

    Let me preface today's experience by saying that I've only used a hotel machine and I don't know if it is different from what you might get at Target. My pods are color-coded: red, green and purple. Let's get the red out of the way because it's decaf and who needs that on vacation. (As a side note green usually represents decaf) If you don't read the instructions and put a 7-ounce pod in but set a 2-ounce cup under it... well use your imagination.

    I did learn how to break down the machine to clean up 5 ounces of spilled foamy coffee. This machine seems silly. The single use idea might make sense in a hotel for cleaning, but I like the smell of brewing coffee just as much as I like the flavor. Hotel room cappuccino from a pod? Nope.

    As vacation coffee pots go, I'll pass on this experience in the future and bring my own nasty single serve pouches. Still wasteful but the flavor is as reliable as a sunrise. Day 301 Love & Light

Day 302 of 365- I Did It   July 18, 2018

      Mary did you know? Today I did an experiment with pain. I've had it intermittently for years and on occasion it has been nearly unbearable. I figured since I was in Colorado, I would take advantage of pain relief in a new way.

      On day 302 I used a transdermal Cannabinoid patch. This is a first for me. I've never used "stick on" weed. I am 100% on board when it comes to the use of medicinal marijuana. I've seen it in action so when this opportunity came, I did not hesitate. My patch was easy to use. I peeled away the plastic backing and stuck it to my hip. Once it was on, I forgot about it. Hours later I didn't ache where I did before. I wasn't stoned or impaired in fact I didn't feel much of a change. I wasn't surprised at all, but I was excited for the relief. Day 302 Love & Light

Day 303 of 365- I Saw It   July 19, 2018

    Mine, mine mine… I had the privilege of dropping 1000 feet below ground to enter the Mollie Kathleen mine. What makes this amazing and special on day 303 is the Mollie Kathleen is the first female owned mine in the United States.

    This adventure takes place during my first visit to Cripple Creek, Colorado. I don't know why I've never been here before. The drive is beautiful, but what isn't in Colorado. As you come around the last curve Cripple Creek is nestled in the valley below. It's like fantasy come to life.

    My mining adventure begins just before entering the city. The entire place feels like a step back in time even though some of the equipment is still in use today. How did I get down 1000 ft? In a sardine can elevator. I'm not kidding. You really get to know your neighbor as the guide weaves you in "Tetris style." It takes two long awkward minutes to get to the bottom. When we hit it I was happy to get out.

The tour is an experience, an authentic walk through the history of mining. Many human beings gave their lives for this mine. As I looked down the miles of winding shafts, I thought about how much manual labor it took to create it.

    The tour is a real treat, and I never felt like I was trapped on some journey to the center of the earth. Following the tour, I had a short walk through town and after dinner I had my very first taste of Flan. One word. NOPE!

    That was a mess of flavors that just didn't work for me. I liked the dollop of whipped cream and the center portion that didn't touch the syrup surrounding it. One & done for sure! If that wasn't enough firsts, I also bumped into a Deer.

    He was sitting in the front yard as we walked through town. It was my first deer with antlers. Oh, but there were three of them eating at leisure from the little aspen trees. I just wanted to pet them, but I didn't want to get my ass kicked by an antlered deer. As experiences go today was full of them. Three for Day 303 Love & Light

Day 304 of 365- I Saw It   July 20, 2018

    Yesterday… I'm not a history buff and most of the things I've learned in school only make a difference on Tuesday trivia nights. On day 304 I took a tour of the history of Cripple Creek at their District museum. This place where the past comes to life is running a scavenger hunt for the summer. What's the prize? A real nugget of gold.
    The quest: to make your way through this amazing museum and answer questions about the history of the area. Whoever started this campaign is a genius because I walked through at a snail's pace and enjoyed every minute of it. The costumes and artifacts made me hungry for simpler times.
    Mining and gold panning intrigues me and the second floor fed my curiosity with samples of mining discoveries. Gold isn't the only thing they search for but who wouldn't want to discover a giant chunk of gold.
    Market price on July 20, 2018? $1223.00 per ounce. It might be worth a few hours in the river with an old pie plate. I may or may not have done that. My ticket to the museum included time in the giant trough panning for gemstones.
    I would still be there now if I didn't have to run off. You don't have to be 10 to disappear in the huge container of ore left over from the mines. As first experiences go this left me wanting more. I should go back and explore the two buildings that I didn't have time to enter. Day 304 was a real gem. Love & Light

Day 305 of 365- I Did It   July 21, 2018

It's still a secret, just not mine, and prepare yourself. Today was all about the one article of clothing I've had a love/hate relationship with most of my adult life.

My Bra. It's the first thing I take off when I get home and the last thing I put on when I go out the door. I've surrendered to the idea that it's a necessary barrier between me and the judgments of society.

FYI... we all have nipples! On my 305th day I went to Victoria's Secret for a proper brassiere fitting. I've been told that this is the place to go if you want to be comfortable in your underwire, which I am not. I walked into the store and asked the salesperson for a fitting. Her question to me, "would you like it right in the middle of the store or in a dressing room?

PANIC! Who wants their breasts measured out in the middle of the showroom floor? Of course I want to go to a fitting room! She asked me a few questions about my current undergarment, which is a basic sport fit. She wrapped me with a measuring tape and ran off to get me a few items to try.

This fitting room is about 150 degrees inside which adds to my level of discomfort. She handed me two articles and after trying both I didn't get the fit that everyone raves about. More bras later and I'm scratching my head to figure out why the side of my boob is sticking out the top of this bra. This isn't quite right and maybe she was using the metric side of that measuring tape. Victoria gets to keep her secrets because I walked out of the store empty handed. I understand my measurements have nothing to do with what I'm comfortable in. This shouldn't be so difficult. Day 305 Love & Light

Day 306 of 365- I Saw It   July 23, 2018

What's to see? Day 306 was my very first concert experience with Third Eye Blind. I'm not a fan of waiting and my adventure happened at the end of the day. As it goes these are the nail biters. What do I do if it all goes to hell?

True confession... I only listened to Third Eye Blind on YouTube in preparation for this experience. I'm not much of a fan. The concert was outside, and the lawn seating created a great stadium view for about an hour, until it started to rain.

Set the stage for this adventure, Littleton Colorado, end of July, pouring rain. I've been here for about a week and when I arrived half of the state was under caution for wildfires. It's been dry as a dustbowl. And yet as I sat with the sun on my face those tiny drops of rain began to fall. This wasn't a light sprinkle it was a freak fest of water soaking through everything. I was squishing in places I just never ever want to.

The rain stopped shortly before the sun set and now it's dark, I'm wet and cold. Sounds like the ideal setting for a concert with a band that I'm not a huge fan of. Perfecto!

The opening act was very entertaining, and they finished playing before the storm. If there is a bright side, it's that lightning never came so the show went on.

As concerts go this is yet another okay experience. I've been to very few life changing performances and I thought maybe this would be one. Nope! The company was beyond great and after everything I wouldn't choose this band, but I will keep the people. Day 306 Love & Light

Day 307 of 365- I Did It   July 23, 2018

This is just too easy. In 2012 Colorado passed amendment 64 regulating Marijuana so sales could be similar to alcohol.

On day 307 I made my first visit to a Marijuana Dispensary. It was an adventure just standing in the parking lot, the cars were rolling in and out. Emerald Fields came recommended so that's where I went. The store was busy even with a few other shops in view.

I was honest with the clerk at the door that I'd never been inside of a dispensary, so super peppy Allen gave me the grand tour. On the street this shop is known as a "cannaboutique." It's adorable and they sell an unbelievable variety of cannabis products.

After the response my body had on day 302, I purchased another transdermal patch. The rest of my browsing took place in the rainbow-colored edibles isle. I had to pause when I saw that Snoop Dogg has a cannabis product line. I decided to experiment with two treats, cocoa for my coffee and a lollypop.

I'll let you know how that goes. As a side note this is an expensive indulgence if you're using recreationally. I paid 25% sales tax on these items, so I guess the state of Colorado is super happy not to have to share that with the Federal government. Day 307 Love & Light

Day 308 of 365- I Saw It   July 24, 2018

    When you see it in action... It's day 308 and I was the photographer at a concert for children. Today was special and I had no idea it would be. My niece is an artist but instead of creating with ink or brush she uses her voice.

    On day 306 I attended a Third Eye Blind concert and for the size of the venue and the sound that bounced around the air, it was nothing like the joy coming from the tiny classroom at a childcare facility. Branik played for five groups of children at two different facilities, and it was inspirational. I've been sitting here trying to find the words to describe what I witnessed.

    Children are so perfectly pure in the way they respond to music. Branik made magic. I watched them smile as the acoustic sound filled their classroom. I wish the world could witness what I did. Day 308 Love & Light

Day 309 of 365- I Ate It   July 25, 2018

Tweezers required... I have been in Colorado for over a week and every time I drive to town, I see rows of cactus plants against the fence line. On day 76 I ate a prickly pear which is the less dangerous treat on top of a cactus plant.

That wasn't enough of a challenge. For my 309th day I foraged for nopales (cactus), cut, cleaned, cooked and ate them. Why? After so many days and experiences this one actually makes sense. I'm in the desert area of Colorado and the plants are growing in the back yard. They should be eaten.

I did a little research and although there are many ways to prepare the pads I didn't want to take any chances with the spines. I remember watching videos of creatures in the wild trying to remove those needles from their little animal faces. I didn't want that on my hands, so I used eighteen-inch tongs through the entire experience.

I was not successful as the base of every spine has an adorable tuft of microscopic fuzz called glochids. These are the little suckers they should warn you about because once they touch you, you're screwed.

I decided to take all the skin off my pads because the thought of swallowing the fuzz FREAKED me out. If you watch the video, you'll see this was a very slow process. I edited it at 20x's normal speed to keep it moving along. Once everything was cleaned and cut, I sautéed them in coconut oil with salt and pepper. They taste wonderful and much like the aloe from day 33 there is a bit of a slime factor. After all the work was done, I read an article that suggests boiling the bits before cooking them. Remember for next time, slime boiling.

I tried to think how I might use cactus in my current recipes, potato salad and salsa came to mind. If I can find the pads at a grocery, I might experiment a little bit more. Day 309 Love & Light

Day 310 of 365- I Made It   July 26, 2018

Let them eat bread. I was having a discussion about health and while weighing back and forth on many topics we stopped on eating habits and real food. I fed my family home cooked meals, made from scratch while being an at home parent. I've baked bread but I've never stopped to think about the ingredients in my bread flour, or more precisely the lack of ingredients in my flour.

I eat bread. I love carbs; two facts about me as a person that will not ever change. On day 310 I decided to make flour for bread. In my head this was going to involve old stone grinders and berries of wheat. I could feel the blisters forming. That's not how this adventure played out. Enter the multi-purpose Nutra bullet. I added a cup of wheat berries to the machine and within minutes I had fresh milled flour.

Why don't I do this all the time? I live near so many grocery stores that carry unmilled grains. Testing the flour was my next step and a very simple bread recipe felt like the right choice. It was amazing, even with a tiny yeast mishap.

The ingredients: water, raw honey, sea salt, yeast and the fresh milled wheat. Simple! About two hours later the most delicious loaf of bread came out of the oven. Day 310 Love & Light

Day 311 of 365- I Made It   July 27, 2018

Extracted... It's my 311th day and I learned how to make tinctures. What the heck is that? I spoke with Janna, the owner of Owl Apothecary about extracting the medicinal properties of herbs using alcohol.

I've been working on pain management since injuring my hip in mid-June. The goal of the afternoon was to mix up a batch of herbs to aid with natural healing. I'm all about the herbs. I could steep the roots and leaves to make tea, but I wanted to make a tincture. What's the difference? Think about the nastiest tea you've ever had. If you were using it medicinally you might need to drink two or three 8-ounce glasses to gain the effect you're looking for.

If you extract the properties of healing by making the tincture you will get the same dose by using only a dropper full. The actual process of mixing is super easy. The herbs are measured and poured into a jar and high proof alcohol is added. I used Brandy. Now it needs to steep.

It'll take about 8 weeks for the alcohol to extract the essential oils and nutrients from the plants. Being patient is just not my thing but I'm sure this will be worth the wait. Day 311 Love & Light

Day 312 of 365- I Did It   July 28, 2018

Bee in my bonnet... The phrase took on real meaning as I tended my first beehive on day 312.

My extraordinary sister Kathleen is a beekeeper. It is something that my family did when I was a child. I remember being swarmed and having my mother pull stingers from my head, which is probably why I've never been inside the hive before. My sister said I used to play with the bees. I don't remember that, but I recall getting shot in the head with the garden hose to get the bees off my head.

That was not my experience today. I had the most exciting time and as I strapped that GoPro cam to my chest I hoped to capture the fun.

We smoked the hive to chase the bees from the frames we were working in. That was CRAZY!! I tried to stay very calm as thousands of bees swooped around our bodies.

"You're not allergic, right?" Great time to ask when I'm wrapped from foot to head in protective gear. Nothing is 100% sting proof as I would learn. We used the hive tool to pry apart the supers (layers of the hive). Each level has a purpose and because this was a first for me, we invaded the entire thing. My sister is doing a hive experiment by placing glass jars inside instead of using the typical frames. My heart was beating so hard I can hear it in the video footage.

Once everything was in place, I was disappointed we weren't going to take any honey, but my sister changed her mind and had me pull out one frame. It was heavy, dripping with honey and bees as I lifted it from the hive. This is when it all went to hell, and I actually did get a bee in my bonnet. I was calm but certain I'd get a sting. That little sucker got me right in the neck. I was not "one" with the buzzing little insects, but I did get to taste that wonderful honey. Day 312 Love & Light

Day 313 of 365- I Made It   July 29, 2018

Hooked… I have wanted today to happen since I started this personal journey. Day 313 I finally got my very first fly fishing rod. Here's the deal, I'm in Colorado, which has always felt like the perfect place to learn to fly fish. I've been visiting this state for 30 years and I lived here in my early 20's but I've never been fly fishing. If I haven't shared this, I LOVE FISHING!

On day 79 I learned how to tie flies for fishing. The experience was free and now I understand why. Bass Pro Shop wanted me to have an amazing experience so that I would return to purchase all my fly fishing needs.

It worked. Today I spent about an hour shopping for the perfect setup for a novice. It was only the beginning. I purchased a 4-piece rod, a reel and all the equipment I would need for a lesson but before I get to go fishing, I need to learn how all the parts come together so I can dance with the fishies.

First order of business: assemble that reel/rod combo and learn how to tie on the ridiculously expensive tiny flies. I do mean tiny. I have a magnifying glass clipped on to my baseball cap. I can't tie that thin filament without it.

We picked up a handy little pocket edition of the Little Red Fishing Knot book and I spent about an hour learning how to tie flies on and join two strands of fishing line together. Mission accomplished and I think I'm ready to have my experience in the water. Stay tuned because it has rained every day since I've been here and the rivers are so muddy I can't fish in them. Day 313 Love & Light

Day 314 of 365- I Did It   July 30, 2018

Caught... If I'm being honest, it was joy, and I am finally one with the universe. Day 314 was the ultimate fishing experience.

The quest for perfect water begins. How do you find great water for fishing in Colorado? Take a long drive to the mountains. If I said it was beautiful you wouldn't understand what my eyes did see. I'd never been down this winding road that led me to gorgeous hills and valleys and even though the road ended, my experience had only just begun.

I was searching for fish. I was also searching for waters clear of the muddy wash coming down from the mountain rains that have hovered above my days in Colorado. There will never be a downside to driving through the Colorado countryside, and not finding a great spot to learn to fly fish. It did take some time. It could have taken all day, and I would have been content.

With the mountains in front of us, we found the perfect location. First challenge: assemble my rod and reel and tie that fly to the line. It should have been easy, but the wind decided I needed another challenge.

By design the line on a fly rod is meant to slip through the ferrules (tiny metal loops). I threaded the thin leader line from the reel to the tip of the rod. It seemed super simple until that damn wind whipped through and sucked my threading out and whipped it through the air. It was funny until it happened a second and third time.

I spent the next hour learning how interesting it is to have the wind blowing against every cast of my rod. I hooked myself on the arm, on the shoe and a few places in between. Did I express how much I love fishing?

Once the line was through, I held it in my teeth until I picked the perfect oversized fly to use as a learning bug. I hiked down the hill to the reservoir and after a short lesson I was released to do my fishing damage. This is full on fishing, and I think I am ruined for life. Once I experienced the rhythm of casting I didn't want to stop.

I had too of course because the leader line is thin, and I snagged everything in the process of learning. I hooked rocks and trees and even caught the remnants of a previous fisherman's loss.

Learning how to tie that cinch knot was a blessing because I did it about a dozen times. I did find my rhythm. I did get hits on my line, and I finally had my first catch while fly-fishing. I didn't want to stop. I'd probably still be out there if I were alone. I'll never be the same. Day 314 Love & Light

Day 315 of 365- I Made It   July 31, 2018

So stuck... The last few experiences have been exciting and so very satisfying but my new adventures in Colorado are coming to an end.

On my 315th day I learned how to make Chinese Dumplings and Tang yuan. Bao Jiaozi is the term for wrapping dumplings. My talented niece, who spent two years in China with the Peace Corps, taught me how to fill, fold and pinch little pockets of meat. Most people call them potstickers but whatever you call them we made almost 70 and it was fantastic to see them all lined up on the counter.

My lesson was quick and once we got into a rhythm it didn't take long to make those dumplings. My niece learned so much about the culture while living in China and although she has cooked for us in the past today's lesson was a definite first.

The dumplings were just a part of the very authentic meal. Tang Yuan was the dessert soup I learned to make. It's an interesting combination of fermented rice juice, goji berries, glutenous rice balls and sugar. It was a sweet treat at the end of the meal. Day 315 Love & Light

Day 316 of 365- I Did It   August 1, 2018

I don't know why I didn't run. This day started with a drive to the Royal Gorge in Colorado. The goal was to experience my first Segway course.

Things didn't go quite as planned. I flew out to Colorado a few weeks ago and didn't rent a car. I've been at the mercy of the drivers I'm staying with and instead of taking me to the Segway course they delivered me to a heart pounding adventure.

On my 316th day I had my first and only ever HELL-icopter ride. I should explain that driving down winding roads makes me nauseous. I get motion sick and that's why there haven't been a lot of 365-day experiences that mess with my equilibrium. If I'm being 100% honest, a helicopter ride was part of my pre 365-day list. I wanted to do this so much but getting sick for the cause didn't have any appeal. The ride launched from Royal Gorge Heli Tours.

I climbed the stairs to the office and the pilot asked if I wanted to take a tour. I laughed and said no! My sister said yes and the decision to ride was made. I watched a safety video. I put on my flotation vest. My heart was beating so fast that I thought fear would win.

It did not! My sister and I climbed in that helicopter, and she was generous (or smart) enough to give me a front seat view. For the first few minutes I was excited and amazed and if you've ever been to the Royal Gorge Bridge this is a great way to feel like a bird above one of nature's heart-stopping creations. Helicopters are funny things.

When the horizon was where my body knew it should be, I loved the ride. As soon as the whirly machine took a turn and I felt like I was flying sideways, the vomit monster started to appear.

If you've been following, you'll remember that I got motion sick playing a VR game on day 98. Reality is so much worse. For safety reasons the protocol for exiting the helicopter is very specific. As we touched down to the landing pad I didn't care a single bit about it. I wanted out!

I don't remember much of the next few hours. My family took me to get a ginger drink in hopes it would settle my nausea. Hell-icopter rides are a NO go for me. I'll stick to long airplane rides with tummy settling Dramamine. Day 316 was quite a ride. Love & Light

Day 317 of 365- I Saw It   August 2, 2018

I usually just drive right through. Leaving Colorado is always hard for me because my heart belongs in that state. I had intentions for this travel day, but they changed when we stumbled upon a beautiful body of water in the middle of Nebraska.

Yep, right smack dab in the "kinda sorta" middle. On day 317 I visited the dam at McConaughy Lake. The experience was both educational and beautiful. The tiny museum had engaging displays outlining the quest for water in the middle of farmland USA.

In a million years I would never have stopped to look at this place. Like I said earlier, when we go to Colorado we drive right through, stopping for two things, gas and bathrooms.

Since I'm up for just about any new experience I decided to make an out of the ordinary stop. This is the second museum that I've been to in the last few weeks, and I was intrigued to learn about the history of irrigation. I found it fascinating that in the span of 50 years circular irrigation was invented and became GPS controlled.

To complete the experience, we drove across the top of the dam. One side was an extraordinary reservoir, and the other was an abundant green landscape. Water is so powerful. Day 317 Love & Light

Day 318 of 365- I Saw It August 3, 2018

Not very rare… I'm in Omaha, Nebraska. I've driven through this city too many times to count and rarely stop for more than gas. On day 318 we stopped for a tour of Omaha Steaks.

The corporate facility does not give tours even though the receptionist gave us a fair amount of info on the area facilities. Maybe if I'd had more questions, she might have made this stop even better.

We did discuss the signs for the million-dollar club posted in the parking lot. You have to sell a lot of steaks to get those prime spots. Did you know there was such a thing? I know you get a pink car for selling makeup; you only get a spot to park a car at Omaha steaks. Hmm, doesn't make me want to sell either.

We were directed to the company storefront a few blocks from headquarters, and I did get the deluxe tour of their freezers where I was given the opportunity to hand over my credit card in exchange for some delicious meaty goodness. My barbeque is going to be very happy. As experiences go, I put this on the same level as the pet expo but not quite as good as the zombie prepping survival fair. Day 318 Love & Light

Day 319 of 365- I Did It   August 4, 2018

Words... A few years ago, I published my first book. It's a short story but the words are powerful, and I wanted to find a way to introduce them to this 365-day experience. This is my 319th day and I used *Dear Kane; what I wish we would have said* to leave a message in a bottle.

Let me start out by saying that I love the idea of finding a message in a bottle floating in the ocean. I've read stories about it and even watched a movie and every time it makes my heart sing (even that Kevin Costner film).

I had planned to deliver this idea to the water when I was in Seattle. I couldn't do it. I have watched so many conservation videos on YouTube and Facebook that I couldn't conscience throwing anything in the ocean even for a noble idea. I couldn't add more garbage to an ocean that is already littered with trash.

That's when this idea was born. I put together a cool, dry land message and rolled it into a bottle. Inside I put a copy of my book, tied with a bracelet from day 283.
I took it to a busy park and left it there for someone to find. I have no idea who might pick it up or even if they will follow the instructions inside, but I hope that they will.

I hope that just one more person comes to see the way that love can build us up and make us strong. Day 319 was my message to a stranger. Love & Light

Day 320 of 365- I Made It   August 5, 2018

It's so Faire. I've been a student many times in the last ten months. On my 320th day I learned how to do leather work. My son set up this experience and I will admit that I was extremely excited to get to work with Sky from the leather shop at the Bristol Renaissance faire. I had two ideas in mind; bracers for shooting that bow I built on day 37 or a leather pouch to wear when I go to faire. I decided I would get more from this experience creating the pouch.

I walked around the shop and selected the leather and accessories necessary to accomplish this adventure. The place is stocked full of everything I needed and so much more.

Sky set me up with a template and tools for creating my new pouch and we modified it so I could also make a belt. I was having the best time and I could have stayed all day to make those bracers too. As experiences go day 320 was up at the top. Love & Light

Day 321 of 365- I Ate It   August 6, 2018

It smells like Christmas. As I foraged through the park this morning, I was struck by the fact that this experience might have been more of an adventure in the mountains of Colorado. On day 321 I brewed pine needle tea.

We had a storm in the middle of the night and as I listened to the thunder my mind started running through the short list of 365-day ideas I have left. My original plan involved sunshine and as of 11:30 am it's overcast, and the sky is still releasing those drops of rain. So, it's Teatime!

I researched my trees to be sure that the pine needles I collected wouldn't create a toxic brew. Like many things I've experienced already, education is key. I selected three needle types mostly because that's what is growing in and around my home. I cut pine, spruce and fir branches. I washed each piece and set the hitchhiking spiders and caterpillars free. I trimmed the pieces to fit inside pint jars and poured boiling water over the top. Each steeped for fifteen minutes.

If you've ever wondered what Christmas tastes like, this is it! All three have very distinct flavors. If I'm in the wild and low on vitamin C I'll look for the long pine needles. The flavor is perfect without needing honey or sweetener. Day 321 Love & Light

Day 322 of 365- I Did It   August 7, 2018

Unicorns just pop up. I am a unicorn. It's my spirit animal and oddly it is also the national animal of Scotland. TRUTH! On day 239 I learned that my recent college graduate would be studying for a master's degree in SCOTLAND.

I will be going there soon and in honor of this life changing event I decided to step way out of my comfort zone and do a virtual race from one end of Scotland to the other.

On day 322 I joined a Unicorn challenge. The name makes me happy even if I just committed to walk 121 miles in the middle of a 365-day challenge of which I have 43 days left. No biggie, I've flown in a helicopter, jumped in a freezing lake and floated at an indoor skydiving park. I should be able to do this walk.

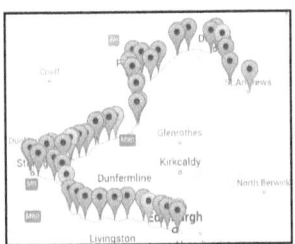

If I'm honest, I haven't been physical since mom got sick in December. I spent so many weeks sitting and talking, I feel blessed for every day I spent with her, but now I have to continue living. My plan is to attack this and average 3 miles per day. With everything I have going aside from the 365-day challenge and writing projects this feels realistic and achievable. Stay tuned. Day 322 Love & Light

Day 323 of 365- I Made It   August 8, 2018

Let the sun shine. The rain has stopped, and the clouds have moved away. I've got the perfect environment for today's experience. On day 323 and I made paper sun art. I saw this in a magazine a few years ago when my kids were home schooling. Just before my adventure in Colorado I purchased all the supplies I would need to make this an experience. I brought it with me on the trip because the sun is always shining there. HA! It rained almost every day. Don't get me wrong, the sun did shine but I had other adventures that came to be. When I felt the warmth of today on my skin, I knew this would be perfect.

I opened the package of supplies and paused to figure out what I was going to use as a subject. I did a test run on a few little dinosaurs, and I had to try my Wonder Woman, because... Wonder woman. I moved on to plants and a beautiful glass snowflake that belonged to my mother. There was a bit of magic to the experience, and the light of the sun exposed the paper creating a negative shadow image. I rinsed each page in water to set the image. It looked like it was washing away but as the paper dried it left something very beautiful behind.

I wish I had 1000 sheets to play with because the process was very satisfying. Day 323 Love & Light

Day 324 of 365- I Ate ItAugust 9, 2018

This... hurt... is... no... good. Look, I'll admit that no part of me really wanted to do what I just did to my body. I have been to this restaurant many times as a vegetarian, which prevented me from ever eating these tiny greasy hot messes.

On day 324 I ate my very first White Castle slider. I didn't eat just one. Oh no! I had a filthy pile of these gems. This is how the mistake happened. I figured I would have the original slider to keep it authentic, and I had to do cheese to balance them out. If I'm choosing those, I should do the bacon, right? After those decisions, it was all downhill. I ordered the veggie burger to satisfy my curiosity. When I saw the chicken/waffle sandwich I threw one of those in for good measure and it felt like I was getting a good sample of the entire menu.

My first thought? No one should ever eat the veggie patty from White Castle. It's possibly the worst thing I've ever tasted on the "meatless" menu at any restaurant. It's my opinion and not a humble one because I had to eat that bacon slider to get the gooey slime of the corn-ish, carrot? and "green thing" out of my mouth.

BACON, who knew it was a pallet cleanser for veggie burgers? The other delightful surprise was the sweet/ salty combo of that chicken waffle sandwich. From the outside this looked risky but turned out to be okay. I knew going into the restaurant that I was putting my digestive system to the test. I've heard all the regretful groans of the White Castle "after party."

As adventures go today was a trip that I will never need to take again. If you're curious about that chicken/waffle sandwich combo just head through the drive up, grab it and go, go, go! Day 324 Love & Light

Day 325 of 365- I Made It   August 10, 2018

This was so on fire. Today is an odd day. I woke up with no idea what I was going to do as an adventure. I have 40 more opportunities to flex the "I've never done this before" muscles and I'm excited and sad. Today's adventure was accidental and an absolute first. On day 325 I made gun powder art.

If I wasn't an artist before today this experience would have solidified my creative street cred. I opened up a half dozen shotgun shells and removed the gun powder from inside. My original plan was to draw a long line and create some kind of boom at the end.

The art was so much better. It did take a little bit of time to sketch my design with the powder. It moves around like sand and started to pick up static. I switched to metal tools, and the problem was mostly solved. As experiences go this is one I will definitely do again. Day 325 Love & Light

Day 326 of 365- I Did It   August 11, 2018

Rainbows and Narwhals... Today was tough and sad. Helping people you love say goodbye is a challenge to write about but when people show up for you it matters. Today I said goodbye to a man who became my father-in-law 25 years ago. He was an interesting person. The fact is, this isn't a first adventure or experience for me because I can't honor this loss the way that I should. I never felt like he belonged to me.

This evening, after all the life celebrating ended for him, I brought my smaller family of four together to play. That's how we celebrate our love for one another. In a few weeks we will scatter off in different directions and everything changes again.

On day 326 we played UNOcorns. This is a lot like Uno but with a unicorn theme. I'm very into unicorns. The big problem with this deck is the addition of a Narwhal card. Actually, they put four of them in to test your relationship with the people around the game table.

I did this to us. Maybe it was the wine, or the abundance of chocolate cake but we had a unicorn throwdown. We got intense, a teeny tiny bit competitive but in the end, there were rainbows...Oh, and unicorns. Day 326 Love & Light

Day 327 of 365- I Ate It   August 12, 2018

I'm judging this YUKKY! I feel very duped by my experience today. I shopped for what I thought would be a delicious treat and a 100% new experience. On day 327 I opened what appeared to be hazelnut candy. The label (written in another language) had pictures of whole hazelnuts so why would I think there was goo inside? I guess I could have Googled it but why? It was going to be a great treat because it had HAZELNUTS!

I adore hazelnuts and especially surrounded by chocolate. The label on this little cone of wonder reads Jedan Je Eurocrem Mini Kornet. What the hell does it mean? I have no clue, but the picture made me believe it would be a paper cone filled with delicious nuts and maybe chocolate.

After Googling it I discovered the marketing pitch is, "ice cream without the cold! This cone is filled with milk and cocoa cream for the ultimate sweet treat without any of the cold!" What? Who does that? Why didn't I Google it at the store? Why is there a picture of a Hazelnut on the package?

So many questions are unanswered when I unwrap this little treasure. First it is cone shaped because this mess is held together inside a sugar cone. Remember, ice cream without the cold?

I call bullshit. This is the inside of an American Kinder Surprise without the flaky balls. Nothing about this is a treat or resembles ice cream. It's so much like Nutella that I ate one bite and could not have any more.

The ingredients are listed in microscopic font after that Google search I read that it contains 4% hazelnuts. 4%, the paper wrapper is going to have more nuts than the entire cone. I took a bite out of the bottom to see if maybe there was a secret nut inside. Nope, no nut. I sliced the cone down the middle in hopes of finding anything that resembled the nut. NOPE!

Those nuts have been liquefied and added to the brown goo in this 50/50 crema cocoa concoction. It was a total bust. If a person wants ice cream just go to Dairy Queen or a local grocery freezer. If you're so afraid of the cold part of ice cream maybe have a glass of warm milk? Day 327 Love & Light

Day 328 of 365- I Made It   August 13, 2018

  Untangled the tangles. I'm filling in the last 37 days with things I've put on the time consuming/messy list. Day 328 was an artistic adventure with ink and string.
On day 7 I learned how to make paper by hand. For many days after I squeezed about a dozen sheets from watery pulp and now, I've got over 100 unique hand pressed pages.
  I had so many plans to make cards and art pieces using repurposed materials and my mother's crafty ideas. Today is the perfect day to put my paper to the test. I pulled out all the artist's ink from day 3, learning to create with a glass pen. I mixed up a batch of colors using red, yellow and blue.
  Today's adventure isn't complicated, but it is unpredictable. I soaked twelve inches of embroidery thread in the ink and draped it over the paper, smashed it between the pages of a book and pulled the string out. These sheets have an interesting texture from the screen pressing process and I hoped that the ink would settle in the little nooks and crannies. I wouldn't call it a perfect success, but I am happy with the final results. I've got plenty of pages to play with. Day 328 Love & Light

Day 329 of 365- I Made It   August 14, 2018

Keeping promises. It's another experience that I wanted to share. Instead of accomplishing this task with my mother I worked with my sister-in-law beside me. On day 329 I made a gourd bowl.

This was an experience that I'd planned back in October of 2017. My mother went to an event and brought a gourd back for me. At the same time my sister mailed me a gourd. Both were unique in shape, which led to very different experiences. On day 160 I made a shakere. Today I cut the other gourd to make a bowl.

I know it doesn't seem complicated, but it was a tiny bit involved. When I discussed this project with my mother it came with a warning, the inside can have mold, wear a face mask. I wore that mask as I cut this thing open. The flesh was dried and flaky and all I could imagine was mold, mold and mold.

I didn't see any, but I finished the cutting and gutting with that mask on. I scraped the inside out, very much like you would if you were carving a pumpkin. When all the cleaning and scraping was complete, I sanded the edges and the inside of the shell. It's pretty wonderful and I kept all the seeds to plant more gourds next spring. Day 329 Love & Light

Day 330 of 365- I Made It   August 15, 2018

Pitched perfectly... I can see a new light as my year comes to an end. In 35 days, I will be 50. I will have honored every day of my 49th year. I can't help but look back and pause at each emotional intersection along the way, love, joy, triumph, pain, loss and death. I guess that is what all these minutes, hours, days, months and years are, a massive mountain of failures and successes. I'm ready to take a very long deep breath and sit in silence for just one day.

But not yet, I've got 35 more things to do. For my 330th experience I got in the sticky business of harvesting pine pitch. Why? This is nature's gorilla glue! Have you ever been out for a hike in the woods, leaned against an old pine tree only to find that you are stuck? That's what prompted this adventure, and I have something wonderful in mind. You'll have to wait to hear about it. Early this morning I went hunting for pine pitch. It's sap that has seeped from the tree and gone kinda funky. It looks like mold. I cut a big chunk from a huge tree and cooked it in a little non-stick pan. It melted like butter and as it simmered it changed from funky to golden caramel brown.

This is where I got to play. I wanted to test the ability to hold things together. This stuff is pretty wonderful. I glued wood together and then I attached fletching to a chopstick. Making flaming arrows just got fun! The rest of the afternoon was spent rolling all that pitch in a ball so I can keep it for the big project. Day 330 Love & Light

Day 331 of 365- I Did It August 16, 2018

Marketing without a cart. I felt like today's experience had great potential. On the 331st day I attended my very first Digital Marketing seminar. I had this idea that I would get to network in a classroom.

I loaded up my backpack with copies of my books, a healthy stack of business cards and promotional materials. The reality of this experience is a little bit, well almost completely the opposite. When I arrived at the site of adventure number 331, I was disappointed that it was at the beach. I'm not kidding. There was sand and canopies and food trucks.

It felt like I set myself up for failure. As I read through the ad for today's event, I realized that it was part of a series of seminars and that mine was being hosted by a pop-up beer garden. This was 100% my first adventure with a pop-up anything let alone a beer garden. There were no plants in the sand and because this was meant to be a 365-day adventure I didn't have any beer.

The problem with an event at the beach is the noise produced by the people who are drinking beer and don't give a crap about digital marketing. I tried to listen closely, but I felt like a frontiersman with the funnel hanging out of their ear as a hearing aid. If I'm lucky I heard every 4th word.

I listened to all four panelists and although some were more articulate than others, they did offer great resources and suggestions. I walked away feeling like this wasn't a waste of time. #hashtagawareness Day 331 Love & Light

Day 332 of 365- I Ate It   August 17, 2018

Nuts, that's not coffee. Day 332 was all about acorns. I wanted to harvest them to make flour but the more I researched this experience the more curious I was about "acorn juice." I asked myself, "can you brew acorns to make coffee?" OH HELL NO! I spent most of the day arriving at this answer. I've never harvested coffee beans but if it's anything like acorn harvesting, I know that I never want to have to.

Praise be to the coffee roasters! My acorn brew began with the collection of about a pound of these earthy nuts. I roasted them in a pan to make it easier to remove the meat from the shell. The process was slow and after I finished I had just over a measured cup of nuts. I debated collecting another bowl full, but I felt I could get what I needed and if it worked I would do it all again.

It worked, if I lowered my coffee standards. Once the shells were removed, I started boiling the nuts. All of the information I read suggested that they would be bitter if I didn't. Most of them were crushed during the shell removal process and I was brewing and cooking at the same time.

No part of this tasted like coffee. If I called it earthy you just couldn't imagine the smell going on in my kitchen. I poured off the first batch from boiling to drink as my "coffee" and I kept the pot full for the next few hours, pouring off until the liquid was light in color. I tasted my brew, and it was not good. I added honey from day 312 with hope that it would improve the flavor, but it was just a waste of that delicious harvest. I'm moving on from this experience. I'll get my coffee from an experienced barista. Day 332 Love & Light

Day 333 of 365- I Made It   August 18, 2018

The wildflowers are in bloom. Day 333 and I went to a cut flower bouquet workshop. I'm not a person who cuts flowers to put in a vase and keep on the countertop. I don't like dead flowers, and I especially don't like cut flowers spilled over the counter by my cats. I tend to keep the plants outside where they are free to grow, flower and rot; circle of life and all that.

The experience started with flower selection. Many of the garden center volunteers brought in cuttings from their own yards. The line of colored flowers made choosing a wonderful rainbow for my own bouquet.

The little trick I learned about stacking the flowers, lay them on top of each other, at the same angle while rotating the entire cluster. It sounds easy but it wasn't and after dropping and breaking some beautiful cuts my bouquet started to take form.

Tip of the day: start with a big clumpy flower like hydrangea. It creates a ball to build around. The entire bouquet is held together by floral tape which I learned how to use and when the entire experience was complete, I felt like the mystery of bouquet making was gone. Day 333 Love & Light

Day 334 of 365- I Read It   August 19, 2018

Words on a page... I am the first to admit that I could never understand any religious text in 24 hours. Not many could. What I wanted to do was end my ignorance about the content. On day 334 I learned about the Quran. Why the Quran? I attended a PRIDE fair yesterday.

It was not a first for me and neither was the very vocal group of protesters screaming on a bullhorn. I thought and felt many things. The first was how vulgar it is to stand in judgment on a city sidewalk without entering to meet a single person inside. I heard hate disguised as religious righteousness. I also felt violated by this kind of Christianity.

As much as any of us has a right to choose a religious affiliation we also have the right not to choose. So today, because I needed to, I opened my mind. I was raised catholic. I've never read the entire bible. I know a person who believes they are better than me because they have. I don't judge, but they do.

How is this better? I watched my parents do their religion. I went with them to build and share. We gave to others quietly all in the name of love. As I started to read the Quran I was struck by the absolute certainty with which the text came directly from the mouth of their prophet. The religion itself has gone to extensive lengths to preserve (word for word) these teachings. If it's in the book, it came from his mouth. There's no John, Luke, Matthew or Mark. There is one word, and it is from the prophet alone. There is a purity in this if you believe.

As I read through the text, I wasn't surprised to see some similarities, all knowing God, these are my commands, follow me or else. Does it make me a better person if I close my eyes and follow any religion? Reading this only created more questions. I don't want to be part of any religion that doesn't respect the imperfection of the human experience. I'm not perfect and I don't expect that from others.

What do I expect? I expect the love that all these religions are meant to be about. When I attend a festival in support of the LGBTQ+ community, why is hate what greets me when I enter the venue? I never understood this as the word of God. I don't understand why the family of protesters couldn't go help someone in need. If they really love their god, they will come inside and try to understand how alike we really are. Love is just love.

I will continue to read this book mostly to try to understand where the differences are that have created so much division. I'm not a follower and it doesn't make me better... just different. Different should be okay. Day 334 Love & Light

Day 335 of 365- I Ate It   August 20, 2018

This was so bad... A few days ago, I harvested acorns to brew a horrible tasting coffee substitute. I'm not surprised that my acorn bread was equally as nasty. These nuts are supposed to be high in protein and loaded with a ton of other vitamins, but they taste worse than dirt.

I slow roasted the nuts after boiling them on day 332. Today I ground them into flour added a few ingredients to bake it like the hard tack I made on day 46.

Everything went so well. The flour sifted fine and was fluffy. I added some of the honey harvested on day 312 along with sea salt and water. I kneaded it, pressed a thin layer across a baking sheet and scored it with the hope that I could break pieces off to serve it. My acorn bread looked amazing. It baked for 20 minutes and smelled a little like nutty tree. The taste was ridiculous and so much like dirt that I couldn't get to the garbage fast enough to spit it out. I decided that I would need to be VERY hungry to ever put this in my mouth again or waste the effort it takes to work those nuts into dough.

Don't try this unless you're very hungry and even then, just eat some dirt. It'll taste the same and you won't have to waste a bunch of time. Day 335 Love & Light

Day 336 of 365- I Did It   August 21, 2018

Start with cutting your nails. I've had quite the adventure in the last 10 months. I've been to some amazing places and done many things I'd never planned to ever try. Through all of it I've been a woman. On the 336th day I'm embracing my womanhood by using an eco-friendly menstrual cup. When I say embracing... I mean full on in my business embracing!

If you're squeamish about discussing menstrual blood and lady bits you might want to stop reading. Shit's gettin' real right now. I've been pregnant 7 times. I've given birth twice and in that 10-year span I've had the hands of many medical professionals up in my lady parts. I'm pretty comfortable with my body but I've never chosen to be THIS comfortable. The Diva Cup is a rubbery reusable cone that captures all the unstoppable goodies that come to most women on a monthly basis. By design, the Diva is meant to keep all the single use tampons and sanitary pads out of the landfill.

It's really gross, I'm not going to lie but they did make a tiny handle to make it easy to pull out. The cup must be folded and rolled to fit and once it's in place it has to be rotated to create a leak-proof seal. Party time! Honest woman moment... I don't want to handle my unused womb and the goo that comes with it but here I am. Day 336 Love & Light

Day 337 of 365- I Made It   August 22, 2018

My aching back... I'm a firm believer that plants are growing in the yard for a reason. Many are considered weeds and because they spoil the purity of the green grass some people nuke them with pesticides.

I'm not one of those people. Today I'm using one of the weediest weeds of them all, the dandelion. On day 241 I made tea with the roots of this plant and although it wasn't delicious, I have kept in on hand.

For my 337th experience I decided to make a body ache soothing dandelion salve. This time the roots are staying in the ground and I'm using the flowers. I harvested about half of a gourd full, which is a measured cup. I rinsed them, drained the water and left them to dry for a while.

To make dandelion oil for the base of my salve I set those flowers to simmer with a coconut and almond oil combo. I'm using food grade ingredients so I can experiment by adding this to tea later. After about 2 hours on a slow simmer, I set this slippery concoction in a sieve to separate the liquid from the solid. My kitchen smells very sweet.

Part one making the dandelion oil. Part two mixing in the beeswax and some peppermint oil. I blended everything together in a double boiler and watched it melt into my salve. Waiting for it to move from liquid to solid is the final step and seems to take about as long as crafting this blog. Day 337 Love & Light

Day 338 of 365- I Made It   August 23, 2018

A labor of love… Today's experience isn't something that was on the list of adventures, but I had a great time doing it. There's a story here so you might want to get a cup of tea.

A few years ago, I published my first book, "Dear Kane; what I wish we would have said." Inspired by a mother's loss, this story explores the old rhyme about sticks and stones and broken bones.

I've used this story as a teaching tool and also to raise funds to bring awareness to the fight against depression and suicide. What does that have to do with today? On my 338th day I learned how to frame a painting. Today was a bit complicated and challenging even after so many experiences. I wanted this to match the perfection of the artwork it was surrounding.

My biggest dilemma was finding a frame that the painting would fit in. The rest of my adventure involved foam board and staples and what seemed like an endless twisting of framing wire. I had two goals in mind, a frame and a result that would hang the painting straight. I was excited to accomplish both. As a side note, kudos to people who build custom frames. They have the patience of angels, particularly for consumers who don't know what they want.

Day 338 was picture perfect. Love & Light

Day 339 of 365- I Did It   August 24, 2018

A little taste of Egypt... To say I have an obsession with the art of ancient Egypt would be an understatement. My creative space is filled with a collection that started over 20 years ago.

On day 339 I attended an open house at the Coptic Orthodox Church, and it was wonderful. Wow, there was so much food, and it was delicious, but the absolute highlight was my tiny cup of Egyptian coffee. The brew was dark and rich with a tiny sprinkle of sweetness. The woman making this drink was so kind and when I asked if she drank it all day say smiled and shared that her sensitivity to caffeine kept her from having a single sip. What was my next thought? That was wise placement by the volunteer coordinator.

I took a tour of the building on my way to the gift shop. Each room down the long hallway had beautiful images outside every door. I'm not into religious icons but I seized the chance to watch an iconographer at work. As an artist this was amazing to see. Out of respect for his work I didn't take pictures, but I really wanted too. As adventures go, I got lost in this one and it was fantastic. Day 339 Love & Light

Day 340 of 365- I Did It   August 25, 2018

    Not so nasty… I spent a few hours practicing my fly-fishing today. I have a large pond on my property and it's a convenient space to learn better casting technique. I never expected to catch anything bigger than a baby bluegill. I was a bit surprised when I snagged a little bass. I could fish all day long and I would still be out there if half of my flies weren't stuck in the tree.

    As I was standing on the edge of my pond, I couldn't help but think about the water that my fish and frogs are living in. It turns out frogs chase flies on string like kittens chase the light of a laser pointer. My pond is a tiny little creature universe. This little ecosystem is spring fed which means the water comes from all over the neighborhood. I started to think about what toxins and other chemicals might be in it.

    On day 340 I learned how to test my water. I scooped up a big glass of pond-y goodness and the color looked more like a urine specimen than potable water and I don't know if I'd ever want to drink from it. I thought I might test it with the goal of tasting it. After watching it move on my kitchen counter, I'm rethinking the entire experimental experience.

    I followed the instructions for the test kit and compared it to my reverse osmosis filtration system. I was surprised to see that the pond water had similar levels to my kitchen drinking water, minus the tiny things swimming in it.

    Pond water is full of living creatures, and I am most definitely NOT drinking any little bitty bit of it. I'm happy to note that it tested negative for pesticides and lead. Yay for that and if I catch monster fish it's good to know it's not toxic to touch when I remove that hook. Day 340 Love & Light

Day 341 of 365- I Ate It   August 26, 2018

Hoppy on the beer bus... On day 282 I started the brewing process by making the wort. I wanted to jump inside that foamy bucket and get lost in the beer's potential. On day 297 I transferred that deliciousness from the festering wort bucket to 50 sterilized glass bottles. I wanted to dive in again, but it would have been a tight fit. Today, day 341 I finally got to dive in and taste that home brewed goodness.

It was delicious. I like beer but I'm not taking up this hobby. I will leave it to the people who are patient and enjoy the science behind the brewing process. I want to enjoy the sport of beer consumption. It's a sport. It has to be. Day 341 Love & Light

Day 342 of 365- I Did It   August 27, 2018

On target... I'm getting very close to accomplishing what felt impossible; 365 consecutive days of first-time experiences. 365 consecutive blog posts sharing what I have done. Set your sights on a target and keep shooting. That's what today was all about. For my 342nd experience, fulfilling a childhood dream, I shot a crossbow.

I have always wanted to do this. ALWAYS! When I was a kid my mother and I watched the adventures of Robin Hood on Showtime. It was magic. In my imagination I was never the damsel, I was always the bow firing, sword waving, crossbow shooting hero.

Today's adventure started with a custom crafted crossbow. The owner brought it out to the property for first time shooting. I was intimidated by the lack of safety features, so I let the owner shoot it. I opted for the modern crossbow, and it turned into an afternoon of FUN! This version had a scope and although the sucker weighed a LOT, I held my own. My very first shot was almost dead center. So, satisfying. This was a definite adventure and although I'm not going to hunt, I would love to continue to shoot for fun. Day 342 Love & Light

Day 343 of 365- I Ate It   August 28, 2018

Roses are red... This was another bittersweet day. I don't have a green thumb, in fact it's shriveled dry earth brown, and I feel the shame of being a plant killer. The vitality bowl that I planted for mom back on day 212 is mostly dead. They were herbs and, in my defense, I cooked with them a few times, but they did shrivel away to crackly death.

That's what makes today difficult. My mother would have loved this experience, and I imagined her beside me sipping Nana tea while I infused the sticky good honey I harvested with the oil of petite roses.

Day 343 was all about eating roses. When my niece and I were sorting through the hundreds of gardening books my mother owned, we found "How to eat a rose." My niece and I decided this would be a 365-day experience, but I was waiting for the perfect blooms. They never came.

Here's another brown thumb moment. I have beautiful wild rose bushes. My mom and I have been caring for them for the last few years. She made suggestions about cutting and fertilizing and with her skills I was able to get that sucker to bloom last year. I was not so lucky in the summer of 2018 and I'm guessing it's because I didn't care for it in early spring. My mother died in April and so did my plans to create the gardens around my home. I had hoped she would be my 365-day sidekick. I miss her every day.

As I stared at the tiny rosebuds that I cut from someone else's plants, I felt my mother's presence. I was planning to make rose water, but it reminded me of sitting in a nursing home, so I went with honey infusion.

I plucked the petals off, I used petite roses and after dropping some bits in the water testing kit I was happy to find them pesticide free. As an FYI, most plants from a florist are grown with added chemistry and my instructions directed me away from cooking with them. I'm pretty sure my roses will bloom after my 50th birthday.

I added about 1/4 cup of honey to the pile of petals and cooked them in a double boiler until the honey was thin. It looked beautiful. According to the recipe I have to wait. Patience, I'm getting so much better. Day 343 Love & Light

Day 344 of 365- I Made It   August 29, 2018

Where my feet fall… I had plans for this experience from day one. I purchased a kit with the idea that I would collect items along my journey. I am 21 days away from entering my 50th year and to honor the past 343 days and some of those who've shared my adventures, I made a mosaic steppingstone.

The kit came with the most important items: concrete and a mold. The instructions for mixing my base material had a warning about keeping the cement on the dry side. It made me a tiny bit nervous, so I added my water a little at a time.

It was perfect and as I spread that "dough like" batter into the plastic mold I started to get excited about this experience. I should back up and share that I traced the shape of my project base so I could lay out my pattern of objects. Every item has purpose or loving intention behind it.

Like I said, this was part of my plan. As I set my stones, I thought about the people who've been my cheerleaders this year, family and friends lending their time and talent and some professional resources to get me to this day. I am humbled and grateful.

I'm not going to run through all the objects, but I will say, if you were a part of my journey, you are a part of this stone. Some things are buried inside, because they sank, or maybe their presence is for me and I will always know they are there; a mustard seed, golf T, fishhook, bottle cap bits, coffee and so many other things are mixed in.

What I can see, brings laughter and tears. In the center, the rose quartz that rested on my mother's chest after her heart went into Afib. She scolded me about how cold it was. The outside temperature that day was Wisconsinably below zero. Her complaint had merit, and we laughed about it.

Her heart was my center, and it seemed appropriate that the end of her life journey would be an integral part of my dwindling days as a 49-year-old person. She would have loved to stir the flower petals in the steppingstone mix. I need to wait 24 hours for this to set, and I plan to pour clear acrylic over the top to seal that #365rockdays rock. Day 344 Love & Light

Day 345 of 365- I Saw It   August 30, 2018

So much wiener… I'm conflicted about today's adventure. I hate hotdogs but I love the Wienermoblie. Truth about the experience today... I saw that vehicle and I did a hard U-turn to go back and get near it. I wanted a picture. Why the obsession?

It reminds me of my childhood and the Oscar Mayer wiener song. Just watch! Don't Judge. I'm sorry that this jingle will be stuck in your head until you listen to that song from Aladdin. I had another plan for today that'll work well for tomorrow because it was an Oscar Mayer Wienermobile afternoon.

Have you ever been inside of this delightful national treasure? In my opinion hot dogs are nasty and I'm probably offending half of my Vegetarian friends by singing the Oscar Mayer song but… IT'S THE WIENERMOBILE!

My youngest kid was along and explained to the staff members how excited I was and shared my 365-day adventures. When I told them, this was day 345 they let me INSIDE! "Just don't sit in the driver's seat." I was like a kid in a Wienermobile. I got my sticker and a whistle, and I felt like I was ten again. Today was ridiculous and childish and AMAZING! Day 245 Love & Light

Day 346 of 365- I Did It   August 31, 2018

This just blows... Remember 8 years old, music class, and the noise from a recorder? Today was worse.

In 2005 I visited Australia and learned how to play the Didgeridoo from an extraordinary aboriginal man. I own that instrument and occasionally I make the dying elephant noise that made him cringe. My cats run and hide because the vibration of the sound freaks them out.

On my 346th day I attempted to play the bagpipes. The experience was tragic for my household. My cats are in hiding and my humans have filled their ears with cotton. This was bad. I am not a bagpiper.

My oldest kid has a practice cantor, which is very similar to the recorder we all played in grade school.

I followed the instructor on the web and learned immediately that I have little to no feeling in the fleshy part of my fingers which makes it very difficult to play because no feeling, no music... just dying elephant that stepped on a Lego brick sound.

Bagpipes aren't for everyone. The way I played them today is for NOONE! The practice cantor is a learning instrument and after making a lot of "noise" I was able to create the sounds that a bagpipe makes. I felt accomplished.

Remember that recorder from second grade? I pulled out the "Hot Crossed Buns" sheet music and played. The video is mostly painful, and I'm embarrassed to say that attempting to use the air filled arm-pumping instrument didn't get easier. Day 346 Love & Light

Day 347 of 365- I Made It   September 1, 2018

Pricked... Baskets are not my thing. I don't have many of them and what I do have came to me as gifts. The rustic style just doesn't appeal to me. I have wanted to weave a bramble basket since late last fall, but all my blackberry bushes were dried and impossible to use for weaving. If I know anything about making baskets, it's that the materials need to be flexible.

Day 347 was my bramble basket weaving adventure. I went out to my mosquito farm to ramble amongst the brambles. I just want to pause for a PSA. I'll suggest one thing if you plan to attempt the bramble basket. Unless you want the tint of blood on your finished project wear gloves to cut and clean your vines.

As I was rambling and swatting mosquitoes, I found a beautiful patch of raspberry bushes, the berries long gone I was left with what felt like an abundance of material to work with. I was so wrong. I cut 7 foundation sticks that I would use as the base to start the weave. My first go around was a terrible disaster. I may have had enough to work with if I didn't start again. I'll admit this sucker is ugly but functional.

I'm still a little proud of the final result because if I did stumble upon a bush filled with berries I could pick and contain them in today's creation. Day 347 Love & Light

Day 348 of 365- I Ate It   September 2, 2018

Energized... Today was a long one. It started with a 3:00am crash of thunder and ended with an 8:30pm downpour. In between those times we held our annual fundraiser to support awareness for depression and suicide. I had a good feeling that today was going to involve exhaustion and I planned ahead. For day 348 I drank my first Yerba Matte energy shot.

The stuff was horrible even though the label read lime tangerine. It tasted more like sour lime rinds. Did it give me a shot of energy? I think it did because I hit a wall at about 5:30pm and most of these tiny bottles promote 5 hours of energy. It's just after 9:00pm and I'm about to crash, 3.5 hours was good enough. The bottle said organic so I figured this would be an okay way to experience this kind of drink. I got a boost even if it was only for a few hours. Day 348 Love & Light

Day 349 of 365- I Did It   September 3, 2018

Quenching a thirst... It's day 349 and I used a Lifestraw. It's been raining intermittently for the last few days and all those drops of water have collected in pools of dark muddy puddles.

I've had the Lifestraw for a while. I wanted to use it in Colorado on a fishing adventure. It never worked out, so today's muddy puddles seemed perfect. The water I collected was pretty gross and I was hesitant to drink it at all. I created a syphon and watched the grey water flow through and out in a collection tube. It was clear and I was a little surprised at how well it worked.

The Lifestraw is advertised for use in areas where water potability might be worse than puddles of rain. I'd rather drink from my reverse osmosis filter, but this straw is compact enough to carry in a backpack. Day 349 Love & Light

Day 350 of 365- I Ate It   September 4, 2018

    I am 15 days away from 365 consecutive firsts. I have had some experiences and adventures but many things I have ingested have been the ultimate confirmation of intuition. Day 350 was all about the ZAGNUT. Have you noticed this candy at the checkout? I have and for 49 years I've avoided it because the flavor/texture combo just isn't appealing.

    The truth is, I love peanut butter but dislike peanuts. I am a huge fan of coconut as a flavor, but the texture of shredded coconut makes me gag like a 5 year old eating lettuce. The Zagnut bar brings together flavors and textures that just don't rock my world.

    First bite, NOPE! Initially it's crunchy and flaky melt away like a Butterfinger but then the coconut texture rolled around to leave a "spit it out" sadness in my mouth. I forced that first bite down and took a second just to make sure I wasn't psyching myself out.

    NOPE! GAG! I'm out. The Zagnut bar just isn't for me and as with most of the 365-day food firsts I'm sticking with those instincts that steer me toward deliciousness. Day 350 Love & Light

Day 351 of 365- I Ate It September 5, 2018

 Irish… We landed in Ireland at 5:00 this morning and it was my first exploration of the airport. If I said it was exciting, I wouldn't be stretching the truth because I had a Guinness for breakfast, and it was delicious.
 The rest of my Dublin experience went quickly, and I did wash that Guinness down with an amazing cappuccino. The next stop was Edinburgh Scotland. By the time we hit the ground we had been up for a very long day. What's the smartest thing to do?
 Take a nap. Did I take a nap? HELL NO, I'm in Scotland. I took a walk through the city dragging a half dozen suitcases, not the best way to tour this town. I did dump the luggage at my hotel/apartment. Did I take a nap? HELL NO, I'm in Scotland. I took my exhausted family to see the Castle in Edinburgh. It was the first time all of us have been there and as we get set to tackle the world in different directions, I saw this as a wonderful opportunity for a family photo.
 My day ended opposite to the way it started with my first frothy mug of Wispa. From the image I thought it was going to be fizzy cocoa. It wasn't, but in my defense the font size on the package required magnified reading glasses, which I did not have. The top of my Cocoa did have pretty iridescent foam. Day 351 Love & Light

Day 352 of 365- I Saw It September 6, 2018

 You're a wizard… I'm a fan of many things and today's adventure was an absolute fan experience. On day 352 I did a walking tour of Edinburgh, Scotland. What did I learn? A LOT!
 More than I'm going to blog about but if you are going to be in Edinburgh, do it! I knew that J.K. Rowling wrote her books while sitting in a restaurant called The Elephant House. It's a cute place but service is at their pace. I learned that J.K. was so broke that she would use their "free paper for students" to write some of the Harry Potter stories.
 Scotland is a beautiful country and this Edinburgh tour led us to many places that inspired J.K Rowling's storytelling. I did not expect to tour a cemetery but after our short walkthrough I felt even more fascinated by her writing process. Maybe I will blog from a cemetery before my 365 days come to an end. That would definitely be a first. Day 352 Love & Light

Day 353 of 365- I Did It   September 7, 2018

Step by step... How do you break up the monotony of a staircase with 246 steps? With a lodge, two halls, a royal chamber and a crown spire. On day 353 I climbed to the top of the Wallace Monument in Stirling, Scotland.

The staircase inside this tower was a narrow spiral of dizzying torture. Used for ascending and descending the structure, passing human traffic felt like hanging from a ladder. My knees got weak and the only support was a carved stone handrail. A stair climb that is certainly for the brave of heart. I'm not going to go in to detail about the history of this landmark because a Google search will answer any questions. What I can share is every step led me to an amazing view of the Scottish countryside.

I was hesitant to do this monument climb as I'd heard about the narrow stairs and worried that the tight space would cause a panic. On the third level of the monument there were metal grates in the floor. I laid my camera over one of the holes and took a shot of the distance between floors. I did get a little rubber legged when I stood up from taking the picture. Some things just induce that fear of falling.

Getting to the top was almost as invigorating as jumping in Lake Michigan on day 104. This was an absolute must see and I am so glad that I pushed myself to achieve this adventure. Day 353 Love & Light

Day 354 of 365- I Did It   September 8, 2018

Just this once… It's day 354 and I moved my grad student into a new life in Scotland. In 1986 my mother was there when I moved in to my first college home away from home. For the next year she would drive for hours to bring me back to the country on the weekend. Those car rides and all of that time together meant so much to me.

I don't think I ever adjusted to being away from the simple life at home. Navigating the big city can be a tiny bit of a drag and that's mostly because public transportation is limiting when it comes to schlepping personal items through busy streets.

We flew to Scotland with four suitcases. Three were filled with necessities my kid would need to start a new life. I've never lived outside of America. This will be my kid's second time making a home in Scotland. The University had a great welcoming team and the space my kid will occupy is cute and very dorm like for a 23-year-old.

It's amazing to be in the space that my kid will call home. This is a master's in philosophy program and the first time ever checking one of my own children into dorm living. I'm excited and sad because our time together will be over the Internet instead of long car rides. Soon all of those "in person" hugs will have to wait. You better believe I'm getting them in while I can. Day 354 Love & Light

Day 355 of 365- I Did It   September 9, 2018

Topping another fear... The last 354 days have involved many experiences that required overcoming fear. On my 355th day I conquered the tower of the Linlithgow Palace. This was no small feat. The structure is ruined and walking through the place is an example of what happens when beauty isn't cared for. I'm not sure about the history behind why this amazing place is crumbling but of all the castles and palaces we've visited in the last week this one is the most explorable.

Why? I'm guessing because there aren't gold leafed walls and crowned jewels guarded by full time staff. There is a beautiful fountain that stands in the center of the courtyard. The water has been turned off and it's creepy as heck to look at.

The buildings are mostly crumbling which makes my experience feel more treacherous. There's a LOT of rusty metal preventing curious adventurers from falling hundreds of feet. I was high and it was windy and there would be video if I wasn't crapping myself because of those two facts. I climbed to the highest point of this palace and as scared as I was at the beginning I was equally as proud to conquer my fear of heights. Day 355 Love & Light

Day 356 of 365- I Ate It September 10, 2018

Today had an interesting flavor… I've been walking around the city of Edinburgh in Scotland for the last week and falling in love with the place my first-born will live. This kid is being brave in ways that I envy.

I can't even touch how much courage it takes to leave all the safety of family to chase your dreams. As part of my 365 days of adventure I enjoyed a few local treats. I'm using the word treat in a loose form because I ate something called black pudding and I really should have Googled the ingredients before putting it in my mouth.

Ingredients:
- 4 cups fresh pig's blood.
- 2 1/2 teaspoons salt.
- 1 1/2 cups steel-cut (pinhead) oatmeal.
- 2 cups finely diced pork fat (or beef suet), finely chopped.
- 1 large yellow onion, finely chopped.
- 1 cup milk.
- 1 1/2 teaspoons freshly ground black pepper.
- 1 teaspoon ground allspice.

I think I'm a vegetarian again. How did my black pudding taste? Like the blood of a pig mixed with seven other ingredients. Not so good.

My blood sausage was served as part of an Official Scottish breakfast. I couldn't eat all of it and shared the plate of food with the rest of my family. What's the next delicious treat? Ginger spiced Pepsi! This is a real thing. If you like ginger beer the taste is so similar, but I couldn't drink it every day. It was a treat. I ended the day with what I'd hoped to have on my Scottish adventure. Thistle Tea

Why? The national animal is the Unicorn. I'm not kidding, and it is magical for me to be in the land of mystical creature appreciation. In a country that honors a Unicorn it only makes sense that the thistle would be the national plant.

There are historical reasons for both, and Google searches will help answer all your questions. I'm focusing on forcing down this tea. IT IS BITTER! This is not a sipping tea and most definitely something to keep on the shelf of medicinal drinks. Maybe I can add my tincture from day 311.
Day 356 Love & Light

Day 357 of 365- I Read It   September 11, 2018

What's the word? Just over a year ago I was having a discussion with my mother about religion. She was brilliant at keeping her journey of faith separate from any organization so much so that all I could ever feel was love. I have felt rejected by the church since realizing that my gender prevented me from becoming a priest. I was 5 years old. Why am I sharing this? On my 357th day I am fulfilling a commitment I made to my mother based in faith but focused on religion. That discussion I had with her circles back to a book she sent to me.

Since December 2017 when mom became ill, I've avoided looking at the book. When I opened it this morning, at the airport in Scotland, I cried because she and I will never have the discussion we'd planned.

I miss her wisdom. I aspire to have the level of faith that guided her through her last days. The book was published on September 23, 1967, almost 1 year before my birth. It's so fitting that it will become one of my final experiences on this journey. On day one of my 365 I took a huge leap of faith that I could make it through the year filling each 24-hour period with something new.

Faith is personal. This adventure has been personal and yet I've shared so many highs and lows in this blog. The Formation of Scripture by Barnabas Ahern was my experience for the day and what an experience it was. I wish mom was sitting beside me so we could discuss all the curiosities this tiny 80-page publication invoked. I am not a scholar. I don't have much use for organized religion, which was the subject of many conversations with my mom.

The Formation of Scripture sounds a little dry but as I continued to read, I was struck by the timeliness of the subject and also by how dated it is and I wondered when mom read this for the first time. Most of today's experience created more questions than answers. I guess I'll have to learn to live with that. Mom planted another seed. She was a master gardener and her green thumb moved well beyond the vegetation of her garden. Day 357 Love & Light

Day 358 of 365- I Made It   September 12, 2018

Sweet... On day 166 I made syrup from the maple trees in my yard. It took about 30 gallons of fresh tree sap to boil down a gallon of sticky goodness. It is my liquid gold.

I bottled that deliciousness and now that we are empty nesters, I'm maintaining this hoard. For my 358th experience I made maple syrup candy. This is where it gets a tiny bit nail bite-y because I covet this syrup. If you've never had it fresh from the back yard you are missing out. It's dark and rich and like nothing you get in a store. I don't want to waste a drop.

I decided to use a half pint jar to make a very small batch. Every part of maple syrup consumption has become special while using my 365-day stash. Cooking the syrup to a candy making temperature was intimidating. When it got to the right thermometer mark, I let it rest (a tiny bit too long... this is the nail bite-y part) and it began to solidify.

If you do a Google search, you'll see that it's meant to look like crystalized sugar, mine looks more like glass. Temperature is so important and I'm definitely not a candy maker. My final result is beautiful, and it melts in my mouth. It's like eating pancakes without the cakes. I'm 100% behind that. Day 358 Love & Light

Day 359 of 365- I Made It   September 13, 2018

Tied up... I bought this embroidery kit many months ago thinking that I could do it while taking care of my mother in the nursing home. I knew from the very beginning what I would make, and it was meant to inspire the fight against cancer. Today it is just a reminder that she is gone, and that fight ended.

I put this on a shelf in May with the intention of letting it go. I'm one week away from accomplishing this personal challenge and if I'm honest many days since my mother's death have been a struggle. She was larger than life. I miss her laugh more than I thought possible. She was supposed to be here at the end of this journey. We were supposed to sip tea, eat cookies and giggle about all of the adventures I had throughout the year.

For my 359th experience I'm making the embroidery wall art. Inspired by the last birthday gift that mom gave to me I'm hoping it isn't too difficult to create. The kit has everything: floss, canvas, needles, washable marking pen and an adorable pair of scissors. I guess the universe felt that I was getting too serious about this experience because the package that my kit came in was ridiculous to open.

I gouged my fingers into the cemented seams and couldn't help but feel the irony of the scissors sealed just out of reach. It was only plastic and cardboard but since I'm in a hotel room today I am 100% without any cutting or slicing implements... aside from the scissors I could not get to.

The packaging did not survive the cardboard and plastic slaughter. I don't know what the manufacturer intended but there was tape on everything.

Among all of the other contents the kit had a card with very basic instructions on stitching. How hard can it be? It's like sewing a Cub Scout badge, right? I've done hundreds of those... twice. Not anything like it at all. I started my stitches loose and it was smart because I had to remove them quite a few times. I feel like this was meant to be a relaxing project. I couldn't get the box open!

Once I drew my plan on the canvas, I mounted it to the rings and went stitch crazy. It never got relaxing and I spent much of my time deciding that I was only ever going to make one embroidery wall hanging. Day 359 Love & Light

Day 360 of 365- I Saw It   September 14, 2018

How do you catch a unique squirrel? Unique up on it. Today was exciting like the wiener mobile was exciting. I wasn't looking for an adorable little creature to cross my path, but it did.

On my 360th day I had a black squirrel encounter. Don't poo poo this. I'm a changed woman. I had no idea black squirrels existed and now I'm ridiculously fascinated by them. The first sighting happened on a side street in Battle Creek Michigan, and I thought I was going to jump out of the moving car to catch it.

After the initial shock of a black squirrel sighting, I knew I needed to capture one of these creatures on video. The hunt was on and like magic there was another poised to frolic across my path. I'm squealing at the thought of this adorable creature, and I don't really even like squirrels.

The rest of my day in Michigan could have gone anywhere after my fuzzy creature encounter and it just got better. I got to put my hands on an amazing weaving loom. Although I didn't get to use it the promise of returning to do it was all I needed.

Day 360 Love & Light

Day 361 of 365- I Did It   September 15, 2018

It's unbelievable that I'm down to my last 5 new experiences. I still have so many things on my list. Today I tried to do something I have never been able to achieve.

Don't laugh. For my 361st experience I learned how to whistle. This is some serious shit. I fall into that small group of people who just cannot whistle. It didn't matter how hard I tried or what technique I used; I could not whistle. For those of you who can I'm sure this seems like nothing. You put your lips together and blow.

Nope! I have been trying this for many of my 49 years. I had some tutelage on achieving this experience and I watched over a half dozen how-to videos. The first few hours there was a lot of wind and spit coming out of my face.

It's embarrassing. My lips are chapped. AND... I learned how to whistle. It's not loud like I want but every time I make the noise the volume increases. I'm having the best time. Maybe it was good that I was on my own today. Day 361 Love & Light

Day 362 of 365- I Made It September 16, 2018

Today I built a floating lantern. The base is made from sticks I cut in my yard and tied together with golden toned hemp rope. It's primitive and as I worked, I couldn't help but think about the raft that saved Tom Hanks in Castaway. I'm not escaping from an island, but I still crossed my fingers hoping that it would float. This is a very special lantern. On the day 7 of this year, I made paper from shredded recycle and today I used it for the lantern walls. My goal, build a floating lantern that I would not feel guilty about if it tips over, sinks or just plain catches fire.

At the end this creation can return to the earth and maybe feed a fish or frog. On day 330 I made pine pitch and on day 362 I'm using it as my glue to hold the lantern sides together. The final addition to my lantern and perhaps the most important part, an orange peel candle that I made on day 122. The fuel was coconut oil, and everything hinged on a tall slow burning flame. I'm very proud of my design and also of assembling it from personal firsts I've had throughout the year.

Today is September 16th. My mother would have celebrated her 80th birthday. As the sun set tonight, I floated this creation in the water and sang happy birthday to my mom. In 4 days, I will turn 50 and it will be the first time I celebrate my birthday without her. I watched the lantern float in the pond for 80 minutes. It was beautiful. Day 362 Love & Light

Day 363 of 365- I Made It   September 17, 2018

Condiments... It's been quite a journey. In the last year I've eaten so many new things and made food that I didn't want to eat. I have confirmed that I've got great instincts when it comes to the flavors that I like. Quite a few of the 365-day taste bud experiences were a bust.

My final food challenge was mayonnaise. Why? I absolutely hate mayo. I know hate is a strong word, but the creamy white substance ruins my sandwich. I've never had a taste for it. I'm a mustard gal and my visit to the Mustard Museum was a perfect adventure on day 294. I purchased a few new flavors, which I incorporated into my mayo today.

I also got to use an immersion blender for the first time and as amazing as this kitchen tool was it got so hot while using it that I had to stop before my mayo was whipped up. The ingredients in this recipe: egg yolk, olive oil, mustard, vinegar, salt and lime juice. All pretty basic and after making it I'm trying to figure out why I don't like the final blending of these ingredients.

I layered all the components, and it looked like a killer lava lamp until the blender hit them. The flavor is a tiny bit heavy toward mustard and maybe that's why I'll like the finished product? It took about 5 minutes to make and because I can tweak the list of ingredients, I might just be okay with homemade mayonnaise.

My final taste bud challenge felt like a win until I actually ate it. It's still mayonnaise and it ruined my delicious bread. Day 363 Love & Light

Day 364 of 365- I Did It   September 18, 2018

  One last creation... The final day of my 40's is almost here and I wanted to create a reminder that this last year was an accomplishment. I didn't do it alone, but every single day changed me.

  That change was made very clear today when I visited the eye doctor and he informed me that my far vision is 20/20 (yay!) but my near vision is VERY NOT 20/20 (boo!). Special gift for turning 50? My prescription doubled and if that wasn't painful enough the Dr. dilated my eyes. I've never had my eyes dilated so I didn't know what to expect.

  Think about this for one minute. I have an adventure to accomplish today and now my world is fuzzy and my new contacts make me dizzy. This should go well. For my 364th experience I made a screen print on a shirt. Back at day 100ish I had planned to visit a screen-printing company, learn how to set up a professional design and make this in a real-world environment. That never happened, well at least not yet, after a little research here's how I did it myself.

  Materials involved? Pantyhose were essential and since I haven't worn a pair of them in years, I really had to dig in the back of the closet to find some. I cut them up and stretched a piece across the embroidery hoop I used on day 359. The design was easy, and you can probably guess what I made. The one element that I was concerned about was Mod Podge. I've seen this in craft stores for years and never used it. I know you can glue crap to make collage art with it but that's the extent of my knowledge until today. I traced the design on my hooped hose material and painted the reverse outline with my Mod Podge. It's raining today. Waiting for the gluey goodness to dry took a long time so I went fly fishing. It's my new obsession. I caught a few bass and after about two hours my screen was ready to go.

  I was hesitant and tested the setup on an old t-shirt. When it worked and I was elated, and I might have done a tiny little happy dance. Yesterday I went to a secondhand store and picked up a sweatshirt to print on.

  I'm 100% happy and as my screen rests in the drying rack by my sink, I'm plotting where else I can paint this wonder woman logo. Day 364 Love & Light

Day 365 of 365- I Did It September 19, 2018

This is it. For the last 365 days I have lived with a vision. I've been focused on a task. So much has been learned and experienced. To be honest I'm a little exhausted.

For my 365th experience I spent the day alone on Lake Geneva having my very first stand up paddleboard adventure. I was hesitant to face the water without a companion but then I realized it was exactly as it should be. This has been a very personal year that I have shared very publicly. It was not what I'd planned on day one but here I am and I'm so different. In February I got a gift certificate for kayaking or stand up paddle boarding. Since I had a kayak adventure on day 233 the decision for paddle boarding was made.

The entire experience... it was amazing and when I do this again, I hope it's as magical. I hoped that I would be able to ride on this paddleboard even if I didn't make it to a standing position. The water around the dock was shallow and so clear that once I hit deep part, I was distracted by what was below me.

When I got to my feet, I was excited. The lake was calm and there were only a few boats on the water. I couldn't have picked a better day. I paddled for a while and felt an overwhelming calm come around me and it felt perfect. I only wish I'd had a fishing pole and the ability to cast from this wobbly board. My 365-day journey began with the words that another author had written and when I read it I had no idea how different I would be. After living with such intention to be better, to do better and to get a little uncomfortable the reward feels as magical as the lake water path I took. Day 365 Love & Light

On Being 50   September 20, 2018

    I'm new at this... being 50. I was quite an expert at those 40's and I banged out 49 like a champ. I learned a lot in the last 365 days and here's a sum up.
    50 observations, tips, thoughts and general life altering experiences:

1. We are all going to fail
2. Drive 100 miles per hour once
3. Only eat acorns in a survival situation
4. Take risks
5. YouTubers are amazing
6. Face your fears
7. Listen more than you speak
8. Just taste it one time
9. Ask questions
10. Trust your instincts
11. Travel by means that let you see small town living
12. We are all going to die
13. Tomorrow comes fast, don't procrastinate
14. Learn from your mistakes
15. Make peanut butter so you'll never have to eat acorns
16. Laugh often
17. Invite a friend for coffee... or tea
18. Failure creates success
19. GO FISHING
20. Value experience
21. Give your time more than your dollar
22. Wear gloves
23. Tell your story
24. Dream big
25. Actions have consequences
26. You matter
27. Be the person you dream to be
28. Stand up on the paddleboard; it's a game changer
29. Share your knowledge
30. PLAY
31. When an opportunity arrives, take it
32. Forgiveness is one sided
33. Always keep your knife sharp
34. Try to inspire

35. Open the door for the person behind you
36. Share your abundance
37. Love who you love and do it with your whole heart
38. Being a non-conforming human being is okay
39. Be brave
40. You have a voice, use it
41. You don't have to fight to communicate
42. The world's full of people who aren't like you, get out and meet some
43. Look up from your phone, unless you're #365day blogging at a Starbucks at 11:40pm.
44. Think before you speak
45. See nature
46. Do the research
47. Eat your dandelions
48. Marijuana is better than OTC
49. You are stronger than you believe
50. Live life one day at a time

That's what I've got. It's been an adventure, and I'm woke. There will not be another 365 days adventure because that was serious work and commitment.
365 consecutive first time experiences,
365 consecutive blog posts,
365 consecutive photos taken (I have 13,000 photos on my phone),
365 minutes of plank position.
Every day, all day this has been quite a ride. I'm going to celebrate my birthday, the first one without my mother. I guess I'll take my own advice and use #39 and 16.
On being 50 Love & Light

Dear Sharon,
  Being the mother of daughters has gifted me with kindred spirits with whom to share the many sides of being a woman. I treasure the moments we've shared and wish for many more, even if it's just a quick cup of tea.
  As you read this book, I hope you find reflections of yourself and of the many women in your life.

God Bless You
Love
Mom
May 2009

MORE BOOKS BY SHARON K. ANGELICI

Rage Room Romance Series

Book 1
CONNED

For Ella Eastman, firefighting is life. She's devoted her body to being the best, but everyone needs a break from reality once in a while. For Morgan Hail, art is life, but she has to make a living. Their lives collide when television fandoms intersect at The Blacktree Comic Palooza.

Morgan's captivating fanart leads to a heated misunderstanding, and a cosplay contest brings these two women together–though only one of them knows the truth. This unlikely pair heats up when their real-world lives collide, but what will happen to their budding romance when Ella reveals her secret identity? And can they find a way to make things work when Ella's job hits a little too close to home? Conned is a story of love, loss, new beginnings, and fandom.

Book 2:
DECONSTRUCTED

After eight years, Ella Eastman has a plan to create the perfect marriage proposal for her partner, Morgan. Inspired by Morgan's to-be-read pile, Ella struggles to incorporate her favorite romance tropes while asking the big question. The ideas pile up, as do the failed attempts to create their once-in-a-lifetime memory. How do you give the perfect partner the perfect memory of a perfect proposal? For Ella, it all seems to come together quite imperfectly. Revisit the Rage Room Romance's chosen family as they unite for Operation Perfect Proposal.

The Alice and Violet Series

YULE BE HOME FOR SOLSTICE

Alice and Violet Book I

Violet and Alice's December road trip is definitely a trial by transport as they set out to deliver the perfect Yule log for the Solstice celebration. This cross-state drive commemorates twenty years of sapphic bliss and three hundred thousand miles on their Subaru Outback named Bess. What happens between home and Aunt Eunice's house is a romantic comedy of errors. Sit back and enjoy this *Planes, Trains, and Automobiles*-style adventure to deliver the perfect Yule log for Winter Solstice.

Available now in print, eBook, and audiobook.

DOUBLE DYNO

Prequel to Yule Be Home For Solstice

Alice and Violet Book II

On a two-week hiking and climbing tour, Al Hadley guides a small team toward high adventure. With her best friends PB and Britt making up the Extreme Adventure Group, the goal is to build confidence and experience for each client. What they weren't counting on was Violet Crest and her amateur adventuring ways.

Weeks of planning and detailed maps can't tame Violet's curious nature. She's determined to make every moment count by capturing as many as possible through her camera lens, testing the boundaries and the patience of AEG's team leader, Al.

Dig into the story before the love story, in this slow burn, opposites attract, adventure and the prequel to *Yule Be Home for Solstice*.

Available now in print, eBook, and audiobook.

-

The Maker Series

MARK OF THE MAKER
(BOOK 1 OF THE MAKER SERIES)

Wildwood Blackstone believed her dream of being a country blacksmith was coming true. When the town of Bannock hires her to restore their abandoned carriage house built in the 1800s, she can't wait to begin.

But there are more than ghosts in Bannock and shortly after her arrival, she discovers this truth. When a childhood friend answers a call for help, Wildwood finds a part of her past that she longed to rediscover. Together they reveal Bannock's secret and uncover the Mark of the Maker.

THE MAGICK AND THE MAKER
(BOOK 2 OF THE MAKER SERIES)

Wildwood Blackstone longed for a life as a small-town blacksmith. She didn't imagine monsters or magick, and she never expected to fall in love with Shay.

Book two of the Maker Series finds the two women tangled together in the dark secrets buried deep in Bannock's small-town history. Is their commitment strong enough to carry them through? Who is the keeper of the Magick? When will Wildwood and Shay uncover the mystery behind the Mark of the Maker?

THE ORIGIN OF THE MAKER
(BOOK 3 OF THE MAKER SERIES)

Wildwood and her girlfriend Shay have uncovered Brigid's secret hidden deep in the earth.

Who is the stranger in the carriage house? How are they there? What do they know about the secret and the power it holds? Can

Wildwood and Shay find the answers and keep fighting the monsters hunting them night and day?

THE LEGACY OF THE MAKER
(BOOK 4 OF THE MAKER SERIES)

In a secret world filled with magick, Wildwood Blackstone has encountered unbelievable mysteries. As the blacksmith in her new hometown, she's survived and endured the call to wield the hammer of the goddess Brigid, but to what end?

Celebrating a year with her girlfriend, Shay, the two continue their search for answers. What lived inside Andrea Peters? How did the entity survive for hundreds of years? Who controlled her all this time?

Their call to be The Magick and The Maker of Bannock comes with more questions than ever, but it might also come with answers to their past. Wildwood and Shay are drawn into endless realms, all of which lead to the Legacy of the Maker.

BEHIND THE EYES

Theirs was a love story for the ages: Rasabel, the captain of the guard, and Isolde, the woman of the territory. In a world of swords and arrows, love could not defend against a cruel curse. For years, they searched for an end.
When the alarm bells of Acadia ring, Rasabel goes home, but she is not welcome. Her path collides with Bylyn, a young thief on the run from the executioner's axe. Their lives are forever entangled.
Can Rasabel and Isolde find hope in the hands of a girl who will do anything to keep her freedom?

DEAR KANE; WHAT I WISH WE WOULD HAVE SAID

Do the words that we say in front of our children build them up or tear them down? This short story explores the consequences of hatred and bigotry when it applies, unknowingly, to someone that you love. There's a time in every relationship when a parent must let go of the dreams they have for their child, so the child can chase what they dream to become.

IMMORTAL HUMAN TRUTH

Immortal Human Truth is a collection of poetry written by the author as she traveled to promote her first book
Dear Kane; What I wish we would have said.
Each section explores experiences with love, injustice, loss, and triumph of the spirit.

SHE BELIEVED SHE COULD

What can you do in a single day? Why haven't you done it yet? Jump out of your comfort zone and dive into life as you follow the author on her journey to achieve 365 new experiences in 365 days.

ABOUT THE AUTHOR

Sharon K. Angelici, she/her, was born in the American Midwest, but her heart and soul belong to the mountains of Colorado.

She began writing as a child, using words to recover from trauma-induced depression. As a member of the LGBTQ+ community, she's an advocate for depression awareness and suicide prevention. In 2016 she published her first book dealing with both subjects, Dear Kane; what I wish we would have said.

Sharon is a full-time lover of life and all things Pagan and Magick. She's an artist and blacksmith, which inspired her to create her Maker series.

www.ingramcontent.com/pod-product-compliance
Lightning Source LLC
Chambersburg PA
CBHW020245010526
44107CB00002B/113